Religion and Cyberspace

In the twenty-first century, religious life is increasingly moving from churches, mosques and temples on to the Internet. Today, anyone can go online and seek a new form of religious expression without ever encountering a physical place of worship, or an ordained teacher or priest. The digital age offers virtual worship, cyber-prayers and talk-boards for all of the major world faiths, as well as for pagan organizations and new religious movements. It also abounds with misinformation, religious bigotry and information terrorism. Scholars of religion need to understand the emerging forum that the Web offers to religion, and the kinds of religious and social interaction that it makes possible.

Religion and Cyberspace explores how religious individuals and groups are responding to the opportunities and challenges that cyberspace brings. It asks how religious experience is generated and enacted online, and how faith is shaped by factors such as limitless choice, lack of religious authority, and the conflict between recognized and non-recognized forms of worship. Combining case studies with the latest theory, its twelve chapters examine topics including the history of online worship, virtuality versus reality in cyberspace, religious conflict in digital contexts, and the construction of religious identity online. Focusing on key themes in this ground-breaking area, it is an ideal introduction to the fascinating questions that religion on the Internet presents.

Contributors: Eileen Barker, Lorne L. Dawson, Debbie Herring, Morten T. Højsgaard, Massimo Introvigne, Mun-Cho Kim, Michael J. Laney, Alf G. Linderman, Mia Lövheim, Mark MacWilliams, Stephen D. O'Leary, David Piff and Margit Warburg.

Morten T. Højsgaard is Internet editor at *Kristeligt Dagblad* (*Christian Daily*) and External Lecturer at the Department of History of Religions at the University of Copenhagen. **Margit Warburg** is a sociologist of religion and Professor at the Department of History of Religions at the University of Copenhagen. Her books include *New Religions and New Religiosity* (1998, co-edited with Eileen Barker) and *Baha'i* (2003).

Religion and Cyberspace

Edited by Morten T. Højsgaard
and Margit Warburg

Routledge
Taylor & Francis Group

LONDON AND NEW YORK

First published 2005
by Routledge
2 Park Square, Milton Park, Abingdon, Oxon, OX14 4RN

Simultaneously published in the USA and Canada
by Routledge
270 Madison Avenue, New York, NY 10016

Routledge is an imprint of the Taylor & Francis Group

Typeset in Sabon by
Keystroke, Jacaranda Lodge, Wolverhampton
Printed and bound in Great Britain by
TJ International Ltd, Padstow, Cornwall

British Library Cataloguing in Publication Data
A catalogue record for this book is available from the British Library

Library of Congress Cataloging in Publication Data
Religion and cyberspace / edited by Morten T. Højsgaard &
Margit Warburg. – 1st ed.
    p.   cm.
    Includes bibliographical references and index.
    ISBN 0–415–35767–5 (hardcover : alk. paper) – ISBN 0–415–35763–2
(pbk. : alk. paper) – ISBN 0–203–00357–8 (e-book)
1. Religion–Computer network resources. 2. Internet–Religious aspects.
3. Cyberspace–Religious aspects. I. Højsgaard, Morten T. II. Warburg, Margit.
    BL37.R44 2005
    200′.285′4678–dc22
                                                    2004030635

ISBN 0–415–35767–5 (hbk)
ISBN 0–415–35763–2 (pbk)

Contents

Illustrations

Figures

Tables

Contributors

Eileen Barker, Ph.D., Dr h.c., FBA, OBE, is professor emeritus of sociology with special reference to the sociology of religion at the London School of Economics. She is also the founder and director of INFORM. Her publications include *The Making of a Moonie: Brainwashing or Choice?* (Blackwell, 1984), *New Religious Movements: A Practical Introduction* (HMSO, 1989), and 'The Scientific Study of Religion? You Must be Joking!' (*Journal for the Scientific Study of Religion*, 1995).

Lorne L. Dawson, Ph.D., is chair of the Department of Religious Studies and an associate professor of sociology at the University of Waterloo, Ontario. He has published many articles on aspects of the sociology of new religious movements, religion and the Internet, and questions of theory and method in the study of religion. Amongst other books, he is the author of *Comprehending Cults: The Sociology of the Internet* (Oxford University Press, 1998) and the co-editor (with Douglas Cowan) of *Religion Online: Finding Faith on the Internet* (Routledge, 2004).

Debbie Herring is a lecturer, academic administrator and doctoral candidate at the Urban Theology Unit, Sheffield and the University of Sheffield. She is also a lecturer at Oxford Brookes University. Her research focuses on the interrelations between theology and cyberspace.

Morten T. Højsgaard, Ph.D., is Internet editor at *Kristeligt Dagblad* (*Christian Daily*) and external lecturer at the Department of History of Religions at the University of Copenhagen. He has published various articles in Danish on religion and information technology. His Ph.D. thesis of 2004 was on networked religion.

Massimo Introvigne, Dr Jur., is managing director of CESNUR, the Centre for Studies on New Religions in Turin. He is also the author of thirty books in Italian (some of them translated into French, German, Spanish, and English) and of more than a hundred chapters of collective books and articles in academic journals. He was the general editor of the *Enciclopedia delle religioni in Italia* (Elledici, 2001).

Chapter 1

Introduction: waves of research

Morten T. Højsgaard and Margit Warburg

> Our Sysop,
> Who art On-Line,
> High be thy clearance level.
> Thy System up,
> Thy Program executed
> Off-line as it is on-line.
> Give us this logon our database,
> And allow our rants,
> As we allow those who flame against us.
> And do not access us to garbage,
> But deliver us from outage.
> For thine is the System and the Software
> and the Password forever.[1]

What does the Internet do to religion? How are religious experiences mediated online? In what ways have religious individuals and groups used and adapted to the emerging reality of virtual culture?

This book addresses some of the questions that can be raised about the various linkages between religion and cyberspace. It is based on the international conference on 'Religion and Computer-Mediated Communication' held at the University of Copenhagen in 2001, and the chapters of the book are selected from the many contributions to this symposium.

At the outset, the conference aimed at addressing three main, interrelated topics within the academic study of religion and cyberspace, and this is reflected in the organization of the book. Part I deals with the terminology, the epistemology, and the history of this field of research. Part II covers various aspects and transformations of religious authority and conflict in the age of the Internet, and Part III contains analyses of religious identity constructions and group formation dynamics within the online settings of cyberspace.

The first studies of religion and the Internet appeared in the mid-1990s, and the very novelty and potential of the subject were grasped with enthusiasm, resulting in what can now be seen as the first wave of research (Kinney 1995; Lochhead 1997; O'Leary 1996; Zaleski 1997). Representing a 'second wave' of research on religious communication online (MacWilliams 2002) , an important aim of this book is to document and discuss what kind of knowledge we *actually* have about the religious usage of the Internet. The far-reaching consequences predicted in the first wave will probably not all come true. However, now that the phenomenon of religious communication *in* cyberspace, *on* the Internet, or *through* computer-mediated communication systems has been with us for some years, new insight should be gained by researching the subject again. The conference, which is the basis for the book, proved that a range of scholars in the field agreed that the time was ripe for a revisit.

Stephen D. O'Leary – a scholar of religion and communication who started the 'first wave' of religious studies related to the Internet – in this book reassesses and evaluates the ideas of his earlier works in the light of the present situation. Having had an optimistic approach in his earlier writings, O'Leary admits that his present analyses of religion and cyberspace tend to have a pessimistic tone. Still, he maintains the basic evaluation of computer-mediated communication as something that 'represents a cultural shift comparable in magnitude to the Gutenberg revolution'.

In the words of Lorne L. Dawson in his chapter, the 'interactive potential of computer mediated communication gives it an advantage in mediating religious experience over conventional broadcast media'. Commenting on cyberspace and the new global communication networks as a whole, Eileen Barker in her chapter of the book declares that any 'student of religion – or, indeed, of contemporary society – will ignore this new variable at his or her peril'. Pondering over her warning, the editors hope that this book may mean that any clever student of contemporary religion will be wise enough *not* to ignore the Internet!

Even the Taliban used the Internet

When the Internet was first set up in 1969, it was primarily used for educational and military purposes, and it could not yet qualify as a public sphere as such. However, as the Internet was supplied with a more user-friendly graphical interface and began to grow significantly in the beginning of the 1990s, the religious usage of the new medium also started escalating.

By the end of the 1990s there were more than 1.7 million web pages covering religion. In comparison there were slightly fewer than 5 million web pages containing the word *sex* on the Internet in 1999 (see table 1.1). By 2004, the number of religious web pages had grown considerably worldwide. There were then approximately 51 million pages on religion, 65 million web pages dealing with churches, and 83 million web pages containing the word *God*. As shown in table 1.1, at the same time there were 218 million, 105

Table 1.1 The number of religious web pages in 1999 and 2004

	Web pages in 1999[1]	Web pages in 2004[2]	Absolute increase	Relative increase (%)
Christianity	610,470	9,140,000	8,529,530	1397
Church	7,102,579	65,400,000	58,297,421	820
Computer	66,316,833	218,000,000	151,683,167	228
Cyberchurch	1,054	19,600	18,546	1760
Denomination	144,250	2,090,000	1,945,750	1349
Faith	2,047,530	37,800,000	35,752,470	1746
God	5,287,260	83,200,000	77,712,740	1470
Politics	3,461,870	58,000,000	54,538,130	1575
Religion	1,794,270	51,800,000	50,005,730	2787
Sex	4,490,310	105,000,000	100,509,690	2238
Theology	482,240	5,490,000	5,007,760	1038

Notes
1 The search was conducted via http://www.altavista.digital.com on 24 May 1999 (Højsgaard 1999: 59).
2 The search was conducted via http://www.altavista.com on 16 November 2004.

million, and 58 million Internet pages containing the words *computer*, *sex* and *politics*, respectively.

If these numbers and their growth are indicative of the priorities of human desires in the age of digital information, religion is doing quite well! Surveys made by the Pew Internet and American Life project indicate that – although religion is not the most popular issue of cyberspace – the interest in this subject area among Internet users has become widespread: in 2001 28 million Americans had used the Internet for religious purposes (Larsen 2001). By 2004 the number of persons in the USA who had done things online relating to religious or spiritual matters had grown to almost 82 million (Hoover, Schofield Clark, and Rainie 2004).

Eileen Barker begins her chapter by addressing this remarkable historical change:

> When, in 1995, Jean-François Mayer and I edited a special issue of *Social Compass* devoted to changes in new religions, there was not a single mention of the Internet or the Web. The nearest approximation to the subject was a chance remark I made about the International Society for Krishna Consciousness (ISKCON) having a sophisticated electronic network that could connect devotees throughout the world . . . Indeed, it was at the ISKCON communications centre in Sweden that I had first set eyes on the Internet, and, although I was impressed by the medium's capacity to enable instant contact with fellow devotees throughout the world, it was at least a year later before something of the full import of this new phenomenon really began to dawn on me.

Today, almost every contemporary religious group is present on the Internet. Even the former Taliban regime in Afghanistan had its connections to this global communication network. Officially, the Taliban had forbidden the use of the Internet. However, in 2001 the foreign minister of the Taliban admitted that they were not against the Internet as such, only against what he perceived as 'obscene, immoral and anti-Islamic material' including sex and politics, which lurked 'out there'. The Taliban therefore sought to establish a control system to guard against such material. They knew that controlling access to the unofficial information and uncensored communication possibilities of the Internet was crucial, as it would give all kinds of opportunities to bypass further control of whom you communicate with and what kind of information you send or retrieve.

Having observed various religious communication activities on the Internet for several years, Anastasia Karaflogka (2002: 287–288) documented that while in 1996–1997 there were 865 Internet pages on the Taliban, by the end of 2001 that number had grown to 329,000 pages. This increase, of course, should be seen in the light of the terror acts of 11 September 2001 in New York and Washington. The extraordinarily high growth rate of the material on this particular issue reflects the inevitable rise of attention and interest in the world public during this period. Likewise, other types of religious information and even ways of using the Internet as such have altered over the years as technology, political affairs, and migration patterns have changed. Some of these changes are documented in the pages of this book. Mia Lövheim and Alf Linderman's call for 'more longitudinal studies' is, indeed, still topical.

Also reflecting the constant evolution of interconnections among religious and electronic networks, Mun-Cho Kim in his chapter sets up a historical model of the various steps that an information society may go through. His model starts with the basic computerization stage. It then goes on to the networking stage. It continues with a flexibility stage, and ends up in a cyber-stage (see fig. 9.1). The networking stage may have begun in 1995, which – according to Manuel Castells (2001: 3) among others – was, indeed, 'the first year of widespread use of the world wide web'. The final cyber-stage, however, is a digitally embedded point that has not yet been reached (and probably never will be).

Addressing his own earlier writings on religion and cyberspace, Stephen D. O'Leary, as indicated above, admits that some of his ideas and attitudes towards the idea of cyberspace as a focal sacred space of the information society have changed over the years. 'Though I do have some positive thoughts and hopes on this topic,' he says, 'I will not apologize if, on balance, I [now] seem to espouse cyber-pessimism. In the light of the terror attacks of the past few years, I have found it difficult to maintain the optimistic tone of my earlier writings. In many ways, I now see my early essays as naive and even utopian.' In 1995 O'Leary thought that the Internet in just a few years would provide a positive and widely used way of experiencing and performing religion. In this book, O'Leary – though still convinced of its importance – expresses doubts about the effects and coverage of the Internet. In the age of digital information, people will still want to meet each other for religious purposes in face-to-face settings. Despite its various virtual representations in cyberspace, the physical Jerusalem, argues O'Leary, will maintain its importance as a holy place and corporeal point of political strife. Besides being a virtual platform for new kinds of religious communication genres, the Internet is also functioning as a supplement to or just a reflection of religion in the modern or postmodern society at large.

If the first wave of religious usage and academic studies of the Internet was filled with either utopian fascination or dystopian anxieties about the surreal potentials of the new digital communication medium, the second wave, in general, tends to be more reflexive and less unrealistic, as it seeks to come to terms with the technological differences, the communication contexts, and the overall transformations of the late modern society. In her doctoral dissertation Mia Lövheim (2004: 267) concludes that uncritical claims about the Internet as something 'new' and separate from other processes in society need to be questioned. Massimo Introvigne, writing for this volume, asserts that while 'celebrations of the Internet as a new and more democratic approach to information were probably premature, dystrophic perspectives of manipulated Internet hierarchies subverting offline hierarchies, destroying responsibility and accountability in the process, need not necessarily prevail'. Common ground for Lövheim and Introvigne – both representing the second wave of research on religious online interaction in this respect – is their shared interest in avoiding either utopian or dystopian extremes in their assessment of the research field. Rather they attempt to focus on the factually situated practice of religious online interaction.

Cyberspace and religion in interaction

Buzzwords without obvious reference to situated practices in general flourish within the literature and the public debate on the Internet and the interactive cultures it has fostered. The culture of cyberspace, for instance, has been characterized by various authors and commentators during the last three or four years by such words and phrases as 'global', 'democratic', 'anti-hierarchical', 'fluctuating', 'dynamic', 'user-oriented', 'virtual', 'visual', 'hyper-textual', 'inter-textual', 'converging', and 'discursive'. The various information and communication technologies that are part of the Internet likewise have been called 'symbols of a *new* world economy', 'voices or mediums of the grass roots', 'reflections of the rise of the network society', 'expressions of the *renaissance* of oral culture', 'the missing link between modern and postmodern mindsets', 'multi-pattern services', 'steps towards a possible future generation of artificial intelligences', and 'interfaces of human-to-human or human-to-machine dialogue'.

One of the most prevalent ideas that permeate these catchy descriptions of cyber culture is the notion of interactivity or interaction. Accordingly, this book seeks to investigate how a range of all these interactive practices and ideas of interaction in cyberspace are situated, constructed, and related theoretically as well as empirically to the field of religion.

As Mark Poster (1995) has summarily pointed out, the Internet by and large can be used either as a television set or as a telephone. In the first case, the Internet *transmits* messages, religious or not, from content provider(s) to content consumer(s). In the second case, the Internet *connects* people from various places. Given the specific focus on interactivity and interaction that goes through much literature on cyber culture, this latter way of perceiving the Internet also constitutes a special concern of the book. The perception of the Internet as a telephone is not only about connections; it is, of course, also about conversational applications, multi-faceted interactions, networks, individual usages and group formations.

Mun-Cho Kim in this book defines the Internet as a medium with great privacy, a focused audience, multi-way direction, and variable temporality. Along with Mark Poster, Kim thus depicts the Internet as being in clear opposition to the mainstream usage or perception of the television set as a medium with low privacy, a broad audience, one-way direction, and delayed temporality (see table 8.1). Mia Lövheim and Alf Linderman, in their chapter on identity formation in cyberspace, add further insights to the understanding of the Internet as a medium that facilitates multi-directed connections rather than one-way transmissions. They use the terms *information exchange*, *interactivity*, and *interdependence* to describe some of the most important aspects or facets that must be taken into consideration before evaluating the religious impact of the Internet. Information exchange is the category they consider the most basic form of connection in this respect. Interdependence is the category they consider as the most advanced form of connection in relation to identity building and group formation on the Internet.

In a similar manner, Massimo Introvigne highlights three foundational aspects of Internet usage – the personal, the interpersonal, and the trans-personal. Personal usage involves externalized information. Interpersonal usage entails objectified information. Transpersonal usage includes imaginary communication and involves internalized information as well. In sum, the level of personal involvement and commitment in religious and/or non-religious communication on the Internet varies, and the evaluation of the religious and social significance of the individual usages of the Internet for religious purposes should therefore also vary.

In this book, many chapters are specifically aimed at studying the varying relationships between religion and cyberspace with special reference to the different religious usages of the Net such as mailing lists, message boards, and news groups. As indicated above, such applications play a key role in establishing, maintaining, and transforming institutional authorities, personal experiences and social interactions across conventional boundaries of time and space.

As such, the total collection of religious materials and interactive applications of the Internet make up a *heteroglossia* of meanings and possible interpretations. No single authority or control mechanism can prevail in cyberspace, and no user can be assured of the stability of his or her identity. In cyberspace there will always be another, perhaps new, way of looking at it. The Internet can challenge plausibility structures, give voice to unofficial sources, and provide communication spots for new horizontal networks. This new global network technology thus offers yet another possibility for citizens in contemporary society who are seeking the freedom to bypass established religious institutions, just as the newly invented printing press provided new means of disseminating religious protest or anti-monopoly material during the Reformation period five hundred years ago.

Despite the potential danger of losing members, in general the religious organizations of contemporary society have wholeheartedly embraced the offerings of cyberspace. It seems to be vital for these groups, as David Piff and Margit Warburg note, to 'make a good appearance before the world'. Data from both international and regional surveys among webmasters for religious organizations indicate that their first priority is to present their group to the general public and to address people not yet affiliated with the group (Wolf 1998; Højsgaard 1999; see also Horsfall 2000). By doing this, these webmasters of religious organizations, however, are merely adding to the complexity, plurality, and information surplus of the field.

Cyberspace, as Dale F. Eickelman (1999) has put it, basically represents a 'multiplication of voices'. Among other things, this multiplication of voices means that conventional or exclusive beliefs, practices, and organizational authorities are being confronted with alternative solutions, competing world-views, and sub- or inter-group formations. In this interactive environment of increasing pluralism, reflexivity, and multiple individual possibilities, new ways of structuring and thinking about issues such as reality, authority, identity, and community are inevitably emerging. And that is, indeed, what this book is all about.

Another X

The study of religion and 'X' (where 'X' stands for some societal category or phenomenon such as gender or the Internet) is typical in the sociology of religion and calls for interdisciplinary research. Depending on the nature of 'X', scholars with backgrounds other than the sociology of religion are not only welcome to contribute to the topic; their particular expertises are invaluable. In this book chapters by sociologists of religion have thus beneficially been supplemented by contributions from disciplines such as communication studies (Michael Laney and Stephen D. O'Leary), law (Massimo Introvigne), sociology (Mun-Cho Kim), and theology (Debbie Herring).

The twelve chapters in the book cover a variety of religious traditions and communication formats. Transformations in Christian Web usage are discussed (Michael Laney, Debbie Herring), and so are analyses of digital communication related to Buddhism (Mun-Cho Kim), Islam (Massimo Introvigne), Baha'i (David Piff and Margit Warburg), and Judaism (Stephen D. O'Leary). A distinctive issue that highlights the innovative potential of the new information technology is the usage of the Internet among new religious movements such as Branch Davidians (Mark MacWilliams), cyber-religions (Morten T. Højsgaard), Scientology (Massimo Introvigne), and Wiccans (Mia Lövheim and Alf Linderman).

Religion and the X of cyberspace is a topic driven by many chaotic forces from globalization to technological innovation. Most likely the Internet itself will continue to undergo fundamental and complex changes with respect to its individual and societal significance. Also, the religious landscape of the twenty-first century will continuously go through alterations and transformations.

With regard to methodology, the diversity or plurality of the chapters in the book is also manifest. Some of the contributions are based on survey analyses amongst religious Internet and news group users (Debbie Herring, Mun-Cho Kim, Michael Laney). Other contributions have interviews with religious online users or editors as their point of departure (Eileen Barker, Mia Lövheim and Alf Linderman, Mark MacWilliams). Various techniques of measuring information flows on the Internet are adopted in another chapter (Morten T. Højsgaard), and, finally, a widespread range of factual contents of religious online communication is analysed at length in the remaining chapters. Not only does Internet research thus involve many interdisciplinary efforts, it is also an area that is irresistibly drawn into multi-methodological studies. It is therefore with good reason that this book has a wide coverage with respect to the empirical areas and the academic background of the contributors.

Towards the third wave

In only a few years, the academic study of religion on the Internet has moved from its first wave of research – focusing on the fascinating, new, and extraordinary aspects of cyberspace – to its second wave that tends to emphasize the diversity of the field and the need to put new findings into a broader historical and social perspective. In the first wave of research on religion and cyberspace, computers and the Internet could (and probably would) do almost anything. The Internet could create new religions existing only in cyberspace. 'Information technology is here,' said David Lochhead (1997: xiv), and it 'is transforming our world. It is transforming us.' 'The computer', said Brenda Brasher (2001: 141) in her first book on the subject, 'reconfigures the content of what we do and redefines precisely who we are.'

In the second wave of research on religion in cyberspace, the significance of computer networks is not neglected, but is put into a more realistic perspective. 'The Internet does not generate religion, only people do . . . The allegedly pure cyber-religious sites *are* being produced and used by persons who do not live their entire lives "on the screen"', says Morten T. Højsgaard in this book. Stephen D. O'Leary – the man who presented the idea of cyberspace as sacred space to the academic public – now asks: 'Isn't the physicality of the place itself something that cannot be dispensed with? How could a cyber-temple ever replace the actual wall of the real one?' Commenting on earlier works by J. Zaleski (1997) and M. Wertheim (1999) among others, the second-wave researcher of religion and cyberspace Patrick Maxwell (2002: 43) correspondingly makes a call for 'broader sociological, psychological, political and even philosophical debates about online identity, online community and related topics'.

A typical first-wave analysis of the Cyberpunk's Prayer – quoted at the beginning of this Introduction – would thus focus on the newness of the vocabulary and the computer-loaded, anti-clerical imagery and sarcasm of this text. An emblematic second-wave interpretation, however, would rather focus on the fact that the structure of the prayer in any case bears close resemblance to the structure of the Lord's Prayer in the Christian Bible (King James Version). The overall framework of the supposed religious transformation formulated in the Cyberpunk's Prayer is thus inescapably of a rather traditional kind. In the first wave, God had become a system operator. In the second wave, God is just like such a Sysop (Højsgaard 2001).

It is, of course, a risky business to make projections about future research. However, we believe that because of its chaotic and complex development, religion and the Internet will continuously be a topic that needs to be addressed by scholars with very different approaches. In the light of that, a *bricolage* of scholarship coming from different backgrounds and with diverse methodological preferences may very well indicate that the topic is maturing academically, and that it is maturing well. The third wave of research on religion and cyberspace may be just around the corner.

Note

1   This prayer – The Cyberpunk's Prayer – was written by Bill Scarborough of Austin, Texas. It was first published in an article by Stephen D. O'Leary and Brenda Brasher in 1996. In a mail correspondence with Stephen O'Leary, Scarborough stated at that time that this prayer was 'not copyrighted. Anyone

is free to quote, repost, or reprint all or part of it' (O'Leary and Brasher 1996: 266).

References

Brasher, B. (2001) *Give Me That Online Religion*, San Francisco: Jossey-Bass.
Castells, M. (2001) *The Internet Galaxy: Reflections on the Internet, Business, and Society*, Oxford: Oxford University Press.
Eickelman, D.F. (1999) 'Communication and Control in the Middle East: Publication and Its Discontents', in Eickelman, D.F. and Anderson, J.W. (eds), *New Media in the Muslim World: The Emerging Public Sphere*, Bloomington, Indiana: Indiana University Press, pp. 29–40.
Hoover, S.M., Schofield Clark, L. and Rainie, L. (2004) 'Faith Online', available from: http://www.pewinternet.org [Accessed 1 June 2004].
Horsfall, S. (2000) 'How Religious Organizations Use the Internet: A Preliminary Inquiry', in Hadden, J.K. and Cowan, D.E. (eds), *Religion on the Internet: Research Prospects and Promises*, Amsterdam, London, and New York: Elsevier Science, pp. 153–182.
Højsgaard, M.T. (1999) 'Gud i cyberspace' [God in Cyberspace], MA Thesis, Copenhagen: University of Copenhagen, Faculty of Humanities, Department of History of Religions.
Højsgaard, M.T. (2001) 'The Cyberpunk's Prayer', in Buck, L., Højsgaard, M.T. and Sigurdsson, L. (eds), *Kristendomshistorie på tværs*, Copenhagen: University of Copenhagen, Faculty of Humanities, Department of History of Religions, pp. 105–125.
Karaflogka, A. (2002) 'Religious Discourse and Cyberspace', *Religion*, 32, pp. 279–291.
Kinney, J. (1995) 'New Worth? Religion, Cyberspace, and the Future', *Futures*, 27 (7), pp. 763–776.
Larsen, E. (2001) 'CyberFaith: How Americans Pursue Religion Online', available from: http://www.pewinternet.org [Accessed 1 June 2004].
Lochhead, D. (1997) *Shifting Realities: Information Technology and the Church*, Geneva: WCC Publications.
Lövheim, M. (2004) 'Intersecting Identities: Young People, Religion, and Interaction on the Internet', Ph.D. Thesis, Uppsala: Uppsala University, Department of Theology.
MacWilliams, M. (2002) 'Introduction to the Symposium', *Religion*, 32, pp. 277–278.
Maxwell, P. (2002) 'Virtual Religion in Context', *Religion*, 32, pp. 343–354.
O'Leary, S.D. (1996) 'Cyberspace as Sacred Space: Communicating Religion on Computer Networks', *Journal of the American Academy of Religion*, 64 (4), pp. 781–808.
O'Leary, S.D. and Brasher, B. (1996) 'The Unknown God of the Internet: Religious Communication from the Ancient Agora to the Virtual Forum', in Ess, C. (ed.), *Philosophical Perspectives on Computer-Mediated Communication*, Albany: State University of New York, pp. 233–269.
Poster, M. (1995) 'Postmodern Virtualities', in Featherstone, M. and Borruws, R. (eds), *Cyberspace/Cyberbodies/Cyberpunk*, Thousand Oaks, California: Sage, pp. 79–95.

Wertheim, M. (1999) *The Pearly Gates of Cyberspace: A History of Space from Dante to the Internet*, London: Virago.

Wolf, C. (1998) 'Going Virtual: The World Wide Web as a Marketplace for Religious Organizations', paper presented at the XIVth World Congress of Sociology, Montreal, Canada, 26 July – 1 August 1998.

Zaleski, J. (1997) *The Soul of Cyberspace: How New Technology Is Changing Our Spiritual Lives*, San Francisco: HarperCollins.

Part I

Coming to terms with religion and cyberspace

Chapter 2

The mediation of religious experience in cyberspace

Lorne L. Dawson

Let us start our brief journey into the heart of virtual religiosity with a litany of obvious but important facts. Religion of every kind, big and small, old and new, mainstream and more exotic, is present online, and in great abundance. There are more religious sites than anyone can seriously hope to catalogue, and thousands of these sites are quite sophisticated in their presentation. Religion is being practised on a daily basis by ever increasing numbers of people, especially young people, through electronic bulletin boards, Usenet news groups, Internet Relay Chat sessions, MUDS and MOOs, and the World Wide Web in general. Recent surveys suggest millions of Americans are turning to the Internet for religious or spiritual purposes every day (see for instance Larsen 2001; Hoover, Schofield Clark, and Rainie 2004). This new forum for religious expression and information is self-organizing, to a degree, as centralized nodes of related links and commercially driven religious 'zines' begin to arise such as *First Church of Cyberspace*, *Beliefnet*, and *BuddhaNet*. If one is so inclined one can read about religion, talk about religion, download religious texts and documents, buy religious books and artefacts, search scriptures with electronic indexes, take virtual tours of galleries of religious art or the interiors of religious buildings, locate churches and religious centres, vote on organizational propositions, see images of religious leaders, watch religious services, watch video clips or whole movies, listen to religious music, sermons, prayers, testimonials, and discourses, throw cyber-runes, and take virtual pilgrimages. But can one be religious or undergo a religious experience online?

Clearly all of the activities listed are part of the practice of 'religion' (however we choose to define it). Yet an element appears to be missing; an element Durkheim perceived to be essential to religious life (Durkheim 1965). Can we *do* religion online, in the more demanding sense of participating in shared religious rites?

Technically the answer is yes, and some people have tried to do so. The opportunity exists to participate in virtual rituals, services, meditation sessions, confessional exchanges, and intercessory prayer groups. But the phenomenon is still rare and we know little about these efforts – their nature or effects. To date I know of only five published academic studies of such practices, though more may exist.[1] The first three discuss, as might be expected, the activities of so-called techno pagans (Davis 1995; O'Leary 1996; Cowan and Hadden 2004: 129–132; see also Brasher 2001: 85–92), while the fourth describes a Jewish 'cyber-seder' (Brasher 2001: 72–78) and the fifth analyses a Christian charismatic service conducted in a MUD (Schroeder, Heather, and Lee 1998). Perhaps other studies will come to light. As this analysis will demonstrate, they are certainly needed.[2]

What will I do in this chapter?

First, I will discuss how and why many analysts have seen the mediation of religious experience online as problematic. The analyses offered to date are fragmentary at best, but certain key concerns emerge from the discussions. Second, I will briefly discuss the four previous studies of virtual rituals mentioned above. These studies provide helpful insights, but they are very preliminary. Third, I will briefly examine the current state of such activities online. At this point I would say that the interactive religious potential of cyberspace remains largely a dormant and untapped capacity. It is difficult to say why this is the case (if indeed I am right), but I believe that part of the answer lies in gaining a better grasp of the nature, limitations, and reality of 'interactivity' on the Internet. I will briefly consider, then, this larger issue, as my fourth point.

Another part of the answer lies in a postmodernist dilemma raised at points in some of the five existing studies of virtual rituals as they try to assess the nature and future viability of virtual religiosity. The medium seems to significantly heighten the reflexivity of participants in rituals, and this reflexivity can appear to be inimical to authentic religious practice. This dilemma sets the initial interpretative context for understanding the mediation of religious experience online. But I believe it needs to be encompassed by a more sociologically sound and less perplexing framework rooted in an understanding of the social, psychological, and communal features of life in late modern society, a society characterized by a more radical measure of reflexivity (e.g. Beck 1992; Beckford 1992 and 1996; Giddens 1990 and 1991).

Doing religion online may well be hindered at present, then, by the combined effects of the physical absence of appropriate interactivity, and the conceptual constraints of heightened reflexivity. Each issue warrants empirical study. But there is evidence that those seeking to practise religion in cyberspace may be reconceptualizing what it means to be religious in ways that pose problems for both conventional religious and social scientific approaches to religious life, while permitting them, nevertheless, to be fully religious on-line. Consequently, when investigating religion in cyberspace it may be wise to distinguish between two related yet distinct sets of questions. First we need to inquire into the ways in which existing and largely conventional forms of religious life are being adapted to this new medium of expression. Second we need to delve into the emergence of new or alternative forms of religiosity online. The concerns overlap, but they are distinct, since there is evidence that cyberspace may be inducing a new way of being religious, or at any rate may be facilitating and accelerating changes in religious sensibilities that are already underway in late modern societies. Developments on both fronts will depend on whether religious experience can be mediated by the Internet, though the experiences in question may be notably different, and hence the religious and social consequences as well.

Is there a problem?[3]

First and most obviously, a consideration of cyber-religious experience leads us to a comparison of the online and offline realities. Can the sacred circles of neo-paganism, for example, be created on the Net? Clearly a problem is posed by the complete substitution of typed words or computer-generated images and sounds for real bodies holding hands in real time. Can the simulated dancing of computer-generated 'avatars' provide the sensate stimulation of real bodies swaying to the rhythm of a chant while circling an altar lit with many candles? The answer hinges on the degree to which this kind of religious experience requires the full stimulation of our senses.

I first encountered the issue of embodying religious experience online in Jeffrey Zaleski's (1997) journalistic exploration of the religious uses of cyberspace. At several points in his book Zaleski expresses strong doubts about conveying the spiritual essence of religious practice, what he calls the subtle energies of *prana*, by the hyper-real simulations of computer-mediated communication. I have since heard other people voice a similar scepticism. Zaleski, however, never examines any actual online rituals, and it is unclear just what he means by *prana* – some vital energy imparted by participation in religious activities.

Part of the problem seems to lie with the strictly textual character of so much computer-mediated communication. Can religious experience be embodied in words alone? In asking this question we must keep in mind that many of the most momentous events in religious history are the product of human encounters with words (e.g., the conversion experience of St Augustine). That is part of the power and importance of scriptures, and the Internet, like the radio and television, can be the vehicle for the delivery of many moving words and images. But in the end what distinguishes the Internet as a medium for religious communication is its potential for interactivity. The act of reading a religious message is interpretative, and in that sense it is interactive. The reader is not just the passive recipient of information. Still, by comparison with the Internet, the printed page, radio, and television are 'broadcast' media. The communication is from the one to the many and, formally, it is a one-way mode of communication. The distinct advantage of the Internet is its capacity for ongoing, adaptive, and two-way interaction (though still largely in typed words).

This problem aside, other commentators have expressed some concern that the medium is even more intrinsically antithetical to religion. Jay Kinney, a student of Gnosticism, observes that the Net is not very compatible with the demands for solitary contemplation and social disengagement that most religious traditions prescribe for true spiritual development. Rather the Internet tends to involve its users in an endless and distracting series of 'addictive facsimiles of life experiences' (1995: 774). In its very form, the World Wide Web inculcates a strong and almost reflex-like preference for heightened visual stimuli, rapid changes of subject matter, and diversity, combined with simplicity of presentation. As Brenda Brasher observes, cyberspace is 'a cool medium that rewards pithy phrases . . . [and] makes unwieldy the extended reflection on the transcendent that religion requires'. It is 'an oversaturated information place' that favours a 'niche knowledge distinctly at odds with the integrated wisdom that religion promotes' (Brasher 2001: 43).

Despite the veneer of active control and of interactivity, then, some critics think the intrinsic values of the Web are much like those of television, with all its debilitating consequences for our habits of discipline and learning. In an excellent story in the *Sydney Morning Herald*, Chris McGillion (2000) drives this point home:

> Interiority, the capacity to step back from places and events and contemplate their meaning is an essential ingredient of the religious imagination. But it is also one of the casualties of an image-driven culture. . . . Internet-generated images . . . invite reaction not reflection, and invite it at the speed of instinctive, rather than considered responses. What we gain in information we lose in insight and, over time, perhaps, in the capacity even to think insightfully.

The intrinsic limitations of the medium can be sensed in other harder to define ways as well. Consider the following passage of conversation between Zaleski and Sheikh Kabir Edmund Helminski. Sheikh Helminski is the chief representative of the Mevlevi Sufi order in North America (the order renowned for its whirling dervishes), and the creator and operator of the elaborate web page of the Threshold Society, a non-profit educational organization affiliated with the Sufi order. At one point in the wide-ranging discussion between Zaleski and the Sheikh their attention turns to the effects of spending long hours transfixed before the glow of the computer screen (Zaleski 1997: 75):

> JZ: . . . I get kind of zoned out when I'm in front of the computer. I find it real hard to stay with myself – not that that's ever easy.
> SKEH: You sort of forget that you have a body.

JZ: Yeah.

SHEK: You forget that you are a living, breathing creature. You enter a mental dimension, a mechanical and mental, technical dimension that is very absorbing and somehow pulls you in. This is a very interesting phenomenon. I don't pretend to understand it, and I've been trying to understand it for about ten years. There's something about the screen – it's mesmerizing, and it absorbs you.

JZ: Absolutely.

SKEH: And yet I don't feel any better for it. I don't think working at the computer returns as much in the realm of quality as working in a garden, or painting, or playing music, or sitting down and talking to another human being. I don't believe that engaging in a conversation in the Internet on a keyboard brings us as much or as many levels of information and experience, touches our heart the way that being with human beings can touch our heart, and touch many levels.

In Brasher's words (2001: 42), the Internet is 'a fantasy universe that stimulates the imagination but ignores the rest of the body, [it] is a non-environment that sucks attention away from the immediate surroundings in which most traditional religious life occurs'.

McGillion worries about this as well. Striking a Durkheimian note, he fears that the Internet 'encourages people to opt out of the kind of flesh-and-blood relationships that are the indispensable condition of shared religious meanings'. If religion becomes detached from real places, real people, and a real sense of shared time and cultural memory, then how can there ever be a significant measure of collective conscience and collective effervescence? Stripped of these embodied elements, the 'suprahuman status of the claims of religion meld into all the other claims on the Net and religion's symbolic powers are undermined' (McGillion 2000). The move of religion to cyberspace may be extending disenchantment and the secularization of the world, in ways unanticipated by its exponents.

The Internet may be ill-suited to the mediation of religious experience, then, because it is a too exclusively ocular, image-driven, textual, change-oriented, individualistic, detached and disembodied medium. As we begin to track the actual uses of the Web for religious and spiritual purposes, we need to keep these concerns in sight. Some would say they go to the heart of religious experience. But the issues are complex, and we must further consider the fact that the nature of religious rites, and the experiences associated with them, vary from tradition to tradition, and even between groups within any one tradition. Moreover, not all rites are the same. I can only allude to the further problems posed by this state of affairs by noting two recent and illustrative news reports. In June of 2001 a top Vatican official, Archbishop

John Foley, told the media that the Roman Catholic Church would soon rule out giving confessions online in a document to be issued by the Pontifical Council for Social Communication. Why? The news report simply states, because confessions require the sacramental context of face-to-face meetings (*Washington Times*, 5 June 2001; received by email from the World Religions News Service). Yet in April 2001 I read a Reuters report on a website from Madras (www.saranam.com) that offers non-resident Hindus around the world the opportunity to perform *puja*, for a price, by means of surrogate worshippers, in hundreds of temples throughout India (Reuters, 5 April 2001; received by email from World Religions News Service). The client receives the receipt from the temple and the *prasad* (i.e., the blessed offering handed out by the priest), and everyone is seemingly happy. Clearly, then, there will be significant variability in the mesh of the Internet and various religious traditions and rites.

Some of these issues have arisen in the four cases studies examined next. But these analyses call our attention to another and perhaps more fundamental concern: the more reflexive nature of computer-mediated communication.

What do we know about virtual rituals?

In a ground-breaking analysis of the first crude attempts to perform virtual rituals, Stephen O'Leary (1996: 803) expresses his doubts about their viability. None the less, as he states:

> In almost all the transcripts [of online neo-pagan rituals] we witness an attempt to recreate or simulate real space in virtual space and to sanctify a portion of this space as a theatre in which spirit is manifested; an establishing of difference with the world outside as well as with other territories of cyberspace; and an assertion of the power of language to bring about wish fulfilment through the verbal act of declaring the wish within the ritual circle. To this extent, they appear as attempts to fulfil authentic spiritual needs now unmet by the major institutions of religious tradition.

Of course, there may be an affinity between neo-pagan practices and the character of computer-mediated communication that cannot be as readily assumed for other religions. In neo-pagan circles it is the practice for different members to create their own and constantly changing versions of the key rituals of the yearly cycle and other life cycle or singular events. Neo-pagans are often compelled by their relative isolation to practise alone, or they choose to practise their religion in solitude. The Internet provides these neo-pagans with a remarkable new resource for accessing materials for creating and modifying rituals, and for sharing their ritual innovations and experiences with others, while continuing to practise on their own. Contemporary neo-pagans engage in a purposeful measure of *bricolage*. They favour the eclectic and creative use of diverse symbols, words, and ritualistic actions to create a transitory sacred space for the inducement of altered states of consciousness where the powers of the imagination are temporarily placed on an equal, if not superior, footing to those of practical reason. They are far less bound in these practices by the dictates of traditional religious or organizational authority. Covens or other groups can be formed and set the standards of their own practice more spontaneously than most other religious groups.

But this is where the problem lies. As O'Leary observes, and Davis (1995) and others (e.g., Dawson and Hennebry 1999) amply confirm, these neo-pagan rituals – especially in their cyberspace varieties – are marked by more than pastiche. There is an attitude of irreverence and a ludic love of parody. They make few cognitive, moral, or even social demands on participants (O'Leary 1996: 803). Rather they bear a resemblance to one of their sources of inspiration – fantasy computer games (see Cowan and Hadden 2004: 130–131). 'This conjunction of reverence and irreverence', O'Leary (1996: 803) states,

> seems to me to be in some ways characteristic of the spiritual situation of post-modern culture, which can neither dismiss religion nor embrace it whole-heartedly, but which ultimately leads to its commoditization along with every other product and project of the past that is not doomed to be discarded in the ash-heap of history.

With these concerns in mind he suggests that 'the options for traditional organized religious bodies in the world of cyber-religion would seem to be limited' (1996: 804).

In passing this judgement, however, O'Leary may be blurring the boundary between three distinct elements of the situation: (i) the intrinsic impact of the Internet as a medium of communication, (ii) the culture of the Internet (and secondarily, in this case, the culture of contemporary neo-paganism), and (iii) the religious motivations and aspirations of modern individuals. He may be ascribing properties that belong to one of these elements to the others. Their interrelationships are complex and difficult to trace.

Hitting upon what I think is the key consideration, O'Leary goes on to say (O'Leary 1996: 804; see also Hanegraaff 1996):

> Rooted in textuality, ritual action in cyberspace is constantly faced with the evidence of its own quality as constructed, as arbitrary, and as artificial, a game played with no material stakes or consequences; but the efficacy of ritual is affirmed, time and time again, even in the face of a full, self-conscious awareness of its artificiality.

In other words, these rituals are marked by a heightened degree of reflexivity – at the levels of self, group, and social identity. They may well be creative expressions, that is, of the kind of institutionalized reflexivity that Anthony Giddens (1990 and 1991), Ulrich Beck (1992), and Scott Lash (Beck, Giddens, and Lash 1994) and others see as the primary feature of life under conditions of radical modernity. Yet these cyber-rituals do seem to be performing one of the traditional functions of religious rituals. As O'Leary surmises, even cyber-rituals contribute to the restructuring and reintegration of the minds and emotions of their participants. But he is not sure to what ultimate end, nor is he sure how durable the effects will be (O'Leary 1996: 804).

From my own dealings with the techno pagan community (The Church of MOO, see e.g. Dawson and Hennebry 1999), I sympathize with O'Leary's interpretative plight. Their practices seem to present us with an interesting modern twist on the age-old tension between reason and faith. O'Leary's analysis, like much work in the sociology of religion, is implicitly informed by the Enlightenment assumption that reflexivity is more or less antithetical to the practice of religion, or at least religious rituals. It appears to be anti-thetical to the mystery and otherness at the heart of religious experience. We know well, though, that some measure of reflexivity has always been displayed by the leaders of religious traditions. This reflexivity is an inherent part of the spiritual quest, and plays a crucial role in the generation and survival of religions. But in the past the reflexive process was a tool in the service of some higher purpose; it was held in check by certain largely unquestioned and purportedly absolute truths. In the realm of techno pagan-ism though, as O'Leary laments, '*literally* nothing is sacred' (1996: 804; italics in the original). So we seem to be left with a postmodernist scenario of reflexivity for reflexivity's sake, and to O'Leary and others this seems to be incompatible with 'authentic' religious activity.

What I mean by this statement will be elucidated further below. But for the moment I will suggest that authentic religious experiences are commonly thought to be crucially independent of human processes of invention. They happen to people and are not the product of human construction – either social or psychological. They are a manifestation of a seemingly ultimate 'other'.

Returning to the experience of the techno pagans, it might be more accurate to say that for them '*seemingly* nothing is sacred'. Harking back to the three aspects of techno pagan practice differentiated above, I would say that their motivations and aspirations are often genuinely religious, but within the confines of a heightened reflexive individualism that reconfigures their operative notions of the sacred. There are indications, as I will discuss below, that certain experiences are being 'sacralized' and taking on the role traditionally accorded to specific sacred objects of worship and doctrines in systems of religious thought and practice. This subtle yet fundamental shift in religious sensibility is in line with a more general shift in religious preferences in many advanced industrial societies that seems to be elevating the cultivation of individual spiritual development and personal religious experience over the cultivation of loyalty to, or protection of, particular religious groups, identities, or systems of doctrines (Dawson 1998; Lambert 1999; Roof 1999). The Internet as a medium is neutral, I would argue, to the presence or absence of the sacred in this world or our lives. In principle nothing automatically precludes the sacred from being manifest in cyberspace, no matter how it is conceptualized. The culture of the Internet, on the other hand, with its individualistic, neo-anarchistic and iconoclastic tendencies, does appear to be somewhat antagonistic to the traditional expression of religiosity, and to favour alternative approaches like those suggested by the thoughts and activities of the techno pagans. In the study of religion online it is very hard to keep these things separate, but it may prove important to do so.

In this regard, when I was re-reading Davis's article on the techno pagans I was struck by some interesting statements made by practitioners that I had failed to adequately appreciate the first time around. Roughly I have three types of statements in mind.

First there are some statements asserting intrinsic links between the practices of neo-paganism and doing things in cyberspace. By way of a simple initial declaration, Davis (1995: 3) reports on his dialogue with the techno pagan Mark Pesce:

> the Craft is nothing less than applied cybernetics. [Pesce says:] 'It is understanding how the information flow works in human beings and in the world around them, and then learning enough about that flow that you can start to move in it, and move it as well.' Now he is trying to move that flow online. 'Without the sacred there is no differentiation in space; everything is flat and grey. If we are about to enter cyberspace, the first thing we have to do is plant the divine in it.'

Moving deeper into the issue, another techno pagan explains why she has adopted the screen name 'Legba' – in honour of a West African trickster god identified with crossroads (Davis 1995: 5):

> 'I chose that name because it seemed appropriate for what MOOing allows – a way to be between the worlds, with language the means of interaction. Words shape everything with incredible speed. If you regard magic in the literal sense of influencing the universe according to the will of the magician, then simply being on the MOO is magic. The net is pure Legba space.'

It may be difficult to decide what these people really mean by these comments, but they make a couple of things clear. They are either in touch with or legitimately questing after a sense of the sacred and they see nothing incongruous about finding it online. My own limited dealings with techno pagans would incline me to this view. In part this seems to be because they are impressed with the power of words or symbols to shape and move people – as stressed in the worlds of computing and magic. The precise nature of the sacred in question is another matter.

There are further hints in a second set of comments, however, that tell us something about their experience of cyberspace as sacred (or at least special). Consider this passage describing Davis's conversation with an advanced techno pagan named Tyagi (Davis 1995: 7):

> These days, Tyagi cruises the Net from four to six hours a day during the week. 'Being online is part of my practice. It's kind of a hermit-like existence, like going into a cave. I'm not really connected to people. I'm just sending out messages and receiving them back.'
>
> But for MOO-oriented magicians like Tyagi, the Net is more than a place of disembodied information. 'Cyberspace is a different dimension of interaction. There's a window between the person who's typing and the person who finds himself in cyberspace,' Tyagi explains. 'If you're familiar enough with the tool, you can project yourself into that realm. For me, I start to associate myself with the words that I'm typing. It's less like I'm putting letters onto a screen and more like there's a description of an experience and I'm having it. It's a wonderful new experiment in terms of magic and the occult, and it connects with a lot of experiments that have happened in the past'.

I find that these comments can be read at two levels, one obvious and one less so. We are coping with rhetoric, but also an earnest attempt to articulate a stunning encounter with the powers of the imagination in a technical medium that fosters reflexive awareness of the continuum between this special place of the mind and everyday life – or how we actually employ the fantastic to guide our everyday lives.

In this regard consider the following comments by 'Legba' (Davis 1995: 8):

> [Davis asks:] 'Do we bring our bodies into cyberspace?'
> Legba does.
> She doesn't differentiate much anymore.
> 'How is this possible?' [Davis asks.] 'Imagination? Astral plane? The word made flesh?'
> 'It's more like flesh made word,' Legba says. 'Here your nerves are uttered. There's a sense of skin on bone, of gaze and touch, of presence. It's like those ancient spaces, yes, but without the separations between earth and heaven, man and angel'.

Then at a later point in the conversation with Davis more is revealed:

> But then she shrugs, refusing to make any questionable claims about online gods . . . 'It works is all.'
>
> I asked her when she first realized that MOOs 'worked'. She told me about the time her friend Bakunin showed her how to crawl inside a dishwasher, sit through the wash-and-rinse cycle, and come out all clean. She realized that in these virtual object-oriented spaces, things actually change their properties. 'It's like alchemy,' she said.
>
> 'The other experience was the first time I desired somebody, really desired them, without scent or body or touch or any of the usual clues, and they didn't even know what gender I was for sure.'

I do not wish to read too much into these brief statements, but I think they are indicative of deeper processes of change that do have a somewhat postmodernist cast. The techno pagans seem to find their explicit or implicit awareness of the postmodern disjunction of the signifier and the signified empowering, and not just in some libertarian and cynical sense, but in a constructive, world-enriching sense. Recognizing this possibility helps to explain not only why they can find the sacred in such a reflexive medium as the Internet, but why they actually are drawn to the Internet as an ideal medium for the expression and experience of the sacred, as they understand it (see Cowan and Hadden 2004: 130–131 as well).

In a series of lengthy personal communications, 'Floyd Gecko', the principal founder and primary leader of the cyber-religion Church of MOO, has given me some insight into the new style of religiosity that may be emerging in the techno pagan community, and perhaps in other online expressions of religion. He makes specific and quite sophisticated links between developments in physics, the philosophy of science, postmodern thought, and the comparative history of religions to justify adopting a completely relativist yet active conception of the sacred. At its core, his view entails a traditional mystical embrace of the joys of paradox and the contradictions of religious language. He denies our capacity to express metaphysical truths, because of the inherent limitations of language. Religious life, he argues, should be about experiences and not beliefs, since no belief can be defended against criticism without eventually indulging in self-contradiction. Yet he simultaneously holds that words, as the primary human mechanism of world-construction, are the only means we have of inducing and sharing the experiences at the heart of religion. No special credence should be given, however, to any systematic or particular set of words, any set of implicit or explicit metaphysical or ritualistic propositions. All that matter are the experiences that are experimentally generated and manipulated by the skilful understanding and use of words and the temporary worlds they create in the minds of individuals. In the classic postmodernist mode, the simulation can be substituted for the reality, yet there is not really a complete collapse of the sign and the signified since the focus is still on some seemingly 'authentic' experience.

Gecko discusses this approach to religious concerns as a form of 'hyper-rationality' that fosters the co-existence, even the integration, of religion and science. He argues that practitioners of this postmodernist style of religiosity should seek to glean ways of being more effective inducers of experience from the study of the findings and insights of the social scientific study of religion.

Whether this highly reflexive and perhaps intellectualized mode of spirituality is something we wish to call religion is a matter of definition, as Floyd Gecko knows. However, he asserts that 'this attitude is not as rare within religious practice as one might assume' (email 7 June 2000), and he points to the exponents of 'Chaos Magic' (e.g., Aleister Crowley, Phil Hine), what he calls urban or scientific shamanism, and such pagan subgroups as the Church of All Worlds and the Temple of Psychic Youth, as well as other more traditional forms of pagan practice. These expressions of religiosity are very marginal, however, so it is difficult at this point to draw any conclusions about the significance of these developments.

Floyd Gecko's comments pose a problem, of course, because they blur the conventional boundaries between data and analysis, the subject of analysis and the analyst. But his analysis is suggestive of the issues to be explored in the face the reflexive religiosity emerging on the Internet. Can we find evidence that his views are shared, explicitly or implicitly, by others being drawn to the Internet for their religious practice? If so, does this mean that the exercise of reflexivity, long a hallmark of detached rational thought, is becoming, by radical extension, a new means of legitimating religious practice or even inducing 'authentic' religious experience? In the process is the experience of reflexivity itself being sacralized? If so, with what consequences?

But what of the other case studies of virtual rituals? Do they lend themselves to such speculations? First, we have Brasher's description of a cyber-seder that was performed on 12 April 1998 at the Lincoln Center in New York (2001: 72–78). This rite was a hybrid in two ways. First, the seder was not truly virtual; rather it was performed in real life on a stage before a large audience, and web-cast (with full video and audio) simultaneously. Second, the rite itself was an experimental blending of traditional and contemporary elements, mixing modern poetry, music, interpretative essays, and film clips with the customary Biblical and Talmudic passages. For the virtual participants there was also an active chat room, which preceded, accompanied, and persisted after the ceremony, and a bank of computers was available for the real-life audience to use as well. The chat room appears to have offered a reflexive forum in which the seder was subject to a running commentary that was educational, critical, and humorous. At one point a question formed online, about the authenticity of merely participating in the ritual via the Internet, made its way to the stage, and was discussed by the real audience. But in many respects this ritual was neither very virtual nor very interactive, and Brasher's presentation is too limited to cast much light on the critical concerns raised about the mediation of religious experience online.

Alternatively, the study by Ralph Schroeder, Noel Heather, and Raymond Lee (1998) deals with a truly virtual ritual, and the authors allude to some of the points raised by McGillion and others. But the interpretative issue of reflexivity may not be as pertinent, because the subject is a charismatic Christian service. They describe how a small and constantly evolving group of Christians have attempted to replicate a charismatic meeting in cyberspace using an online multi-user virtual world. The meetings happen in a three-dimensional computer-generated church where participants can move around and interact in the form of human-like avatars that operate from a first-person perspective on the world. After their analysis of the main features of the social interactions and text exchanges of a typical E-Church meeting, Schroeder *et al.* (1998: 11) conclude:

> Unsurprisingly, there are both similarities and differences [between the E-Church world and a conventional church service]: many practices and modes of communication – the formal structure of the meeting, some of the content, as well as the roles – are transferred from real world services into the virtual world. Some practices, however, are transformed by the technology, and may detract from the sense of a religious gathering; verbal exchanges become shorter, emotional solidarity with co-participants is weaker, and there is less orderliness to prayer meetings. But the technology also brings certain gains: the virtual church allows for more candid exchanges between participants, it enables a kind of access from all over the world that is not available in conventional services, and it permits experimentation in the use (and prior to that, the design) of the virtual space that is less constrained than a church in the real world.

The role of reflexivity in the online experience of religion is highlighted more directly in Cowan and Hadden's (2004) brief analysis of another neo-pagan ritual performed by six women using the Online Wiccan Rituals website (http://go.to/OnlineWiccanRituals). The experience of the ritual as 'authentic', they suggest, is closely tied to the 'exuberant online decon-struction' of the ritual carried out by the participants after its performance. In this way a key measure of shared meaning is attributed to the ritual experi-ence post hoc. The ritual and its later embellishment are facilitated, they speculate, by a convergence of 'the imaginative nature of Neopagan ritual itself and the dramaturgical character of the e-space environment' (Cowan and Hadden 2004: 130).

Clearly virtual manifestations of religious practice, like the ones surveyed here, warrant more study, particularly as they proliferate (if they proliferate). Of course, it remains an open question how common they are on the Net in the first place. Regrettably, none of the studies cited here moves beyond a mere textual analysis of these ritual happenings. We need true qualitative studies of virtual rituality, entailing real-time participant observation and face-to-face interviews with those involved. There may be many different ways in which people are utilizing and responding to these situations. These differences need to be delineated. Beyond this, no one has tried as yet, to my knowledge, to analyse a virtual ritual from the vantage point of a systematic theory of ritual. A semiotic or rhetorical analysis of virtual rituals or services could prove most enlightening. We have every reason to believe that the results will vary between different kinds of rituals and religious traditions, and thus an entire new field of comparative study awaits exploration.

In every case, I surmise, research will be guided by the suspicion that the conspicuous reflexivity induced by doing things in cyberspace runs counter to religious authenticity. But if we can turn this metatheoretical suspicion into a research question we may discover that radical reflexivity is compatible with genuine religious experience, under a transformed conception of the sacred. The introduction of a new way of mediating religion is rendering many of the conventional ways of thinking about religion problematic for both the religious and social scientists. We need to pause and investigate these implications. This is especially the case if the reflexivity and consequent changes in religiosity found on the Internet are mirroring and extending a more generalized 'spiritual reflexivity', to borrow Wade Clark Roof's term (1999), born of the social conditions of late modernity.

But what do I mean by 'authentic' experiences? Let us return to the issue. Technically, of course, social scientists have no means of differentiating authentic from inauthentic experiences, religious or otherwise. The terms are normative, evaluative, and culturally relative. Religious experiences in particular are troublesome since they entail a claim to real encounters with some phenomena that is by definition beyond the scope of scientific analysis – the sacred, the transcendent, or the supernatural. Debates about the authenticity of a religious experience are seemingly the preserve of theologians and the religious. Yet the apparent authenticity of a religious activity or experience will play a determining role, I suspect, in whether the Internet will become a forum for core religious activities and serious religious engagement. Consequently, those wishing to study this possibility must come to grips with the 'authenticity' of religious experiences as a key descriptive category, explicitly or implicitly invoked by the people they are studying. This has always been the case in religious studies. But the shift from the 'real world' to the 'virtual' highlights the methodological dilemma as the heightened reflexivity of life online magnifies the significance of the authenticity issue.

If there is evidence, as O'Leary suggests, that virtual rituals can be efficacious at times, that they can be transforming, then presumably it is because they are authentic, in some sense, for those involved. This may be hard for other religious people and social scientists to perceive, however, because the criteria of authenticity have shifted along with the change in religious sensibilities from a focus on the sacred as a specifiable, if mysterious, presence in this world – a thing of some sort – to an experience or state of mind that is intrinsically valued, that is sacralized, somewhat independently from how it is symbolized.

For traditional believers authenticity is tied to notions of an experience of the real sacred, which usually entails contact with a power assumed to be external to the religious actor. There is an acceptance of a commonsense differentiation between appearances and reality, and an assumption that the contact with the sacred is a serious matter (i.e., not playful or irreverent). Inauthentic religious phenomena merely mimic the appearances of real ones. To the extent that social scientists talk about people's judgements of authenticity they more or less subscribe to the same commonsense distinction, while bracketing any judgements about the reality of the judgements or the phenomena on which it is premised (i.e., the (w)hol(ly) other). Since Durkheim at least, most social scientists are disinclined to assume that these judgements are simply complete cognitive errors. They may be off the mark but they are not totally unfounded. Social scientists have searched for some human or natural experience to account for these judgements. For Durkheim and later sociologists of religion, the reality of these judgements, and hence their real power, rests with the social processes thought to be at the heart of religion. The 'reality' of religious experience resides with the reality of society as the actual, if unrecognized, object of worship. But for some contemporary practitioners of religion, like the techno pagans briefly discussed here, both the traditional religious and the Durkheimian conceptions of the foundations for these experiences seem to have fallen by the wayside. For them the sacred need not be a real other, not even in the reduced sense of the power of sociality itself. They are content to work with a simulacrum. In true postmodernist manner the 'appearance' can stand in for the reality, if it generates the desired experience (whatever that may actually be). The experience itself, though ill-defined, has been sacralized.

With time, of course, Durkheim may be proved right. In the absence of embodied social effervescence online, cyber-religion may prove little more than an intellectual chimera. It may be 'inauthentic' for everyone. But the nature and degree of social interaction required to create and sustain a religious experience may be changing in important ways. It seems as likely now as ever that William James (1902) was wrong when he famously pronounced religion to be what people believe and do in their solitude. Religion, no matter how reflexive, is still a social phenomenon. Thus I suspect that the amount of interactivity permitted, or simply happening, online will have a significant influence on whether people think they can have an 'authentic' religious experience in cyberspace. The degree and type of social interactivity required, though, may be changing.

What is happening online?

But just how much virtual religiosity is there out in cyberspace? The task of measuring and describing what is happening on the Net in terms of religion has barely begun. I know of no efforts to systematically gauge the degree of real religious interactivity happening online, especially in the form of virtual rituals. In the limited time available to me, and with the helpful suggestions of some colleagues, I explored twenty sites of supposed virtual religion. The results are not encouraging, but the Internet is still in a highly formative stage of development. At this time let me just make five summary observations.

First, most of what I have said about mediating religious experiences in cyberspace could have been said in 1998, because the landscape of virtual religion has not changed much. There is a great deal more religious content online, but a sort of standardization has set in that has minimized the 'interactivity' that uniquely marks the Internet – in both of the assumed senses of that term: there is limited opportunity for the direct and meaningful interaction of people, and there are often fewer site linkages promoting the innovative interaction of sites and ideas. For whatever reason – perhaps the commercialization of cyberspace (as I speculated previously, see Dawson 2001) – the web pages of many religious groups have become more professional. That is, they are beginning to increasingly resemble 'zines' – hypertext magazines, or maybe popular encyclopaedias. The potential of the new media is being forced into the familiar form of the old media. Interactivity has been reduced to providing email feedback, the electronic equivalent of letters to the editor, or entering chat rooms where the level of discussion is often less than inspiring or even informed or coherent. Other features may allow one to post a request, for intercessory prayer for example, and to receive some limited acknowledgement of the request or offers of counselling. What is missing is much in the way of ongoing, communal interaction.

Second, many of the sites of supposed 'virtual religion' recommended or referenced in academic literature, the popular press, course outlines found on the Internet, or on other religious web pages, are only metaphorically virtual at best. They are often sites like those described above, or they may have a 'virtual temple' which turns out to be little more than a posted image of some deity or building interior. You can make an offering to the picture on your computer screen in lieu of a statue of the deity in your home or office. In other words, these virtual temples are static and differ little from the religious images ripped from calendars and magazines and tacked to the walls of households throughout the third world.

Third, the few extremely sophisticated, extensive, and multimedia sites that I have encountered are largely educational in nature, and not sites for the active practice of religions (e.g., Ancient Egyptian Virtual Temple, Virtual Church).

Fourth, many of the twenty sites I was referred to are no longer operating, or not operating fully or properly, or have not been updated for some time.

Fifth, only two of the sites, both neo-pagan, came close to offering the kind of virtual and interactive religious experience I am interested in investigating. In addition to being compendiums of information and links to other neo-pagan sites, these web pages offered detailed instructions on how to perform rituals, archives of past rituals, including online rituals, complete with transcripts in some cases. In one case, gatekeepers were in place, with the intimation that the right people may gain access to additional ongoing and planned events.[4]

Why does 'interactivity' matter?

If in fact the potential for the virtual practice of religion in cyberspace is not being met, the problem may lie with the limitations of 'interactivity' in general in cyberspace. Interactivity – or at least the potential for interactivity – is what most distinguishes the Internet from all other modern mass media. Computer-mediated communication is a group phenomenon; it is inherently social. But it is actual interactivity that draws people into the social life of the Net and binds them to any ongoing social activity. True interactivity is thought to emulate face-to-face conversation, though there is a continuum of interactivity even in face-to-face situations. The Internet has the capacity to draw near to the interactivity of offline relationships, unlike most broadcast communication. But the actual exchanges initiated in cyberspace may vary greatly. To what extent do the messages typed into cyberspace relate to each other in sequence? To what extent do posted messages display their relatedness to earlier messages in some exchange? To what extent do the turns taken in a cyberspace dialogue constitute a continuous feedback loop fostering the comprehension of a shared interpretative context, one that facilitates the emergence of new jointly produced meanings? Or is much of the interaction in cyberspace closer to the reactive or declarative end of some hypothetical continuum of interactivity? There will be a difference, I suspect, from site to site on the Internet, and the reasons for the differences need to be identified and understood. Can there be religious life, is there collective effervescence in cyberspace, without genuine interactivity? We need to investigate, systematically and empirically, the nature and the extent of the interactivity in the religious realms of cyberspace (cf. Rafaeli and Sudweeks 1998).

This line of inquiry, however, raises many fundamental questions. Is face-to-face conversation, for example, the logical base model of interactivity?

Why and in what ways? How is interactivity actually related to religious experience? How much interactivity is necessary? What kind, under what circumstances? With changing social conditions, is the nature of the relationship between interactivity and religious experience changing? If fewer or different kinds of interactivity are operative in late modern society, what are the consequences for religious experience? These are sweeping and complex questions, but ones which the studies of religion in cyberspace bring to the fore in unique ways.

Most immediately we need to investigate the literature on the nature of face-to-face interactivity before we can make significant comparisons with computer-mediated interactivity. If differences emerge from such a comparative analysis, what are the implications? Is computer-mediated interactivity different from other forms of mediated interactivity, like telephone calls for example? If so, in what ways, and with what significance? Research into the nature of email and Internet Relay Chat is beginning to delineate some differences. Online communication is marked by some distinctive features which users may seek to mute or take advantage of, but which no one can avoid altogether: anonymity, multiplicity, and disembodiment, and the problems they entail (e.g., impersonal communication, loss of inhibition, deception, and stereotyping). Little can be said about these features in this limited context, but the elimination of many social distinctions, the lack of physical and social cues, and the asynchronous and textual nature of most computer-mediated communication tends to produce a more freewheeling, brief, even abrupt, uninhibited and rhetoric-driven style of interaction. The style often strikes people as impersonal, and in another manifestation of this limitation commentators have noted a tendency for some people to experience the Internet as a licence to talk without end, without fear of interruption or concern for whether others wish to listen to them (Guy 2002). Yet many users have also asserted that the Internet allows them to be more open, personal, and intimate, more self-expressive than in any offline context. Investigating the nature and ramifications of these differences is a major undertaking that has only just begun (e.g., Crystal 2001). In the process I think it will become clear, as James Slevin concludes (2000: 175), that 'more than with any other medium, individuals using . . . the Internet have to actively negotiate mediated experience and endow it with structures of relevance to the self'. It is a complex medium open to many different expressive uses and abuses. But as Slevin's observation drives home, one thing is probably true – in all of its manifestations it inculcates a greater measure of reflexivity, of active participation in meaning construction, than more traditional media.

At present the innovative capacity and consequences of computer-mediated communication are probably held in check by a tendency to understand new media in terms of more familiar old media (cf. McLuhan 1964). In the limited number of decent qualitative studies available of social relations online we see, contrary to initial expectations, that users are seeking to establish continuity between their online and offline lives. They seek, consciously and subconsciously, to replicate many aspects of the latter in the former, and they often turn to an online existence to exert control over facets of their changing or ambiguous lives offline (see Blanchard and Horan 1998; Dawson 2000: 35; Dawson 2002; Fox and Roberts 1999; Markham 1998; Parks and Roberts 1998; Rheingold 1993). This may account, for example, for the curious and disappointing dominance of simplistic and self-ascribed sexual and gender stereotypes in online forums (O'Brien 1999). In the face of the anonymity and the disembodied character of life in cyberspace, people are inclined to revert to stereotypes to quickly secure and offer the information and trust needed to allow for a meaningful interaction. It also seems that the stereotyping allows them to indulge in the kind of idealized sexual and gender relations rarely encountered any longer in their offline lives. But most likely with time and increased usage the desire to turn life online into a simplified replica of life offline will diminish and the innovative potential of the medium will be better grasped and utilized.

In general, if our offline life is becoming ever more reflexive – institutionalized reflexivity is becoming an ever more dominant and pervasive feature of daily life – then the virtual world offers an excellent and safer forum for experimenting with some of the more disturbing and extreme consequences of this reflexivity. In the process, however, our level of comfort with this reflexivity will increase. In the religious context, as indicated, one of the consequences might be an evolutionary shift in our symbolic grasp, and hence experience, of the sacred (Bellah 1970; Dawson 1998; Lambert 1999; Roof 1999). It is in this sense that O'Leary may be right in suggesting that traditional religions are less likely to find the Internet hospitable. It is probably not accidental that the studies discussed above dealt with the neo-pagan and charismatic communities – realms of religious innovation in our age.

What have we learned?

What conclusions can we draw from this preliminary analysis of the mediation of religious experience in cyberspace? First, there may well be intrinsic reasons why cyberspace is not well suited to the mediation of at least traditional understandings of religious experience. As a medium it may be too exclusively ocular, image-driven, textual, change-oriented, individualistic, detached and disembodied. But these suspicions have yet to be systematically explored. Second, from the few studies available of online rituals it is apparent that cyberspace may be better suited to the needs and orientations of some religious traditions than others. There does seem to be a particularly good mesh, for example, between the medium and the message in the case of contemporary neo-paganism. Exactly why this is the case awaits further investigation. Third, the root of the problem for many forms of religious life may be the extraordinary measure of reflexivity encouraged by use of the

Internet and the creation of religious simulacra in cyberspace. Just how is this reflexivity fostered, and what are the nature of its consequences for such processes as the transformation of personal identity, the formation of communities, and the rise and exercise of religious authority? These are key concerns of the ongoing sociology of the Internet. Fourth, some forms of virtual religion may be indicative of a shift in our comprehension of 'the sacred', for want of a better term. Alternatively, the flagrant reflexivity of the Net may just be making what has always been the case more manifest. Fifth, in any event the mediation of religious experience seems to depend on a crucial measure of interactivity, off or online. So the investigation of interactivity in cyberspace should play an important role in the study of religion online. The interactive potential of computer-mediated communication gives it an advantage in mediating religious experience over conventional broadcast media. But the interactivity that happens online tends to heighten our reflexivity, which jeopardizes our sense of the 'authenticity' of the religious experiences people are claiming. This is not necessarily so, however, if the character of what constitutes an 'authentic' experience has changed, in part because of the great institutionalized reflexivity of life in late modern societies. But even a newly conceived and reflexive religious experience still seems to require a critical amount of interactivity to generate the emergent properties that lie at the heart of the new sense of the sacred evoked by Floyd Gecko and others. The key question then becomes how much interactivity and of what kind? This is yet another open-ended issue to be explored further. Sixth, and lastly, whatever the potential of the Net to mediate religious experience, it is not happening much yet. The problem lies, I suspect, with the impediments to greater interactivity in cyberspace. At present, for many of us, the technical demands of experimenting with creating a sacred place in cyberspace are too intimidating and the limitations of typed exchanges too restrictive. Plus the dominant culture of cyberspace at present is just too glib and reactive (in its style of interactivity). The development of religion in cyberspace depends on maximizing the potential of the Internet for more complete and satisfying forms of interactivity. How this can be accomplished is yet another fit subject for research.

Notes

1 Since writing this chapter I have encountered two additional essays (Fernback 2002; Larsson 2003). Both studies, however, are quite limited, largely descriptive, and add little to the analysis provided here.
2 I have had little opportunity to track down virtual rituals and subject them to analysis since I first broached the question of whether religious experience can be created or mediated online (Dawson 2000, 2001). I am restricted at this point to extending my previous comments by clarifying the broader context in which I think such analyses should occur and specifying more accurately the issues at stake. Certainly there are now many more sites facilitating such activities,

e.g. Lady Gueneva (http://www.ladygueneva.com), Raven's Quest for Celtic and Pagan Spirituality (http://www.ravenquest.net), including ones offered by the Methodist Church of Great Britain (Shipoffools.com) and the Anglican Church of England (http://www.i-church.org).

3   The following discussion reiterates some passages used in previous publications (Dawson 2000, 2001, 2002), but the bulk of the analysis is original.

4   Since writing this chapter I have become aware of a cyber-religion that came into being and conducts almost all of its activities online, Kemetic Orthodoxy (Krogh and Pillifant 2004a, 2004b).

References

Beck, U. (1992) *Risk Society*, London: Sage.

Beck, U., Giddens, A., and Lash, S. (1994) *Reflexive Modernization*, Stanford, Calif.: Stanford University Press.

Beckford, J. (1992) 'Religion, Modernity and Postmodernity', in B. Wilson (ed.) *Religion: Contemporary Issues*, London: Bellew.

Beckford, J. (1996) 'Postmodernity, High Modernity and New Modernity: Three Concepts in Search of Religion', in K. Flannagan and J.C. Jupp (eds) *Postmodernity, Sociology, and Religion*, New York: St Martin's Press.

Bellah, R. (1970) *Religious Evolution. Beyond Belief*, New York: Harper and Row.

Blanchard, A. and Horan, T. (1998) 'Virtual Communities and Social Capital', *Social Science Computer Review*, 16 (3): 293–307.

Brasher, B. (2001) *Give Me That Online Religion*, San Francisco: Jossey-Bass.

Cowan, D.E. and Hadden, J.K. (2004) 'Virtually Religious: New Religious Movements and the World Wide Web', in J.R. Lewis (ed.) *The Oxford Handbook of New Religious Movements*, New York: Oxford University Press.

Crystal, D. (2001) *Language and the Internet*, Cambridge: Cambridge University Press.

Davis, E. (1995) 'Technopagans: May the Astral Plane be Reborn in Cyberspace', *Wired*. Available from: http://www.wired.com:80/wired/archives/3.07/techno pagans_pr.html [Accessed in January 1998].

Dawson, L.L. (1998) 'Anti-Modernism, Modernism, and Postmodernism: Struggling with the Cultural Significance of New Religious Movements', *Sociology of Religion*, 59 (2): 131–151.

Dawson, L.L. (2000) 'Researching Religion in Cyberspace: Issues and Strategies', in J.K. Hadden and D.E. Cowan (eds) *Religion on the Internet: Prospects and Promises*, Amsterdam, London, and New York: Elsevier Science.

Dawson, L.L. (2001) 'Doing Religion in Cyberspace: The Promise and the Perils', *The Council of Societies for the Study of Religion Bulletin*, 30 (1): 3–9.

Dawson, L.L. (2002) 'Religion and the Internet: Presence, Problems, and Prospects', in P. Antes, A. Geertz, and R. Warne (eds) *New Approaches to the Study of Religion*, Berlin: Verlag de Gruyter.

Dawson, L.L. and Hennebry, J. (1999) 'New Religions and the Internet: Recruiting in a New Public Space', *Journal of Contemporary Religion*, 14 (1): 17–39.

Durkheim, E. (1965) *The Elementary Forms of Religious Life*, translated by Joseph Ward Swain, New York: The Free Press.

Fernback, J. (2002) 'Internet Ritual: A Case Study of the Construction of Computer-Mediated Neopagan Religious Meaning', in S.M. Hoover and L. Schofield Clark (eds) *Practicing Religion in the Age of the Media: Explorations in Media, Religion, and Culture*, New York: Columbia University Press.

Fox, N. and Roberts, C. (1999) 'Gps in Cyberspace: The Sociology of a "Virtual Community"', *The Sociological Review*, 47 (4): 643–671.

Giddens, A. (1990) *The Consequences of Modernity*, Cambridge: Polity Press.

Giddens, A. (1991) *Modernity and Self-Identity*, Stanford, Calif.: Stanford University Press.

Guy, C.F. (2002) 'You've Got Soliloquy', *Globe and Mail*, 28 September, F6.

Hanegraaff, W.J. (1996) *New Age Religion and Western Culture*, Leiden: E.J. Brill.

Hoover, S.M., Schofield Clark, L., and Rainie, L. (2004) 'Faith Online'. Available from: http://www.pewinternet.org [Accessed 2 May 2004].

James, W. (1902) *The Varieties of Religious Experience*, New York: Longmans, Green.

Kinney, J. (1995) 'Net Worth? Religion, Cyberspace, and the Future', *Futures*, 27 (7): 763–776.

Krogh, M.C. and Pillifant, B.A. (2004a) 'Kemetic Orthodoxy: Ancient Egyptian Religion on the Internet: A Research Note', *Sociology of Religion* 65: 167–175.

Krogh, M.C. and Pillifant, B.A. (2004b) 'The House of Netjer: A New Religious Community Online', in L.L. Dawson and D.E. Dowan (eds) *Religion Online: Finding Faith on the Internet*, New York: Routledge.

Lambert, Y. (1999) 'Religion in Modernity as a New Axial Age: Secularization or New Religious Forms?', *Sociology of Religion*, 60 (3): 303–333.

Larsen, E. (2001) 'CyberFaith: How Americans Pursue Religion Online'. Available from: http://www.pewinternet.org [Accessed 10 August 2003].

Larsson, Göran (2003) 'On-line Rituals: A New Field of Research, Neo-pagan and Muslim Cyber Rituals', in T. Ahlback (ed.) *Ritualistics*, Stockholm: Almqvist and Wiksell International.

McGillion, C. (2000) 'Web of Disbelief: Religion Has Staked a Big Claim in Cyberspace, but Has It Done a Faustian deal?', *Sydney Morning Herald*, 23 December [Retrieved from the *World Religion News Service*, 22 December 2000].

McLuhan, M.H. (1964) *Understanding Media*, London: Routledge and Kegan Paul.

Markham, A.N. (1998) *Life Online: Researching Real Experience in Virtual Space*, Walnut Creek, Calif.: AltaMira Press.

O'Brien, J. (1999) 'Writing in the Body: Gender (Re)production in Online Interaction', in M.A. Smith and P. Kollock (eds) *Communities in Cyberspace*, New York: Routledge.

O'Leary, S.D. (1996) 'Cyberspace as Sacred Space: Communicating Religion on Computer Networks', *Journal of the American Academy of Religion*, 64 (4): 781–808.

Parks, M.R. and Roberts, L.D. (1998) '"Making MOOsic": The Development of Personal Relationships On Line and a Comparison to their Off-Line Counterparts', *Journal of Social and Personal Relationships*, 15 (4): 517–537.

Rafaeli, S. and Sudweeks, F. (1998) 'Interactivity on the Nets', in F. Sudweeks, M. McLaughlin, and S. Rafaeli (eds) *Network and Netplay: Virtual Groups on the Internet*, Menlo Park, Calif.: AAAI Press/MIT Press.

Rheingold, H. (1993) *The Virtual Community: Homesteading on the Electronic Frontier*, New York: Addison-Wesley.

Roof, W.C. (1999) *Spiritual Marketplace: Baby Boomers and the Remaking of American Religion*, Princeton, NJ: Princeton University Press.
Schroeder, R., Heather, N., and Lee, R.M. (1998) 'The Sacred and the Virtual: Religion in Multi-User Virtual Reality', *Journal of Computer Mediated Communication*, 4 (2) [Available from: http://www.ascusc.org/jcmc/vol4/issue2/schroeder.html].
Slevin, J. (2000) *The Internet and Society*, Cambridge: Polity Press.
Zaleski, J. (1997) *The Soul of Cyberspace*, San Francisco, Calif.: HarperCollins.

Chapter 3

Utopian and dystopian possibilities of networked religion in the new millennium

Stephen D. O'Leary

My purpose in this chapter is to consider the impacts of communication technology on religious belief and practice in the twenty-first century. Since the publication of my two essays 'The Unknown God of the Internet' (O'Leary and Brasher 1996) and 'Cyberspace as Sacred Space' (O'Leary 1996), I have continued to research the ethical and cultural issues related to the question of religious technologies. This chapter will attempt the (admittedly risky) task of extrapolating from current trends into the foreseeable future of religion and computer-mediated communication, and perhaps even humanity itself. Though I do have some positive thoughts and hopes on this topic, I will not apologize if, on balance, I seem to espouse cyber-pessimism. In the light of the terror attacks of the past few years, I have found it difficult to maintain the optimistic tone of my earlier writings. In many ways, I now see my early essays as naive and even utopian.

In the piece co-authored with Brenda Brasher, for example, we considered the ongoing redefinition of the boundary between machines and humans, and celebrated the figure of the 'cyborg' as an emblem of contemporary spiritual liberation. That the cyborg – in Donna Haraway's influential definition, 'a cybernetic organism, a hybrid of machine and organism, a creature of social reality as well as a creature of fiction' (Haraway 1991) – has become an important symbol of our age is evident both from the films and novels of popular culture and from the reams of cultural studies scholarship that have emerged to grapple with the cultural, political, and ethical problems of the human–machine relationship.[1] While it may be true that we are all, in one way or another, becoming cyborgs, I am now decidedly more sceptical about whether this will ultimately prove an improvement in and beyond the human condition. I stand by the assessment in my early work, in which I argued that computer-mediated communication (CMC) represents a cultural shift comparable in magnitude to the Gutenberg revolution. However, I am now considerably less optimistic about the future that this revolution portends for both religion and humanity, and considerably more wary of the sort of technological determinism that says, whether we like it or not, the transformation from the human to the cyborg is inevitable, and we must either get on board or be left behind. I think it is important to stress that there are significant choices ahead of us; that our adoption of certain new communication technologies is neither inevitable nor advisable; and that the decisions made by both the developers and users of new technologies will have a profound effect on who we are, and what we will become.

Virtual ritual and the physicality of religious experience

I will return to the topic of cyborg religion at the end of this chapter. First, I want to examine trends in online religion since the mid-1990s, and to use these trends as a springboard to a discussion of the possibilities and limitations of technology as an aid to or medium of spirituality. As a starting point for this, let me note that the two early essays alluded to above were both written either before, or in the early days of, the rapid expansion of the World Wide Web. Both focused primarily on text-based religious communication, and devoted attention primarily to email discussion lists and textual rituals in chat rooms. The conclusion of 'Cyberspace as Sacred Space' featured the following prediction (O'Leary 1996):

> As we move from text-based transmissions into an era where the graphic user interface becomes the standard, and new generations of programs such as Netscape are developed which allow the transmission of images and music along with words, we can predict that [the available resources of] online religion will [expand beyond text to include] iconography, image, music, and sound – if not taste and smell . . . Surely computer rituals will be devised which exploit the new technologies to maximum symbolic effect.

To some extent, this prediction has been fulfilled. The Internet has indeed transformed religious communication by making possible a far greater array of visual and aural symbols than was possible in the early days of CMC. Yet, as I prepared to write this piece by reviewing hundreds of religious websites, I was struck by how few of them come close to fully utilizing the inherent capabilities of this new medium.

Consider, for example, a Yahoo! Pagan website that claims the title: 'Official Site for Online Wiccan Rituals' (www.angelfire.com/folk/wiccasi novess/Main2.html). Founded in October 2001, the primary features of the site are regular weekly web-based chat discussions and participatory real-time rituals available after the performance in transcript form. What I find curious about this page, and the rituals it displays, is that (if we take this page as in any way typical) the Web has made very little difference to the actual ritual practice of pagans online. The texts and conversations are presented with fancier and more colourful graphics, but there are no sound files, no three-dimensional graphics, and no attempts to use the more advanced capabilities provided by Java applets, Flash animations, or video in any format. As the following excerpt indicates, this page presents no real advance beyond the chat-room rituals available on the Compuserve network that I analysed in my 1996 essay (Sinovess 2002):

> Sinovess: Purification/Protection Ritual
>
> Sinovess: ** All cast the circle by lighting the 2 White Altar Candles and the 1 Purple Energy Candle. Then light the sandalwood incense (If not available, improvise) **
>
> Sinovess: HP/S [High Priestess/Shamaness]: 'With flame and smoke this rite begins.
>
> Sinovess: 'To raise our powers from within'.
>
> Sinovess: 'Elemental spirits of old'.
>
> Sinovess: 'We call thee forth to guard and behold'.
>
> Sinovess: ALL: 'Here and now we join as one'.
>
> Sinovess: 'Until our magick deeds are done'.
>
> Sinovess: 'Positive energy now prevails'.
>
> Sinovess: 'To she who turns the wheel we hail!'
>
> Sinovess: ** All raise their arms up toward the sky Imagining you are hold hands with the person next to you Say in unison: **
>
> Sinovess: 'Hail the goddess!'

Two points are worth noting about this excerpt, which apply to most of the rituals available at this and other similar sites. First, the ceremony is still text-based. Ritual action is accomplished by a combination of keyboard and utterance, with an attempt to synchronically link the voices of actors by means of written textual cues. Second, the ritual requires both physical acts in the offline world and an active exercise of the imagination, requesting that participants light candles and incense and imagine holding hands, chanting in unison, etc. One may not have the incense required, and one cannot actually hold hands with the others in the virtual circle. But as in the rituals performed in the Compuserve chat rooms a decade earlier the virtual/textual invocation of the physical elements of ceremony is considered to be both necessary and valid. No attempt has been made to augment the sense of sacramental presence with the use of web cams, animated representations of candles, or avatars. My point is simply that while there are technologies available that would greatly increase the sophistication of the spatial representation and sensory impact of online rituals, these have (in most cases) not been adopted by their practitioners. It may even be the case that participants in these rituals prefer the textually invoked imagination as a vehicle of ritual action to the virtual embodiment of the ritual's physical and sensory elements.

A visit to the virtual sanctuary of Reverend Charles Henderson's First Church of Cyberspace (www.godweb.org) shows that Christians have done little to surpass the online pagans in the use of available technology for ritual purposes. Reverend Henderson has received a substantial amount of attention as the founder of the first Christian church based entirely in the virtual realm of the Internet, and is widely quoted as a cutting-edge exponent of online religion. Yet his website offers little to the spiritual seeker beyond audio files of hymns and transcripts of sermons on seasonal and topical issues. The virtual sanctuary displays a variety of iconic Christian images with a repeating animated loop of a burning flame; it does not attempt to simulate the sacred space of an actual altar or sanctuary. Other mainline Protestant denominational churches have embraced the Internet, using live web casts to expand the audience for their regular Sunday worship services. The Peachtree Presbyterian Church of Atlanta, Georgia, broadcasts its well-attended Sunday services to an audience of 1600 web viewers (www.peachtreepres.org). Yet this hardly seems to be a substantial innovation, since it essentially duplicates the function of television in bringing religious services to wider audiences.

If we examine websites that present non-Christian religious traditions, we find a similar approach to relating the virtual world with physically embodied ritual. At www.prathana.com one for instance can find Online Hindu Temple Services. For a small fee ($45 US), payable by an online credit transaction, one can purchase ritual performances 'such as Pooja, Archana, Prarthana, and Homam to the presiding dieties [sic] at the following temples: Tirupati, Palani, Thirunellar, Guruvayur'. *Homams*, or fire rituals, are *poojas* [devotions] performed for a particular deity by invoking Agni, the God of fire. Available ritual options at this website include *Ganapathi Homam*, a ritual 'dedicated to Lord Ganesh, to improve family bondage, to win over enemies, to overcome disease and to achieve a planned objective without any hindrance'. One can also purchase *Mruthyunjaya Homam*, 'dedicated to Lord Shiva to avoid untimely death and for extending life time'.

Another experiment in online religion can be found in the numerous Jewish websites that focus devotions on Jerusalem's Western Wall, the last remaining structure of the Second Temple. For centuries, Jewish prayers have centred on the Holy City and the Temple in particular. As one devotional website for 'Prayer at the Western Wall' explains (Tornopsky 2001):

> Where the Holy Temple, Beit HaMikdash stood has always been considered the 'shortest route' to G-d's [sic] ear. Certainly, prayers said in any part of the world will reach G-d. But it is said that 'G-d's Presence' in this world was situated specifically in this holy place. This is, so to speak, G-d's abode. As such, petitions made in this place have less 'travel time' than petitions made elsewhere . . . One tradition going back

hundreds of years is to place a prayer, written on a small piece of paper, or Tzetel into a crack in the Wall . . . Perhaps one is asking for a speedy recovery for a sick person, another may be seeking his soul mate, yet another may be asking for G-d's guidance for a personal problem. No matter what the petition, a feeling that one's burdens are being shared and will be alleviated is often felt after the tzetel, with sincere prayer, is inserted into the Wall.

This website (along with many others) offers believers in remote locations around the world the opportunity to place a Tzetel in the wall by clicking a button and filling in a form on one's web browser (unlike the Hindu site above, the service is offered free of charge). Other devotional services are also available:

> If you would like, you may fill out the following form and have your own petition inserted into a crack in the Wall. You may also request that Kaddish (prayer for the departed) be said for a loved one, or for Torah learning to be done in the 'credit' of a specific person. Tehillim (psalms) can also be said on your behalf. You may also request that a mishaberach (welfare prayer), prayer for a speedy recovery, be said for someone . . .

In both the Jewish and Hindu examples, we find religious devotees using the Internet to offer a performance of religious rituals at a physical site of worship. While prayer, devotion, and contemplation may be performed while surfing the Web, the rituals themselves remain offline. One sends a fee, presumably by an electronic credit transaction, or fills in a form, and the ritual is performed at the physical temple in faraway India or at the Wall in Jerusalem. This may be a transformative experience for believers who use the Web to perform a devotional ritual, but there is an evident importance attached to the physical space, the lighting of a fire in the actual temple, or the paper stuffed into the crack in the Wall. It is a considerable leap from this to what we may consider the next step: the cyber-temple, the virtual Jerusalem, where cyberspace is itself the location of pilgrimage and the focal point of devotion. Is it possible to imagine that Jewish people could ever come to accept and practise a purely virtual enactment of this ritual? Isn't the physicality of the place itself something that cannot be dispensed with? How could a cyber-temple ever replace the actual wall of the real one?

And yet . . . I know one observant Jew, a friend with whom I have visited Jerusalem, who refuses to pray at the Western Wall. He believes that the fixation on the architectural remains of the ancient temple represents a kind of idolatry, a fetishization of the physical accoutrements of worship that diverts attention from the Divine. He might, perhaps, be attracted to the idea of a virtual temple, which conceivably could focus the attention in a different way from a two-thousand-year-old pile of dusty rocks. This may be farfetched. But it is possible to conceive of a 'virtual Jerusalem' that is the site of a very different kind of pilgrimage and prayer from those that are now conducted. And it may be that such a development could provide something in the psychic economy of world religions that would operate as a counter-force to those who seek to gain control of sacred grounds by means of military force, whether in Jerusalem or Ayodhya.

I hold this out as an imagined possibility, a potential, a vision of what may happen as we see more attempts to sacralize portions of cyberspace. I am not, however, sanguine about the prospects for building the New Jerusalem in the virtual realm, at least not in the near future. Given the intensity of political and religious conflicts over sacred space in Israel (between Jews and Muslims) and in India (between Muslims and Hindus), it seems much more likely that the primary uses of the global Internet will be to fan the flames of religious hatred. Finally, the designers of online worship are nowhere near close to exploiting the latent capabilities of the World Wide Web, as it now exists. The state of the art in virtual religion will have to become considerably more sophisticated in its presentation of the visual, aural, and symbolic dimensions of religion to create a serious experience of the virtual sacred.

Let us assume, however, that further steps will be taken in this direction, that as a new generation comes of age for whom the Web is a fully natural-ized symbolic environment, we will see artists, designers, and worship leaders collaborating to extend religion further into the digital realm. What will happen to our spiritual senses when the next step is taken, i.e. when rituals are performed purely in the realm of the virtual? We may lose the smell of the flowers or the smoke in the ritual fire offering, but will the ritual necessarily be any less efficacious for its practitioners if the flowers are cyber-flowers and the flames are cyber-flames? And if the full sensory experience of the ritual is diminished by its reduction to the text, sound, and imagery now possible on the Web (I don't think we're ready for networked smell-o-vision), what in turn may be gained by working within these limitations, and what are the possibilities for transcending them?

The physical sign and the spiritual signified

For a sense of what can be done to design a virtual space in which ritual can take place, it may be more useful to examine the world of computer games than religious websites. Although most of the products of the multi-billion-dollar computer game industry are relatively trivial, often focusing on little more than mind-numbing violence, the sheer volume of investment in the creation of virtual realities is staggering, and has produced some interesting experiments. In games such as 'Myst' and 'Black and White' we find sophis-ticated visual landscapes and an enveloping sense of place in which it is not too difficult to imagine ritual action. Many children have spent weeks exploring the world of the 'Harry Potter' computer game. As they have found their way through the mysterious building and grounds of the Hogwarts School for Witchcraft and Wizardry, they have solved puzzles, mixed magical potions, and cast spells. The virtual environment of this game is highly detailed and realistic, calling to mind a sort of Gothic cathedral/labyrinth. As I watched my own children (or rather, their game avatars) enter virtual chambers lit by torchlight in order to struggle against the magic of the evil Lord Voldemort in this game, I was struck by how similar the world of the game was to a temple or church, and by how little of this sort of sophisticated design can be found in web pages devoted to online religion.

Of course, such games require millions of dollars in development costs, and are a decidedly commercial enterprise. So far, no church or religious organization at least to my knowledge has seen fit to make this kind of massive economic investment. Yet computer games do offer an indication of what online religion could become with the right designers, motives, and resources. As one game designer puts it, 'Religion and games . . . may seem like strange bedfellows. But they have more than a little in common' (Cameron 1997).

Even if such a fusion of religion and virtual reality does take place (and again, I do not predict this any time soon), the limitations of the medium present serious obstacles. I do not believe that any cyber-ritual – even one that makes full use of the latent capabilities of current Internet technology – will ever be able to replace ritual performance in a physical sacred space. Even with the best graphics, sound, and three-dimensional simulations, the participant in such rituals remains too much of a spectator, separated from the virtual space by the box on the desk. As one observer, a game designer whose credits include lead design on 'The Sims Online', has put it, 'No matter how good the graphics, it's still peering through the keyhole of the computer screen into another room where the ritual takes place, rather than being in the room. With online rituals we are still at arms-length from the sacred space' (Michael Sellers, personal communication, 7 July 2002).

While sceptical about the future of virtual ritual, this man nevertheless went on to offer a reflection on the physical nature of religious experience that may prove relevant. Recalling mosaic labyrinths on the floor of medieval cathedrals (which were meant to serve as a symbolic enactment of pilgrimage to Jerusalem), he suggests more expansive possibilities for religious enactment (Michael Sellers, personal communication, 7 July 2002):

> While the physicality of walking the labyrinth path embedded in the floor of the Cathedral was entirely different from that of the actual journey to Jerusalem, for many worshippers it nevertheless brings a significant sense of peace, spirituality, and inspiration. It is a spiritually acceptable substitute for the actual journey – not because of the distance traversed, the physicality, but because of the changes brought about on the inside of the pilgrim . . . This leads me to recall that the physicality of sacred

ritual is only the sign, not the thing signified, which means that we may be able to find other signs, other experiences, that lead the mind and spirit to similar signified realities.

I think that this – the relationship between the physical sign and the spiritual signified – is the crux of the issue that will have to be debated and resolved by those who wish to lead a significant portion of their religious lives online. Some will refuse to accept the absolute separation of signifier and signified; Catholic theology, in particular, holds that in the sacrament of the Eucharist the signifier (bread and wine) becomes that which it represents (the body and blood of Jesus). For this reason, the Catholic Church is not likely to ever admit the validity of virtual sacraments. But for those whose religious observance does not include Eucharistic devotion, or for whom the physical elements of ritual and sacrament are nothing more than arbitrary signifiers, there are still a multitude of possibilities to be explored. If there is any possibility of an auspicious alignment of cultural, spiritual, and economic forces, the coming decades may yet reveal some interesting experimental collaborations between web designers, theologians, and worship leaders.

Millennial hopes and the microchip

In this section I want to consider the utopian – and even apocalyptic – implications of the computer revolution, and to conclude with a reconsideration of the cyborg as an emblematic figure of religious transformation. I begin by noting that my focus in the study of religious communication has from early on been the discourse of millennial and apocalyptic movements. My first book, a study of Christian apocalyptic rhetoric, paid scant attention to questions related to technology. Some time after this book was published, and after my two essays on religion and CMC came out, I discovered a book by David Noble called *The Religion of Technology* (Noble 1999). This book makes what is to my mind a persuasive case for the thesis that the origins of technological innovation in Western societies lie in a millennial hope for the transformation of the world. If Noble is correct in arguing that the project of Western technological development was motivated in large part by the ancient hope of a miraculous regeneration of society according to a divinely ordained prophetic plan, then we must sit up and take notice. For it is a truism that the millennial prophecies of past ages have all been disappointed, that the aspirations of prophetic dreamers through the ages have forced us, time and again, to confront the disparity between hope and reality.

Perhaps one measure of our maturity is the degree to which we can accept the perpetual disappointment of our millennial dreams. With this principle in mind, let us re-examine the millennial aspects of our contemporary fascination with computer technology. First, and most obviously, there is the way that Christians have interpreted technological innovations, from Gutenberg to the Internet, as providing an opportunity for the fulfilment of the 'Great Commission'. At several points in the canonical scriptures, Jesus enjoins his disciples to preach the gospel to the ends of the earth. This commandment is explicitly linked to the 'Last Days' passage in Matthew 24:14, that reads as follows in the King James Version: 'And this gospel of the Kingdom shall be preached in all the world for a witness unto the nations: And then shall the end come.' It is surely significant that Christians have interpreted any new advancement of communication technology as a fulfilment of this prophecy. The printing press, no less than the Internet, was seen in its time as both a compelling sign of the completion of the 'Great Commission' and the advent of the 'Last Days', and as an instrumental tool for the completion of the divine plan.

With regard to the idea that communication technology allows for the completion of the Great Commission, it is enough for this sceptical scholar of millennialism to note that the media-saturated cultures of the industrialized West are still not the norm. Pockets of aboriginal and non-literate peoples still remain; printing, television, and the Internet are still out of the reach of millions, and (given current global economic configurations) are likely to remain so for decades if not centuries. As well, the fundamentalist backlash against the modernization of mass-mediated industrial society will continue to be a powerful force for the foreseeable future.

Nevertheless, the millennial dream that communication will transform the world continues to have force. Consider the following prophecy from media theorist Marshall McLuhan: 'The computer . . . holds out the promise of a technologically engendered state of universal understanding and unity, a state of absorption in the logos that could knit mankind into one family and create a perpetuity of collective harmony and peace' (McLuhan and Zingrone 1995: 262). These words, which eerily anticipate the claims made for the Internet by a variety of technological enthusiasts, were uttered in McLuhan's famous *Playboy* interview, at the end of the transformative decade of the 1960s. The chronology is important, for it indicates a certain prescient mysticism that was typical of that era. In hindsight, however, I agree that the promise remains viable, but the reality will be somewhat problematic. The potential to realize McLuhan's vision may be there, implicit in the technology, but I believe it will take more than the technological capability to make this dream a reality. Osama bin Laden and his associates seem to be adept in the uses of technology, but evidently have little interest in the project of knitting humanity into one family and creating a perpetual collective harmony.

My last example of the millennial hope driving the computer revolution comes from Nicholas Negroponte. Author of the cyber-manifesto *Being Digital* from 1995, columnist for *Wired* magazine, and director of the MIT Media Lab, Negroponte was one of the chief cheerleaders of the technological boom of the 1990s. In a 1997 lecture presented as part of the Millennium series at the Getty Institute in Los Angeles, Negroponte said that, with the aid of computer technology, 'I actually believe you will see things like world peace through better communications'. Speaking of medical uses of the microchip, he went on to say that within the next three decades, 'the deaf will hear and . . . the blind will see' (Negroponte 1997). What makes me interested here are the explicit parallels to religious source material that invoke (whether consciously or unconsciously) the language of millennial prophecy. The coming of the messianic kingdom is predicted in Isaiah 35:5–6: 'Then the eyes of the blind shall be opened, and the ears of the deaf shall be unstopped' (see also Matthew 11:4–5).

Perhaps Negroponte is correct. Maybe computer technology will truly bring about the messianic miracles. But I'm not holding my breath for these things to happen – and even if they do come to pass, I believe that there are critical questions that must be asked.

What Negroponte's vision requires of us is that we accept and integrate computer technology into our physical selves – that we become cyborgs. What will become of humanity as we evolve into such cyborg creatures of the future? The technological imperative is pushing us into a redefinition of humanity. What begins as an incremental improvement – sight for the blind, hearing for the deaf, and ('the lame shall walk') locomotion for the paralysed – will inevitably turn into a fundamental mutation of human being. If I endorsed the cyborg in my earlier essay as 'a fascinating and desirable addition to human community', I must now stand back and ask, what will we have lost when the transition to the cyborg self is completed? What will we gain, and what will we give up, as we allow ourselves to be implanted with chips that will improve vision, enable hearing, and ultimately allow unprecedented extensions of the human lifespan?

Conclusion: the cyborg body in the new millennium

The January 2000 issue of *Wired* may be an indication of where we are heading – or of where certain forces want to take us. This issue of the magazine, which appeared in the wake of the deflated fears of the apocalyptic catastrophes that would supposedly result from the Y2K computer bug, led us to believe that we will (within the next century or so) be able to extend the human lifespan to 150–200 years – and ultimately, perhaps, indefinitely. Author Brian Alexander writes that 'A growing number of scientists agree that humans are poised for a breakthrough in longevity and what might be called "human reparability" – a new era that will not only raise the maximum age, but also deliver unimaginable new methods for preserving and even redesigning our own bodies' (Alexander 2000). This type of computer-engineered life extension may lead to a technological 'denial of death' – to use Ernst Becker's (1997) famous phrase – that reduces all previous efforts in this regard to insignificance.

I suspect that along with life extension, the move towards the cyborg body will also involve significant efforts to remove the final barriers between the world of virtual reality and direct sensory experience. The logical extension of the quest for experience that is both virtual and 'real' is to eliminate the computer screen and plug human brains directly into cyberspace, with electronic attachments wired straight into the human skull. This vision, which was first presented decades ago in Aldous Huxley's classic dystopian novel *Brave New World*, may actually be not far from developments in the near or distant future. A popular variant of this virtual-reality fantasy has been articulated in some of the fictions, which inspire current cyber-advocates such as Neil Stephenson's influential novel *Snow Crash* (2000) and William Gibson's famous *Neuromancer* (1995). While such innovations (which would tend to eliminate the barrier between the virtual and the 'real') may be technologically feasible, I cannot help but think that they would involve too great a sacrifice. If acceptance of a wired connection directly into the brain is the price we will have to pay for experiencing 'virtual' reality as indistinct from the 'real,' then I for one will opt out of this future. I don't want to live beyond a normal human lifespan (though I may change my mind as I approach my seventh and eighth decades), and I'd rather maintain the distinction between the world of sensual experience and the virtual world.

In sum, my attention to the millennial and apocalyptic aspects of computer technology has fostered a profound scepticism about the claims now being made for the brave new world that is supposedly coming into being. McLuhan, Negroponte, and *Wired* magazine have promised us in different ways that technology will bring the oneness of humanity, collective harmony and peace, the extension of life, or the promise of avoiding death in a perpetually regenerated body. I think we have good reason to doubt that these millennial dreams are capable of fulfilment, or that we should pursue them even if they are feasible. Whether online religion will have a viable future for humans who choose to resist the temptations offered by the cyborg remains to be seen.

Note

1   For an introduction to the various cultural products that feature the cyborg and to the literature these have spawned see for instance Brasher (2001: 140–159), Featherstone and Burrows (1995), and Gray (1995).

References

Alexander, B. (2000) 'Don't Die, Stay Pretty', *Wired Magazine*, available: http://www.wired.com/wired/archive/8.01/forever.html [Accessed 1 August 2002].
Becker, E. (1997) *The Denial of Death*, New York: The Free Press.
Brasher, B. (2001) *Give Me That Online Religion*, San Francisco: Jossey-Bass.

Cameron, C. (1997) 'Games Lamas Play', available: http://home.earthlink.net/
~hipbone/ GameLama.html [Accessed 1 August 2002].

Featherstone, Mike and Burrows, Roger (eds) (1995) *Cyberspace/Cyberbodies/
Cyberpunk*, London: Sage Publications.

Gibson, W. (1995) *Neuromancer*, New York: Ace Books.

Gray, C.H. (ed.) (1995) *The Cyborg Handbook*, New York: Routledge.

Haraway, D. (1991) 'A Cyborg Manifesto: Science, Technology, and Socialist-
Feminism in the Late Twentieth Century', in Haraway, D. (ed.) *Simians, Cyborgs,
and Women: The Reinvention of Nature*, New York: Routledge, pp. 149–181.

Henderson, C. (2002) 'Sanctuary', available: http://www.godweb.org/sanct.html
#prayers [The website was launched in 1994; the actual page was accessed on
1 August 2002].

McLuhan, E. and Zingrone, F. (eds) (1995) *The Essential McLuhan*, New York: Basic
Books.

Negroponte, N. (1997) 'Being Global', Lecture at the Getty Institute, Los Angeles,
available: http://www.mit.edu:8001/people/davis/NegroponteLec.html [Accessed
1 August 2002].

Noble, D.F. (1999) *The Religion of Technology: The Divinity of Man and the Spirit
of Invention*, New York: Penguin.

O'Leary, S.D. (1996) 'Cyberspace as Sacred Space: Communication Religion on
Computer Networks', *Journal of the American Academy of Religion*, 64 (4):
781–808.

O'Leary, S.D. and Brasher, B. (1996) 'The Unknown God of the Internet: Religious
Communication from the Ancient Agora to the Virtual Forum', in Ess, C. (ed.)
Philosophical Perspectives on Computer-Mediated Communication, Albany: State
University of New York Press, pp. 233–269.

Online Hindu Temple Services (2002) Available: http://www.prarthana.com/
[Accessed 1 August 2002].

Peachtree Presbyterian Church (2002) Available: http://www.peachtreepres.org/
[Accessed 1 August 2002].

Sinovess (2002) Official Site for Online Wiccan Rituals, available: http://www.
angelfire.com/folk/wiccasinovess/Main2.html [Accessed 1 August 2002].

Stephenson, N. (2000) *Snow Crash*, New York: Bantam Doubleday Dell.

Tornopsky, A.J. (2001) 'A Prayer at the Western Wall', available: http://www.
shemayisrael.co.il/kotel/ [Accessed 1 August 2002].

Chapter 4

Cyber-religion

On the cutting edge between the virtual and the real

Morten T. Højsgaard

One of the new words that have been brought into the study of religion in contemporary society along with the emergence of cyberspace is 'cyber-religion'. The point of this chapter is exactly to address and discuss key questions that relate theoretically as well as empirically to this new issue, concept, or phenomenon of 'cyber-religion'. Does the Internet generate religion? If so, what are the characteristics of the sort of religion that stems from or has its primary location in cyberspace? What is, in fact, a 'cyber-religion', and how is it distinguishable from other types of religion and cyber cultural communication? These are the key questions that the following conceptual delineations, phenomenological juxtapositions, and case studies will focus on.

Conceptualizing 'cyber-religion'

As a concept, 'cyber-religion' has been defined in various ways since the academic study of the relations between religion and cyberspace was initiated in the mid-1990s. Some scholars have used the concept in a very general sense to describe *any* kind of religion that is mediated via the Internet. An example of this all-embracing approach is Brenda Brasher's (2001: 29) definition of the term. 'At its most basic', she states, 'cyber-*religion* refers to the presence of religious organizations and religious activities in' cyberspace. Other analysts have perceived the phenomenon in more specific or exclusive ways. Lorne L. Dawson (2000: 29), for instance, reserves the expression 'cyber-religion' to those 'religious organizations or groups that exist *only* in cyberspace'. Anastasia Karaflogka in turn has coined the phrases 'religion *on* cyberspace' and 'religion *in* cyberspace' in order to distinguish, at least discursively, between the diverse perceptions of 'cyber-religion'.

'Religion *on* cyberspace' in Karaflogka's terminology thus refers to 'the information uploaded by *any* religion, church, individual or organisation, which also exists and can be reached in the off-line world' (Karaflogka 2002: 284–285, emphasis added). Contrarily, 'religion *in* cyberspace' refers to religion 'which is created and exists exclusively in cyberspace, where it enjoys a considerable degree of "virtual reality"' (Karaflogka 2002: 285; see also Thursby 2003). In the first case, the primary function of the Internet is to mediate information on religious contents and activities that has already been established or defined by various religious traditions outside cyberspace. In the second case, the Internet rather functions as a creative or formative environment fostering new religious contents and activities online. In between the all-embracing 'religion *on* cyberspace' and the exclusive 'religion *in* cyberspace', Karaflogka then puts such intermediate phenomena as cyber-churches and cyber-synagogues, which contentwise belong to well-established religious traditions, but formwise are closely tied up with the new interactive and user-oriented reality of cyberspace (Karaflogka 2002: 284–286; see also Maxwell 2002: 349–350).

Materializing 'cyber-religion'

It has been estimated that there are more than one million single web pages with a religious content on the Internet (Beckerlegge 2001: 224, Dawson 2000: 28, Helland 2000: 206, and table 4.1 on p. 53 below). Anastasia Karaflogka's distinction between religion *on* and religion *in* cyberspace undoubtedly represents an achievement, when it comes to systematizing this vast amount of religious material on the World Wide Web. From an epistemological point of view her perception of 'cyber-religion' as something that *exists exclusively* in cyberspace, however, is problematic. To be more precise, the epistemologically questionable presupposition of her definition is the idea that religions may have an essence or existence on their own independent of human existence, and this presupposition does not seem to fit very well with the tradition within the secular study of religion of perceiving religions as synthetic constructs of human thoughts, acts, organizations, etc. (Arnal 2000: 22). Following this line of thought, religions are only located or mediated (not existing) in cyberspace because 'somebody at some stage did something', i.e. started the communication, set up the programme, designed the web page, bought the server, or moderated the listserv, just to mention a few of the possibilities. Accordingly, a genuine example of a religion that has been set up in cyberspace without at least the initial interference of a human being remains to be seen (Brasher 2001: 30). The allegedly pure cyber-religious sites *are* being produced and used by persons who do not live their entire lives 'on the screen'.

In spite of these epistemological objections, 'cyber-religion' in factual praxis has become a distinct part of the vast field of digital communication that humans design, participate in, and relate to at the beginning of the twenty-first century. An articulate demonstration of this is the references to websites with a specific cyber-religious linkage in various indexes of religion online that can be found both in print (e.g. Bunt 2001: 124) and on the Internet (e.g. Thursby 2003; Yahoo! 2003). In table 4.1 a number of such indexed websites with a cyber-religious affiliation are summarized. The table contains tentative figures for how long these websites have been present on the Internet. These figures are based on data from an international web archive. Moreover, the table includes exploratory data on the dispersion degree of the cyber-religious sites in 2003. The dispersion degree is measured in this case by an aggregated number of links on external web pages referring to the indexed cyber-religious sites. All these figures and data are intended to provide an overview of the materials that have been consulted during the preparations for and the analyses included in this chapter.

Now, based on comparative examinations of the listed cyber-religious websites (table 4.1) and reconsiderations of the conceptual framework set up by Lorne L. Dawson, and Anastasia Karaflogka among others, I shall continue my explorations of 'cyber-religion' by presenting a model of the cyber-religious field at large. Following that, I shall report the findings of a more specific study of one of the cyber-religions listed in table 4.1, namely Digitalism. This religion has been selected for this investigation because it comes very close to manifesting all the central characteristics of 'cyber-religion' as presented both within the conceptual framework above and within the larger model of the cyber-religious field that will be presented below.

Modelling 'cyber-religion'

The religious sites that are listed in table 4.1 all seem to have their primary location in cyberspace. In this way they all qualify for the exclusive designation or interpretation of 'cyber-religion' that has been put forward by Dawson and Karaflogka. When it comes to the question of how to distinguish 'cyber-religions' from other types of religion and cyber cultural communication, the issue of location alone, however, does not seem to provide sufficient analytical tools for comprehending the phenomenon in a satisfactory way. In order to reach a more comprehensive understanding of the cyber-religious field at large, I propose a model with three analytical parameters or dimensions by which I can assess the degree to which a religion could be characterized as a 'cyber-religion'. These three parameters are mediation, content, and organization (see fig. 4.1).

The mediation parameter of this model of the cyber-religious field to some extent parallels the issue of location as raised by Karaflogka. Thus, the mediation dimension spreads from 'virtual communication' at the centre of the model to 'body-centred communication' at the periphery. As we have seen, the prototypical 'cyber-religion' is mediated exactly through virtual communication *in* cyberspace. Contrarily, some traditional types of religions (some of which are not even present *on* cyberspace yet) are mediated primarily through body-centred communication *outside* cyberspace during religious services, rituals, meetings, conversations, etc. In between these opposite positions, we find a number of intermediate, entwined, and parallel

Table 4.1 Selected websites with a cyber-religious affiliation

Name and URL[1]	On the Internet at least since[2]	Dispersion degree[3]
Church of the Subgenius http://www.subgenius.com/	3 December 1998	46,781
Church of Virus http://virus.lucifer.com/	10 June 1998	10,376
Cyber-Voodoo http://www.cyber-voodoo.com/	24 January 2001	13
Deify Yourself! http://www.tftb.com/deify/	17 August 2000	202
Digitalism http://digitalism.8m.com/	3 November 1999	60
HyperDiscordia http://jubal.westnet.com/hyperdiscordia/	23 March 1997	9,800
Kibology http://www.kibo.com/	3 December 1998	4,582
Kemetic Orthodoxy http://www.kemet.org/home.html	25 December 2001	148
Reconnecting.CALM http://www.reconnecting.com/	30 December 1996	324
Technosophy http://www.technosophy.com/	1 December 1996	533
SpiriTech Virtual Foundation www.geocities.com/~spiritechuk/	21 February 1999	171
The New House http://thenewhouse.org/	3 December 1998	184
Virtual Church of Blind Chihuahua http://www.dogchurch.org/	5 December 1998	4,284

Notes
1 The names and web addresses are based on Bunt (2001), Thursby (2003), Yahoo! (2003), and selected results of searches conducted on 10–12 August 2002 on combinations of 'cyber', 'virtual', 'religion', and 'religiosity' at www.google.com.
2 Some of the sites contain information on the time of their first appearance on the Internet, but it has not been possible to verify this information in a consistent way, and for that reason all the dates are based on comparable searches only in 'The Internet Archive' (www.archive.org) containing data from 1 January 1996 up to the present.
3 Based on data from the 'Link Popularity Check' application on www.marketleap.com. The data in each cell of this column represent an aggregated number of links to the indexed cyber-religious sites registered in the search engines 'Alltheweb', 'Alta Vista', 'Google' (AOL), 'HotBot' (Inktomi), and 'MSN' on 1 October 2003.

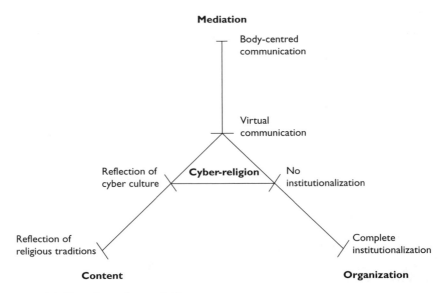

Figure 4.1 The cyber-religious field.

communicative systems at work in most religions (cf. books, booklets, letters, radio programmes, television sets, videos, telephones, etc.).

As suggested above, the mediation parameter, however, cannot function as the *sole* criterion for defining (or the *single* way of describing) the characteristics of 'cyber-religion'. The content as such is of great importance as well. In this connection, a remarkable trait that can be found on many cyber-religious sites is the continual attempts to oppose or to provide alternatives to central ideas of major religious organizations and traditions. Many cyber-religions are thus also deliberately satirical about the worldviews and belief systems of such established religions as Judaism, Christianity, and Islam. Accordingly, the deity of the Church of the Subgenius is not a metaphysical entity, but a pipe-smoking middle-class American called Bob (www.sub genius.com). Likewise, the saint of the Church of Virus since 1996 has been the founder of the evolution theory, Charles Darwin (see Sørensen 2002 and http://virus.lucifer.com/saints.html). At another web page related to Kibology, the content or beliefs of this movement are presented as a matter for public decision brought about through a 'scienterrific' electronic survey analysis (www.kibo.com/survey/survey-2.shtml). 'You may bring your dogma, but only if it doesn't bite', an entry message pronounces on yet another cyber-religious website (www.dogchurch.org), and the first part of the statements of beliefs at the same site reads: 'I believe that the members of the Virtual Church of Blind Chihuahua believe all kinds of different things' (www.dogchurch.org/indexfrm.html).

Traditional religious figures such as Moses, Jesus, and Allah in most cases thus have no high standing within cyber-religious Web presentations. Rather, fascination with technology, role-playing, satire, relativistic identity constructions, experiments, and imitations, as well as an outspoken antipathy towards existing religious credos, rituals, myths, and ethical codes, prevail (Beaudoin 1998: 146; Dawson and Hennebry 1999: 35; Karaflogka 2002: 285). 'There is no single factor in human life more important than technology', a precept of the cyber-religion Technosophy reads, 'and yet most users have little or no idea of how technologies work or even that their own bodies are sophisticated collections of technological systems' (http://www. technosophy.com/precepts.html). In short, the core content of the cyber-religious field seems to resemble the dynamic, fluid, user-oriented, technology-driven, and anti-hierarchical culture of cyberspace itself, whereas typical representatives of established religious traditions would tend to be rather sceptical towards what they might perceive as a pop-oriented, postmodern, secular, or even susceptible cyber culture. The content dimension of the cyber-religious field model reflects these opposite points of view by placing the 'reflection of cyber culture' at the centre of the field and the 'reflection of religious traditions' at the periphery.

The last parameter of the cyber-religious field model has to do with organizational matters. This parameter spreads from 'no institutionalization' at the centre of the model to 'complete institutionalization' at the periphery. A significant point here is that the authors on most cyber-religious sites seem to subscribe to the idea that their religions are *not* seriously institutionalized. 'Organized religion tames the idea of God to support its existence and to affirm its cultural milieu', J.A.H. Futterman (from the Virtual Church of the Blind Chihuahua) critically asserts (www.dogchurch.org/indexfrm.html). Accordingly, many proponents of 'virtual religiosity' have been reported to oppose what they perceive as the static features – traditionalism, conservatism, economic bureaucracy, anti-idealism – of the large organized religions in the offline world (Beaudoin 1998: 145–155). 'Any religion that relies on ecclesial authority and hierarchy, as well as on sacraments, is going to have a hard go on the Net', proclaimed Jeff Zaleski (1997: 100) in his influential book *The Soul of Cyberspace*. Relying first and foremost upon the voluntary engagement of individuals more or less fortuitously coming across their sites, the designers of cyber-religions seem to be focusing primarily on transmission and testing of ideas and thoughts rather than promotion of sacral institutions, hierarchies, or sacraments.

Despite the widespread idea of anti-institutionalization within the cyber-religious environments, a number of the cyber-religions that have had active followers for some years now appear to be starting to institutionalize. In Kibology and Church of Virus, for instance, a stable communication culture and the somewhat persistent profile of the participants in the discussions have developed in relation to news groups such as alt.religion.kibology, alt.

religion.kibology.orthodox, and alt.religion. kibology.second-coming as well as on various so-called virian email lists (see Sørensen 2002). The founder of the Church of the Subgenius, after all, earns a living by selling anti-religious goods via the Internet (Ringgård 2002). And on the Deify Yourself! site the editor boasts of the fact that the site is updated once a week (www.tftb.com/deify). All those activities and features do require some degree of logistics, organization, or institutionalization, and therefore, as time goes by, one might expect that at least some of the cyber-religions that succeed in attracting the interest of Web users may turn into more and more complex, hierarchically structured institutions.[1] Following this line of argumentation, the kind of Internet-mediated religion that would come closest to being located solely in the virtual realm of cyberspace would be a 'cyber-religion' that did *not* succeed in attracting human followers and thus eventually was put down, forgotten, or erased by all – except on the hardware memories of some international Internet archives.

In sum, the prototypical 'cyber-religion' is mediated or located primarily in cyberspace, its contents reflect the main features of the postmodern cyber culture, and it is only sparingly organized as well. Within the cyber-religious environment at large there is solid opposition towards traditionally structured religious institutions, but still 'cyber-religion' as such addresses the same type of questions about legitimations of ethics and the meaning of life and death that are habitually designated as belonging to the religious field. Accordingly, the cyber-religious jokes about, peculiar imitations of, and opposition towards conformist religion in contemporary society can be hard to distinguish structurally from other religious trends or expressions in postmodern society. Some of these trends or expressions of the religious landscape within contemporary society have been summarized by sociologist of religion Yves Lambert (1999) as 'this-worldliness, self-spirituality, dehierarchisation and dedualization, parascientificity, pluralistic, relativistic, fluctuating, seeking faiths, and loose network-type organizations (indeed, religion without religion)'. Many of the core characteristics of the cyber-religious field that have been presented and discussed above seem to be covered by these keywords. In any case, an apt example of these demarcations of the cyber-religious field can be found on the particular website of Digitalism.

Exemplifying 'cyber-religion'

The first version of the Digitalism website that was stored at The Internet Archive (www.archive.org) is dated 3 November 1999 (see table 4.1). According to this version of the site, Digitalism was founded in 1995 by a person called Peter Holmgren, and the website was set up in 1998 (see http://web.archive.org/web/19991103010131/http://digitalism.8m.com/). According to the following accessible versions of the site in The Internet Archive, the Digitalism website, however, was made already in 1996, and

it was last modified on 23 May 2000 (see, for instance, http://web.archive.
org/web/20010202031200/http://digitalism.8m.com/). I will use this latest
version of the site, which can be found outside the archive as well (at http://
digitalism.8m.com), as the primary basis for the following analysis. The
domain name of Digitalism as such is commercial (it ends .com), but the
content of the site mainly addresses topics that are 'free of charge' and have
more or less obvious religious connotations as well, such as 'creation', 'life
itself', 'death', 'unity', 'occultism', 'Armageddon', and 'God'. The more
detailed explanations and interpretations given at the site on these topics,
however, are not obviously religious.

'There are no mysteries in Digitalism. Only facts and answers', a central
sentence reads at the Digitalism website (http://digitalism.8m.com). 'The rules
that exist are only rules made by humans through history', it is declared in
another sentence, and in the Q and A (question and answer) section of the
site, the answer to the subject area entitled 'God' simply is: 'This page is under
construction' (http://digitalism.8m.com/cgi-bin/framed/2141/quefram.htm).
By and large, there is a peculiar mixture of demythologization, rational thinking, pragmatic philosophy, and utilitarian ethics involved in the Digitalism
web project. 'And to coexist with each other,' an argument on the site, for
instance, goes, 'we need a set of rules. But we shouldn't state that some
rules are more righteous than others. Rules and laws are merely a concept
to protect us from ourselves. We feel that kindness, compassion and love are
what can serve mankind best' (http://digitalism.8m.com).

Graphically the website (still referring to the latest version updated in
2000) seems to be inspired by science fiction. The background colour is black.
The texture and the icons are harsh green. Endless combinations of the
computer basic digits one and zero make up the background. The audio
material on the site is techno-oriented and computer-fashioned. And in the
link section there are eighteen references to other websites on how to design
and produce virtual reality applications, while there are no links to any
traditional religious groupings or institutions whatsoever.

So, were it not for the initial headlines and demarcations of topics such
as creation, life itself, and God, the average reader or the user of the site
would hardly think of describing this website as a religious one at first sight.
None the less, if we take a closer look at the ways in which the virtual reality
components are employed on the website, there seems to be a sort of
metaphysical aspect to it. 'You, as a person, is [sic] now on level 1', the introduction to the philosophy of Digitalism states, and it goes on: 'When you
enter VR [Virtual Reality] you will enter level 0. The question is now; is there
a level 2?' (http://digitalism.8m.com). In other words: The life you are living
now as a person can be compared to level 1 in a computer game or a virtual
reality simulation. When you die, the game or the simulation is over: 'Death
is only a return to the body itself. A return to the real life' (http://digitalism.
8m.com). This condition is level 0 at the outset, but when you understand

or perhaps accept this, you might be able to go through to level 2 or even higher. Hence, Digitalism seemingly retells or reinterprets the classical Buddhist teachings of *samsara* or reincarnation.

Once this line of thought is perceived, the vast amount of virtual reality links and features on the site suddenly make more sense: for the virtual reality applications can thus possibly be interpreted as a new set of religious tools, a new religious means of heightening the awareness among potential followers of the fact that life is a virtual reality game, and death is only the beginning of the real reality. The neutral or even secular digital technology in this manner becomes an integral part of a reflective process of re-enchantment or virtualization of the material world and vice versa. The virtual becomes real, and this reality of the virtual in turn is interpreted as the ideal. The 'new science of digitalism says that the universe itself is the ultimate computer – actually the only computer', Kevin Kelly (2002: 182) wrote, on the interplay between computing and metaphysics within contemporary society.

This interpretation of the religious content of the Digitalism website is supported by background information on Peter Holmgren, the founder of the 'cyber-religion', that can be found at the 'old' version of the site. In this version of the site from the late 1990s, the author thus admits (http://web. archive.org/web/19991103010131/http://digitalism.8m.com/):

> The first faint thoughts of Digitalism was [*sic*] born in 1983. It started with a Buddhistic [*sic*] equation: A man woke up one morning. He remembered being a butterfly in his dream. He then asked himself the question: 'Am I the butterfly dreaming that it's a man or did I dream I was a butterfly?' This was so inspirering [*sic*] for Peter Holmgren, that he started looking at the world with a completely renewed Attitude.

What at the outset looked like a new type of religiosity, with the cyber culture and the computer world at its centre, in this way turns out to be rather a re-invention of a central religious tradition. Accordingly the sources of inspiration for the epistemological theme in Digitalism concerning the reality of the real seem to be much older than the world of digital communication in which and by which that theme is mediated.

Interfering with 'cyber-religion'

Now, what about those 2.4 million members worldwide that the latest version of the Digitalism website claims? Are they virtual entities or real persons? Is the number just a joke, a fake, or is it a sensible figure?

Unfortunately, I cannot provide a definite answer. It is easy to become a member. You just have to press a button. And after you have pressed this button, there is in fact no button to press if you do not want to be a member any longer. Furthermore, there are no restrictions tied up with being a member of Digitalism (http://digitalism.8m.com):

> We don't ask you to do anything special but to relax and be yourself. You don't need to pray or do special things every day. Your existence and search for your truth is enough for us. Enjoy what you have and be happy about the little things that happen to you. The more details you uncover in life, the nearer you are to the truth. We discovered that life is so much easier to live if you bring joy, happiness and compassion to your surroundings. It's up to you . . .

The version of the site that was stored on 3 November 1999 moreover contains the message that 'Digitalism . . . is fast growing. By now there are almost 120.000 members World Wide' (http://web.archive.org/web/199911 03010131/http://digitalism.8m.com/). According to the Danish journalist Allan Wahlers (2000: 53), this number had grown to 532,000 members at some stage in 2000, and in 2003 the figure was as high as 2.4 million. These are some of the observations that might support the idea of perceiving the membership figure as sensible at least to some extent.

The fact that the number of members worldwide has been fixed at least since 7 October 2000 (http://web.archive.org/web/20001007040809/ http://digitalism.8m.com/) indicates that the issue should not be taken too seriously. In order to test what would happen with the membership figure, if the membership form was filled in and sent out, I decided to test the case on 13 February 2001. As an academic trying to be objective I was not fond of filling in the form with my own name. So I decided to make Santa Claus, aged 99 and with the email address santa@e-box.dk, a member of Digitalism. It turned out to be no problem submitting the form, but nothing happened to the membership figure. Afterwards, however, I was struck by the thought that without being really aware of it, I had in fact become quite involved in the reality game, the epistemological conundrum, of Digitalism: I pressed the button on this specific date. I reinvented the name of Santa Claus for this occasion. Being deeply curious, I must admit that I really wanted to see this digital membership ritual being performed as well. But still, I did not think of my subsequent action as really being my own. I have not finished pondering on why this was so, but the process convinced me that 2.4 million is not an exact figure of the membership. Had it been so, there would probably also be more than sixty external web pages worldwide – as is now the case – containing a link to the web address of Digitalism (see table 4.1).

Incidentally, I found out later through a short email interview with Peter Holmgren, the founder of Digitalism, that he is, in fact, Danish. Although Digitalism in principle addresses an international audience within the global cyber cultural environment, the Web designer and initiator of this 'cyber-religion' has thus got his own connections outside cyberspace to a specific country and a language spoken by no more than six million people. No matter how virtual Digitalism seems to be, it thus did not come about without some interference with material history and real-life experiences.

Contextualizing 'cyber-religion'

A notable work of art is René Magritte's painting *Ceci n'est pas une pipe* from 1926. The painting, habitually designated as belonging to the surrealistic tradition, calls into question the validity of the supposedly real by portraying a pipe in combination with the painted words 'This is not a pipe'. In a similar vein the concept of 'cyber-religion' calls into question established ideas about the authenticity of religiosity. What is it, in fact, that constitutes religion, religiosity, or religious interpretations of the real?

Considering the idea of a virtual Jerusalem, where cyberspace itself becomes the focal point of devotion and the location of pilgrimage, Stephen D. O'Leary in this volume asks:

> Is it possible to imagine that Jewish people could ever come to accept and practise a purely virtual enactment of this ritual? Isn't the physicality of the place itself something that cannot be dispensed with? How could a cyber-temple ever replace the actual wall of the real one?

Admittedly, religions whose primary locations, contents, and organizational structures are tied up with the virtuality of cyberspace are rare. Most religious communication on the Internet is *not* cyber-religious; it is rather about real people, actual places, established institutions, and so forth.

None the less, a 'cyber-religion' such as Digitalism in a quite notable manner seems to be leaving out the central question of location. It is based on virtual communication, it reflects ideas and concepts of postmodern cyber culture, and it does not seem to be institutionalized in any significant way either. As such, it does not display a substantial number of the features that are typically assigned to the major religious traditions of the world. At the same time, however, it does, as we have seen, resemble or reconstruct some aspects of a Buddhist worldview, and also, it readdresses certain questions on ethics and the meaning of life in a way that seems to have religious overtones. In this sense, Digitalism as a representative of the prototypical 'cyber-religion' might sociologically be considered a 'religion without religion' (to use the terminology of Yves Lambert) or surrealistically be labelled 'this is not a religion' (to use the phraseology of Magritte).

By ascribing such general descriptions to the cyber-religious field, the specifics or the uniqueness of the phenomenon, however, seem to wither somewhat. Representatives of the cyber-religious field themselves would probably be comfortable with being classified as new entities, as they in the main favour evolution, innovation, and free choice without any conventional constraints on the individual. But to be reasonable, cyber-religions should be seen in an appropriate context – that is in light of or in connection with the overall dynamics and transformations of religion and religiosity in contemporary society at large. And if this context is taken into account, then at least some of the newness, particularity, and (perhaps even) oddity of the cyber-religious field start to evaporate. Of course, the religious trends of the modern and postmodern world are not uniform (Berger 1999; Bruce 1996). Notorious traits of the religious landscape within contemporary society, however, reportedly are the very virtualization of religion and culture, the intensified interplay of scientific, artistic, and religious approaches to life, and the prevailing struggle between secularizing and counter-secularizing forces that the cyber-religions so exactly reflect.

John Naisbitt (2001: 13), having researched the lives of cultural leaders in the arts, in media, and in business as well as academics and theologians, describes contemporary society at large as a 'Technologically Intoxicated Zone . . . defined by the complicated and often paradoxical relationship between technology and our search for meaning'. The indicators of this state of affairs, as far as he sees it, are that people in contemporary society seem to prefer 'quick fix, from religion to nutrition . . . fear and worship technology . . . blur the distinction between real and fake . . . love technology as a toy . . . live [their] lives distanced and distracted' (Naisbitt 2001: 13).

In line with this, Mark C. Taylor, writing on the basis of analyses of art, literature, philosophy, politics, economics, and popular culture, perceives the cultural environment of contemporary society at large to be of a virtual and religious nature at once. 'Processes that have long seemed natural and relations that have long seemed material now appear to be information processes and virtual realities', Taylor (1999: 3) asserts (see also Kelly 2002: 182). 'With the inexorable expansion of various electronic technologies, all experience is mediated by tangled media networks until the hyper-reality of contemporary culture renders reality virtual', he further notes (Taylor 1999: 133). Thus, in short, to Taylor the real of the present either has proved or will prove to be virtual, and in a 'myriad ways . . . virtual culture is about religion' as well (Taylor 1999: 6).

'Modernity', explains Peter L. Berger (1999: 7) in another piece of work on the religious landscape of contemporary society, 'undermines all the old certainties; uncertainty is a condition that many people find very hard to bear; therefore, any movement (not only a religious one) that promises to provide or to renew certainty has a ready market'. Such a market might be found within leading segments of the contemporary youth culture, the Generation X, who, according to T. Beaudoin (1998), have strong preferences for the ideas and practices of virtual faith (expressed, for instance, via movies, music, sports, fantasy games, mobile phones, and computer networks) rather than the worldviews and customs of traditional religions.

Concluding 'cyber-religion'

The Internet does not generate or construct religion on its own, only people do. But while they are doing so, they make use of and they are influenced by the technological possibilities as well as the social, political, and cultural conditions of their time. In some cases, then, the communicative possibilities and conditions of the Internet have had such a remarkable impact during this process of religious construction that the type of religiosity that has come out of the process can be duly designated as 'cyber-religion'.

'Cyber-religion', at its basis, is mediated or located primarily in cyberspace, its contents reflect the main features of the postmodern cyber culture, and it is only sparingly organized as well. Within the cyber-religious environment at large there is, as we have seen, a solid opposition towards traditionally structured religious institutions; but still, 'cyber-religion' as a phenomenon addresses the same type of ontological and metaphysical questions that religious institutions and traditions have usually done.

The cyber-religious field, moreover, is characterized by such features as role-playing, identity constructions, cultural adaptability, fascination with technology, and a sarcastic approach to conformist religiosity. 'Cyber-religion' calls into question customary notions of the real and established distinctions between religion and science as well. By doing so, 'cyber-religion' seems to express or reflect some notable religious and cultural developments within contemporary society at large. These developments among other things have to do with the escalating virtualization of religion and culture, the intensifying interplay of scientific, artistic, and religious approaches to life, and the prevailing struggle between secularizing and counter-secularizing forces.

Yves Lambert in 1999 productively classified the noteworthy trends and characteristics of the religious landscape of today's world. His catch phrases and keywords, as indicated above, constitute an apt summary of the social and religious dynamics at stake within the virtual field of cyber-religiosity as well. In sum, 'cyber-religion' is thus about 'this-worldliness, self-spirituality, dehierarchisation and dedualization, parascientificity, pluralistic, relativistic, fluctuating, seeking faiths, and loose network-type organizations (indeed, religion without religion)'.

Note

1 For a parallel example and further discussion on institutionalization within new religious groupings on the Internet see the chapter by Mia Lövheim and Alf G. Linderman in this volume.

References

Arnal, W.E. (2000) 'Definition', in W. Braun and R.T. McCutcheon (eds), *Guide to the Study of Religion*, London and New York: Cassell, pp. 21–34.

Beaudoin, T. (1998) *Virtual Faith: The Irreverent Spiritual Quest of Generation X*, San Francisco: Jossey-Bass.

Beckerlegge, G. (2001) 'Computer-mediated Religion: Religion on the Internet at the Turn of the Twenty First Century', in G. Beckerlegge (ed.), *From Sacred Text to Internet*, Aldershot: Ashgate, pp. 219–280.

Berger, P.L. (1999) 'The Desecularization of the World: A Global Overview', in P.L. Berger (ed.), *The Desecularization of the World: Resurgent Religion and World Politics*, Grand Rapids, Michigan: William B. Eerdmans Publishing Company, pp. 1–18.

Brasher, B. (2001) *Give Me That Online Religion*, San Francisco, Jossey-Bass.

Bruce, S. (1996) *Religion in the Modern World: From Cathedrals to Cults*, Oxford: Oxford University Press.

Bunt, G. (2001) *World Religions*, London: The Good Web Guide Limited.

Dawson, L.L. (2000) 'Researching Religion in Cyberspace: Issues and Strategies', in J.K. Hadden and D.E. Cowan (eds), *Religion on the Internet: Research Prospects and Promises*, Amsterdam, London, and New York: Elsevier Science, pp. 25–54.

Dawson, L.L. and Hennebry, J. (1999) 'New Religions and the Internet: Recruiting in a New Public Space', *Journal of Contemporary Religion*, 14 (1), pp. 17–39.

Helland, C. (2000) 'Online-religion/Religion-online and Virtual Communitas', in J.K. Hadden and D.E. Cowan (eds), *Religion on the Internet: Research Prospects and Promises*, Amsterdam, London, and New York: Elsevier Science, pp. 205–223.

Karaflogka, A. (2002) 'Religious Discourse and Cyberspace', *Religion*, 32, pp. 279–291.

Kelly, K. (2002) 'God is the Machine', *Wired*, 12, pp. 180–185.

Lambert, Y. (1999) 'Religion in Modernity as a New Axial Age: Secularization or New Religious Forms', *Sociology of Religion*, 60 (3), pp. 303–333.

Maxwell, P. (2002) 'Virtual Religion in Context', *Religion*, 32, pp. 343–354.

Naisbitt, J. (2001) *High Tech * High Touch: Technology and Our Accelerated Search for Meaning*, London: Nicholas Brealey.

Ringgård, U. (2002) 'Church of the Subgenius', available from: http://www.dr.dk/skum/ulandp1/arkiv/2002september.asp [Last revision: 29 September 2002].

Sørensen, T. (2002) 'Church of Virus', MA Thesis, Aarhus: Department of the Study of Religion, University of Aarhus.

Taylor, M.C. (1999) *About Religion: Economies of Faith in Virtual Culture*, Chicago and London: The University of Chicago Press.

Thursby, G.R. (2003) 'Virtual Religions', available from: http://www.clas.ufl.edu/users/gthursby/rel/virtual.htm [Latest revision: 13 May 2003].

Wahlers, A. (2000) 'Troen på Internet' ['Faith on the Internet'], *PC Planet*, 9, pp. 52–55.

Yahoo! (2003) 'Cyberculture Religions', available from: http://dir.yahoo.com/Society_and_Culture/Cultures_and_Groups/Cyberculture/Religions/ [Accessed 1 August 2003].

Zaleski, J. (1997) *The Soul of Cyberspace: How New Technology Is Changing Our Spiritual Lives*, San Francisco: HarperEdge.

Part II

Religious authority and conflict in the age of the Internet

Crossing the boundary

New challenges to religious authority and control as a consequence of access to the Internet[1]

Eileen Barker

It is a whole new world. When I started my research into new religions in the early 1970s, there was no World Wide Web. When, in 1995, Jean-François Mayer and I edited a special issue of *Social Compass* devoted to changes in new religions, there was not a single mention of the Internet or the Web. The nearest approximation to the subject was a chance remark I made about the International Society for Krishna Consciousness (ISKCON) having a sophisticated electronic network that could connect devotees throughout the world (Barker 1995a: 168). Indeed, it was at the ISKCON communications centre in Sweden that I had first set eyes on the Internet, and, although I was impressed by the medium's capacity to provide instant contact, it was at least a year later before something of the full import of this new phenomenon really began to dawn on me. But it was not until 1997 that I actually wrote something about the difference that electronic communication was making to the new religions (Barker 1998). Now it seems almost impossible to believe that the Internet is such a recent phenomenon.

But although the omnipresent computer has become taken for granted as part of our everyday life (in at least most of the English-speaking developed world), it is clear that the difference that it has made to the functioning of new religions is far from being fully charted. Some excellent work has been done on the battles that are being fought for the attention of non-members by both the movements and their opponents on their respective websites and the various electronic discussion groups that argue about the achievements – good and/or bad – for which the movements are responsible (Mayer 2000). Less has been written, however, about ways in which the internal functioning of the movements has been affected by the new medium or how it has challenged some of the features of religions that have been associated with the sociological concept of the sect – a type that overlaps in many respects with that of the new religious movement.

In this chapter I am not concerned with the *content* of the Internet, let alone with whether or not the content is accurate. Nor am I concerned with the virtual communities that have come into being as a result of the exis-tence of cyberspace, let alone with whether community life is enhanced or diminished by virtue of its being virtual (Wellman and Gulia 1999). The communities with which I am concerned were already existing at the time the Internet became so widely available, and the authority structures with which I am concerned were originally instituted in real communities of new religions – they are not those imposed by the owners or controllers of websites, BBSs,[2] MUDs[3] or any other Internet group, community or network (Kollock and Smith 1999). What I am concerned with is how one kind of 'real' new religion, with one type of authority structure, finds its authority structure being affected by the arrival of cyberspace.

New religious movements (NRMs)

If we want not merely to describe but also to understand how the Internet can affect NRMs, it is first necessary to understand the movements themselves, some of the challenges that they face, and how they have dealt with these. It is, however, of crucial importance to stress from the start that one cannot generalize about new religions. They differ from each other in every conceivable way – in their beliefs,[4] practices,[5] organization,[6] lifestyle,[7] attitudes,[8] and their relations with the rest of society (Barker 1995c). They certainly differ widely in the extent to which, if at all, they make use of computers and the Internet. In fact, almost the only thing that they are likely to have in common is that they have been called a 'cult', a 'sect' or an 'NRM'. There are, none the less, certain features that one can expect to find in a considerable number of the movements *just because they are new*[9] – and it is because of these that the introduction of the Internet has had some consequences that do not apply, at least in so stark a manner, to older, more established religions.

What, then, are these characteristics that might affect a new religion's vulnerability to processes associated with the Internet?[10] First, and almost by definition, the movement's membership will consist of a large proportion of converts. Next, we can expect new religions to change more rapidly than older religions. And then, being new, the movement is likely to be offering its members something novel – an alternative to mainstream society. This can lead to two consequences of relevance to our present concern. Firstly, non-members who do not share its beliefs and/or practices are likely to object and try to convince converts (especially if these are relatives or friends) that their joining the movement was not a good idea. Secondly, although converts are typically enthusiastic about their new religion, their new perspective on life is likely to be more fragile than that of people who have been brought up with a way of looking at things that is shared by most of those with whom they come into daily contact. This means that founders of new religions are likely to feel the need (1) to protect their followers from outside influences and (2) to ensure that, within their movement, the new way of seeing things is being constantly reinforced and, if need be, enforced.

Coping with the outside

It has been suggested that the precariousness of an NRM means that individual members need to be protected from disruptive influences. The information to which they are exposed needs to be carefully regulated and, thus, communications that they have with or from sources other than the leadership need to be carefully regulated. This regulation is facilitated if 'The Truth' that the movement proclaims is unambiguous and uncomplicated, with a clear delineation between dichotomies such as good and bad, right and wrong, and true and false. As such a polarized worldview could be endangered by qualifications or questioning, any middle-way option or ambiguity is likely to be demonized as part of the bad, the false and/or the satanic alternative.

Throughout history new religions have typically expected a high level of commitment from converts to their movement, and this has frequently involved not only a renunciation of their previous life but also a denunciation of those associated with it.[11] It is certainly not only new religions that will try to restrict the influence that the rest of the world might have on their members,[12] but the tensions that arise from the need to preserve their 'otherness' mean that new religions are likely to introduce censorship to a relatively high degree. This may involve the banning of television, books and various other sources of alternative (to the alternative) worldviews, and, perhaps most importantly, controlling contact with non-believers.

One way of dealing with dangers from without is to intensify their apparent threat by drawing on the dichotomous worldview to create a strong distinction between 'us' (the membership) and 'them' (the rest of the world). This may involve a geographical boundary, the movement living in a closed community having little or no contact with other ways of seeing the world – as was the case when the Peoples Temple moved to Jonestown, Guyana (Hall 1987). More frequently it is a social boundary that defines 'us' as homogeneously godly and good, and 'them' as homogeneously satanic and evil. The movement is seen as a person's principal source of identity – that is, a person is seen, first and foremost, as a member (or not a member) of the group; and if he or she *is* a member, it is the group, rather than the individual, that is of prime importance.[13]

While *non*-members (including relatives and erstwhile friends) may be portrayed as satanic, the boundary between them and members can be strengthened even further by defining *ex*-members as particularly evil. They are reviled and, frequently, shunned. Stories are circulated about the terrible misfortunes that have befallen those who have renounced 'The Truth' – they have, one hears, contracted cancer, been in a horrendous road accident or, perhaps, committed suicide. They belong unambiguously to the other side of the boundary and any communication with them will be defined as polluting and treacherous. Not that the ex-members themselves are likely to want to make contact with their erstwhile movement when it is clear that 'you are either with us or against us'. Not infrequently they had slipped away in the dead of night or 'escaped' without telling anyone in advance, anxious to avoid the pressure to which they knew they would have been subjected had they voiced the doubts that led them to depart. The divide can be even more insuperable if the former member has been 'deprogrammed' or counselled by persons who select only negative characteristics of the movement, having themselves a dichotomous worldview so far as new religions or 'cults' are concerned (Barker 2002).

However, complete isolation from potentially disruptive influences is usually impossible without resorting to physical restraint – something that happens only in rare instances.[14] Several movements allow their members to visit friends and family, but have a rule that members should not venture 'outside' without at least one other member accompanying them.[15] Furthermore, new religions are likely to need some sort of communication with the outside world for economic and other reasons, not least of which is a commonly felt requirement to attract new members.[16] And then, in order to ensure that potential converts have the opportunity to hear the message that the movement has to offer, it may be felt necessary to impose on them a degree of social isolation; they may be urged to visit the movement on its home ground, where they will be 'protected'. The visitors may find themselves constantly surrounded by members, and, should they initiate a discussion with another non-committed visitor (or, if they have just joined, with a fellow noviciate), a senior member will be present to monitor and, if deemed necessary, redirect the conversation. They may even find that a friendly member accompanies them to the bathroom.[17]

Coping with the inside

In many ways it is more difficult to control the day-to-day interactions between members than it is to control outsiders' access to insiders. During its early stages a new movement is likely to have a relatively small membership and primary, face-to-face interaction between the members and the founder/leader is possible. If, however, the movement is successful in attracting more members, communication and authority will have to be mediated through indirect channels. As part of their ideology, sects have frequently claimed that the community has a democratic character with the members being 'a priesthood of all believers' – and, with everyone equal in the sight of God, any organizational structure is neither necessary nor desirable (Wilson 1970: 34). In practice, however, there frequently emerges a patterned structure of relationships which consists of a charismatic leader at the apex transmitting information and commands to trusted lieutenants who, in turn, pass the information down a hierarchical chain of command to grass-roots level. The structure allows for little in the way of horizontal exchange of ideas or information, and any upward communication is likely to take the form of either reporting back or requests to the spiritually superior for elucidation of correct practice and/or 'The Truth'.

Not only are founders of new religions seen as the fount of the new wisdom, their followers frequently accord them a special kind of authority because of what is perceived as their unique, divinely conferred gift of grace (charisma). This results in the leaders being bound by neither rules nor tradition, with their authority extending over all aspects of their followers' lives – from, for example, pronouncements about what kind of clothes the followers should wear, and what kind of food they should eat or not eat, to where they should live and whom they should marry. It follows that charismatic leaders are unpredictable and are not accountable to anyone – except, perhaps, to God. While all kinds of authority figures can frequently persuade others to perform actions that they would not otherwise perform,[18] God's seal of approval being stamped on the charismatic leader adds an extra dimension to the authority s/he wields. One does not question such authority.[19]

The hierarchical authority structure helps to formalize relationships between those above and those below. Members are expected to obey those above them, and are unlikely to demean themselves by confiding in those below, whom they are expected to monitor on a constant basis. Obedience to the leadership is supposed to be unquestioning to the extent that there is (as in the military) an ethic that loyalty is expected even if the immediate leader (officer) is wrong. If, the argument goes, everyone were to do whatever they as individuals felt was right then nothing but chaos would result. Much better to let God (or someone in a position of top command) correct the person making the mistake and keep the strength of the group intact.

Divide and rule

One of the more hazardous challenges for the leadership comes from the potential development of strong social bonds between members of the same horizontal level in the hierarchy. A familiar method of preventing the formation of dissident small groups is to 'divide and rule'. This may involve regular transfers between centres or even countries, thereby breaking up groups that seem to be exhibiting a degree of independence that threatens to disrupt the smooth implementation of the leader's wishes.

Couples may be prevented from developing too close a relationship at the expense of loyalty to the leadership or the group as a whole. One way is to ensure that unmarried members of the opposite sex cannot be in each other's company without the presence of a chaperone, another is to send one partner in a marriage away on a mission.[20] In some groups there is a strict enforcement of celibacy.[21] Another ploy is the constant exchange of partners, whether this be wife swapping or regular mass orgies.[22] Sometimes a leader has instituted divorce and remarriage to a more reliable partner;[23] sometimes the leader has chosen partners who do not even speak the same language and/or who have little, apart from their devotion to the leader, in common;[24] sometimes marriage partners have been encouraged to fantasize about their relationship as being really with the leader or even with Jesus, thus minimizing the dyadic focus of a relationship by transforming it into a vehicle which reinforces the leader's authority.

A variation on the practice of separation between sexual partners is the promotion of a worldview in which women are not expected to have opinions about ideological or political matters, let alone voice any thoughts they may have on the way in which the movement operates. Or, to take a slightly different approach, children may be taken away from their parents either altogether or for much of their socialization, thereby reducing the likelihood of the growth of strong family ties or of the transmission of alternative worldviews to the next generation but, rather, fostering the growth of strong community loyalty.[25]

Even when a friendship is struck up between members, the friends may have to be very careful about what they confide to each other. It is not only those who are in positions of authority who contribute to the control of the movement through reporting disruptive elements to the leadership. It may be part of the ethos that each member is expected to ensure that his or her peers are not undermining the integrity of the movement by straying from the official beliefs or not behaving according to the expected norms – and this, it is maintained, is for the sake of the miscreant as much as for the group itself. Occasionally, as in Rajneeshpuram, electronic surveillance has been introduced to make possible the policing of even casual comments passed between members (Milne 1986).

None of this is to suggest that individual members do not question the authority of their movements – they clearly do, which is one reason why there are so many ways in which the leaders try to control any questioning. But there can be little doubt that one of the most effective ways in which the movements operate control is through peer pressure. Experiments by Solomon Asch (1959) have shown how people can come to doubt the experience of their own senses when everyone else in a particular situation appears to 'see' something different from them. How much more can this be the case when it is not the relative length of a straight line (as in an Asch experiment) but the correctness of a theological tenet which is at issue? However, as Asch also shows, it only needs one other person to 'see' what the subject sees for the latter to be given the courage to admit to seeing the same as that other one person – which explains why the formation of partners and friendships can be seen to pose such a threat to group solidarity.[26]

When members of a movement find themselves in a situation in which they have doubts about the truth of a belief or the correctness of an action, and it appears that these doubts are not shared by any other members, there are various possible outcomes. As we have seen, one is that the doubter reaches the conclusion that he or she is wrong and the group right. Another is to suppress the feeling or to put it in a 'pending tray' to be taken out and examined at some future (probably unspecified) time. Yet another response is to move to the margins of the movement where, while remaining protected from the demonized Babylon that lies beyond the boundary, the doubter can escape the intensity of total involvement – it is, after all, possible that he or she still accepts other aspects of the movement's beliefs or practices, and/or perhaps the doubter has developed a dependence on the movement through fear or gratitude or a complicated combination of emotions, experiences, and friendships.

It is also possible that the doubter will, sooner or later, decide to make a complete break with the movement and return to the outside world, perhaps without discussing his or her doubts with any of the other members. However, so long as individual doubters decide to stay in a new religion with a dichotomous worldview and a strong authority structure, they are likely to remain silent or continue to pay lip service to what is communicated from the top of the hierarchy, and thus to reinforce the peer pressure on others (who may be harbouring similar concerns) to appear to accept 'The Truth' and to go along with the movement's practices.

None the less, there have been doubters who have been courageous enough to test the waters by voicing their opinion – perhaps setting up a small resistance movement, which might even publish its own underground periodical. Such moves have, however, tended to result in repression in one form or another – and possibly the expulsion (and demonization) of the ringleaders and others who refuse to return to the fold. Occasionally this has led to schisms when dissidents have left *en masse* to form their own new group.

It should, however, be stressed once more that control of information is never complete and all manner of new challenges are likely to surface,[27] making it necessary for the leadership continually to reassess the situation and, when necessary, introduce new measures to reinforce its authority – or, eventually, to decide to accommodate to the changing membership and/or outside society.[28]

The new challenge of the Internet

As already intimated, the arrival of the Internet has introduced a multitude of changes in the life of most religions in the West and elsewhere around the world. It might be thought that the advantages for new religions that want to disseminate their alternative worldviews would be considerable, and indeed, there certainly are advantages. But these same advantages extend not only to their competitors, but also to their opponents – and, while the movements can present outsiders with the information that they wish others to have about them, the rest of the world can introduce not only non-members but also the movement's members to alternative sources of information about the movement and its leadership.[29]

The rest of this chapter is concerned with the challenges posed to those features of new religions I have outlined in ideal typical form in so far as the Internet enables their members to obtain alternative information, both from the outside world and from unofficial sources within the movements themselves.

Assuming that members have access to a computer connected to the Internet, there are several ways in which they can access new knowledge. It may be by looking at the range of non-interactive information presented on websites, including the 'anti-cult' and 'counter-cult' sites that attack the practices and beliefs of NRMs.[30] It may be by participating in or lurking[31] on a message board or in a chat room where a discussion is being conducted about the NRM. It may be by subscribing to an email list or simply through one-to-one communication by email.

Undermining the plausibility structure

First, and most obviously, the Internet offers a new *content* to the available knowledge, or (to use the language of Berger and Luckmann (1967)) new additions to 'everything that passes for knowledge' in the social reality that confronts the individual – including not only new information that claims to be of a factual nature, but also opinions, values, and, perhaps most importantly of all, questions. This new information can alter the general perspective of the members in much the same way that turning a kaleidoscope can introduce a new patterning that alters the entire gestalt of the picture one perceives. By doing so, the 'plausibility structure' or social base required for maintaining the 'esoteric enclave' or 'sub-universe' that the movement offers its members is undermined (Berger and Luckmann 1967: 104–105; Berger 1969: 45).

Next, the new *medium* by which the information is communicated can introduce a radical *restructuring* of the internal functioning of the movement.[32] On the one hand, the medium can permeate and thus weaken the boundary between the movement and the outside world, thereby blurring the distinction between 'them' and 'us'. On the other hand, information that is communicated directly within a horizontal network of members, rather than being channelled down the vertical hierarchy, poses a radical challenge to the restrictive control imposed by the leadership.

Most of the controversial NRMs that have been attacked in the media have provided responses for their members to many of the accusations that have been made against them. It is unlikely, however, that all the members will have been prepared for all the skeletons that the movement will have locked up in its cupboards but which their opponents provocatively dangle on a hostile website. Such information need not by itself result in an individual member doing anything that would undermine the movement as a whole. S/he may react, on the one hand, by assuming the information was false, or, on the other hand, by deciding to leave the movement. But once the information is *spread* (and is known to have spread) among several members, the situation can change quite dramatically. For this reason, it is the interactive aspects of the Internet that can pose the greatest threat to a movement's status quo.

In other words, a shift in the beliefs, attitudes, or knowledge of individuals is of interest to the undermining of a social plausibility structure only to the extent that it involves and/or leads to shifts in patterns of relationships. It is then that one can observe the movement, rather than particular individuals, undergoing a radical change.[33]

Horizontal interaction

Access to email is not always easy, but it provides a safer means of communication between separated friends than letters, which can be intercepted, or telephone calls when someone else might be at the other end and, perhaps, monitoring what is being said – quite apart from their being an expensive method of contacting people in another country. The individual member may obtain, say, a Hotmail address employing a pseudonym and either visit an Internet café or use a private computer when no one is watching, carefully deleting the evidence. In this way, private contacts can be maintained with geographical distance no longer being the barrier it was to confidential exchanges.

What has then frequently happened is that snippets of information and/or opinions have been forwarded to other trusted friends and, eventually, a network has been built up in which gossip is exchanged, ideas thought through, and opinions tested. Then, once a critical number of members are communicating with each other in this way, a more formal email list or discussion group on which the exchanges can continue might be created.

There are numerous variations of the scenario in which horizontal networks form and develop at the margins of the movement. One such variation involves communication between young people who have grown up together in the movement.[34] They will have learned who are the likely 'moles' and who can be trusted to keep the secrets of their own 'peer-group sub-sub universe'. Thus, in some ways, the second generation may have developed a protective barrier against the stringent controls to which their parents will have been subjected[35] – they, unlike the converts, will have a ready-made *group* constituency, rather than being a *category* of isolates with, merely, the potential for group formation.

Permeating the boundary

Some chat rooms and message boards are carefully monitored; in others, there appear to be no restrictions on what anyone can say – and anyone can say it. Some are restricted to current members, and these may include or exclude those in the hierarchy and/or from different cohorts. Others are open to (perhaps founded by) former members. Yet others embrace complete outsiders.[36] Sometimes access is possible only with a secret password; in other situations anyone who manages to discover the electronic address can join in.

In these electronic networks there is no preordained status distinguishing participants and deciding who can say what. Pseudonyms can be used and new personalities assumed – neither sex nor age need be revealed. Even the boundary between 'them' and 'us' may be ignored. It is here that, rather than merely receiving 'The Truth' in the form of wisdom and instructions, there is a genuine possibility for there to be a community of equals. Tentative innuendoes can be picked up and elaborated, gossip can flow around the world in no time at all to be denied or confirmed – or both, but the criterion for assessing its truth is no longer an official pronouncement from above – it can be an assertion from the member who was there, or the confession of the former member who was involved in the plot, provided a false alibi or was asked to fudge the accounts.

While the occasional underground newspaper in the past has criticized second-level leadership,[37] it was unlikely to question the charismatic leader. On electronic discussion groups, however, exposés, and even the ridiculing of leaders, are not uncommon.[38] Scandal once it is on the Net is difficult to contain – whether it concerns the sexual proclivities of Sai Baba or Roman Catholic priests, the accusation can spread like wildfire – no longer a hushed whisper but a literal broadcast.

Discussion can swerve in almost any direction. Anxieties may be taken out of the 'pending tray' – possibly by someone else bringing up the repressed topic, but also by the individual who has longed to ask but never dared, fearing possible punishment for being so stupid, doubting or disloyal. No longer need doubting individuals feel that they are the only ones with questions to ask; no longer need they feel afraid to risk exploring misgivings or disaffection. The woman who has felt guilt at her resentment that men are given the credit for the work she does finds other women who have been harbouring similar feelings. The teenager, who was sexually assaulted and never dared admit it, finds that others have undergone similar ordeals.

Of course, not all members will be affected in the same way. Those who had already some concerns are likely to have these confirmed by what they find on the Internet. Others who do not accept the gossip at the time may, none the less, have the seeds of doubt planted in their minds and become more open to questioning and alternative views in the future. While some will air their doubts without identifying themselves,[39] others 'come out of the closet' and openly contribute to the new 'universe of discourse'. The very variety of positions one can find will, in and of itself, undermine the homogeneity of the group that the leadership has been so anxious to preserve.

Former members

While it is true that some of those who have left an NRM have been deprogrammed, sought refuge in and/or contributed to the so-called anti-cult movement, many, indeed the vast majority of former members, have not done so. Some, especially those who had not been in the movement for long, have just slipped back into 'normal society', but others have had more difficulty in adjusting to life on the outside and may miss much of the idealism or friendship that they encountered in the movement.

The communication between the two 'sides' that has been facilitated by the Internet is far more subtle and effective in eroding the 'them/us' boundary than the heated exchanges that take place between members and anti-cultists, when each side is reinforcing a dichotomous worldview. Old friends can continue their friendships and recognize that each may have a point of view to express, and, even if there is not total agreement, there can be agreement on some matters and agreement to disagree on others. The electronic discussions enable members to communicate with people who are familiar with the beliefs and practices of the movement, and who have shared, and perhaps still share, the same ideals, hopes, values, and fears that they themselves hold. The former members have, however, concluded for reasons that they are eager to share with the members that the NRM has not got all the answers and may even be counterproductive in bringing God's Kingdom on earth – or whatever the stated goal of the movement might be. The fact they have not experienced some terrible punishment provides just one more piece of evidence that the picture built up by the leadership may not be entirely reliable. Indeed, the former members may seem not all that different from the members themselves – they are merely people with similar interests on the other side of the divide.

One of the reasons why members have not left the more closed new religions is that they have feared that, having broken ties with the outside society, they have literally nowhere they can turn. Such fears can be experienced even more deeply if members have been born into the movement and know no one on the outside. If, however, it is possible to have contact with former members over a wide geographical area, then leaving the movement appears less of a jump into an unknown satanic wilderness, and the perceived difficulties of life outside the movement can appear less daunting. Former members may offer practical advice about how to succeed in the 'outside' society. Such advice might include suggestions about where to live (perhaps an offer to doss down on an erstwhile fellow-member's sofa for a short period); on how to get social security or work; on how to procure further education; or on how to open a bank account.

On the other hand, members may no longer feel the need to leave as they may feel far more comfortable at the margins of the movement, knowing that there are other members asking similar questions and experiencing similar doubts. And, moreover, that they have a means of communicating with like-minded friends on *both* sides of the watered-down boundary between the movement and the rest of the world.

Controlling the Internet

As one might expect, leaders who want to preserve the culture and structure of their NRM are not going be unaware of the problems that the Internet can add to their maintaining the invincibility of the movement's beliefs and practices, and various tactics have been employed in attempts to curtail the disruptive influences of the Web.

Just as some movements have placed an outright ban on radio and television, so has the use of computers been banned, sometimes being defined as 'of the devil'. As ever, however, attempts at censorship have on occasion increased the attractions of the forbidden for the curious. Other attempts to control potential damage are made by limiting the length of time that members can spend on a computer, or restricting what they can look at – either by fiat or by introducing special software that acts as a 'net nanny' and monitors and/or filters or denies access to particular sites or discussion groups.[40] Another method, especially when children are involved, is to allow use of the computer only when someone else in authority is present and can observe what is being accessed.

Then, of course, control can lead to counter-control, and if the pressure becomes too great on a discussion group webmasters can introduce new passwords that are distributed only to trusted participants so that lurking leaders or tittle-tattlers are excluded from further discussion.

Other consequences

It would, however, be wrong to give the impression that the effects of the Internet are all in one direction. There is, indeed, a mirror-image version of the situation I have been presenting in this chapter, for the Internet can be used to reinforce, or even as the principal component in achieving, an 'old-style' top–bottom control by the leadership. The fact that information can be transmitted instantly around the globe facilitates the reporting of intelligence to, and the receipt of directives from, leaders, who can thereby assemble an overview of the situation and not have to rely on lower-level locals making decisions based on partial information (of the situation) or understanding (of the movement's beliefs and goals). Although the advantages of a local understanding may well be lost in the process, the directness of the Internet bypasses the potential dangers of intermediaries adjusting the message through a form of 'Chinese whispers'.

Use of the Internet to exert control in a manner that might otherwise have been impossible can be illustrated by the 'cult career' of one young man who became involved with what has been termed an abusive, high-control religious group. James (not his real name) was a committed Christian who was studying linguistics at an Ivy League university, having decided to devote his life to translating the Bible to enable the Scriptures to be available to 'unreached people groups'. Then his brother introduced him to Tariq, a Pakistani evangelist who was recruiting students at Wheaton, a Bible-based college. James continued with his studies, but for the next two months he would join Tariq and others on the Internet on an instant messaging pro-gramme in a prayer service from 5.30 to 9.30 every morning and whenever he was not eating, at classes, or engaged in some other activity permitted by his new spiritual teacher.

On graduating, James went to live with the group, and soon he, his brother and a couple of other members were sent to Pakistan on a two-month prayer journey.[41] Each morning they would email Tariq to tell him what they had been doing the previous day and to receive further instructions. The general exchanges were conducted with all four members gathered round the com-puter, but then Tariq would ask one of them to leave, or would address them on a one-to-one basis, finding out what the others had been doing and giving instructions for extracting forced confessions and administering punishments – which would include severe beatings as well as periods of fasting and/or isolation in the bathroom.

The remarkable thing was that the four never communicated to each other on a horizontal level – beyond discussing mundane matters – and some of them would even go beyond the dictates of their leader by, for example, suggesting that they did not need to stop their prayer vigil for lunch because God/Tariq would not want them to. None of the others would risk showing their lack of commitment by mentioning that they were hungry or did not feel that it was necessary. Even when not logged on, it would seem that the electronic medium created and preserved the image of the Big Brother omni-science and omnipotence of Tariq despite the fact that, physically speaking, he was literally half way round the world.

Of course, the effects of the Internet for new religious movements are not confined to strengthening or weakening authority and communication structures. As already mentioned, the Web can provide a useful means of advertising a movement's wares. Internally, it has been used selectively to enhance home schooling, and to enable purchases to be made without going to (worldly) shops. One function that is of growing importance is the Internet's use as a medium for dating. Children brought up together in a communal situation tend to see each other as siblings. The Web provides a means of contacting a potential spouse elsewhere within the movement, thus lowering the risk that young people will leave altogether in order to find a partner. The Family International is particularly interesting in the uses it has made of the Internet. Apart from the fact that their children all learn to use it at an early age for educational purposes, several of them have developed professional abilities in skills such as creating and maintaining websites. The movement also provides a comprehensive electronic religious news service (see www.wwrn.org).

Furthermore, it should be stressed that, while the Internet may help to separate sheep from goats,[42] if the movement has reached a certain level of development the Internet can provide a push in the direction of denominationalization.[43] Not all horizontal communication is necessarily disruptive; it can be perceived as integrative and leading to an enrichment rather than a fragmentation of a movement's culture (Horsfall 2000: 177). The Internet can enable the leadership to have access to a more honest appraisal of developments in which the movement is likely to flounder and those in which it might have the opportunity to flourish. Some of the leadership have started issuing responses to critical attacks on the Internet not merely through denial and/or suppression, but also by acknowledging mistakes and incorporating new approaches to the movement's beliefs and practices.[44] New structures have been introduced, allowing a greater degree of autonomy at the local level, and diversity of approaches has been celebrated rather than repressed – up to a point; there is always the danger of an excessively 'anything goes' *laissez-faire* resulting in the original *raison d'être* being lost, which can result in schisms or an exodus from the liberalizing movement.

Concluding remarks

This chapter has attempted to indicate some of the ways in which new religions face certain challenges that are not so pressing in older religions, and how the Internet can undermine some of the responses that they (the new religions) have traditionally used to maintain their alternative beliefs and practices. More specifically, it has suggested that a strong vertical authority structure, which controls the content of the culture from the top, and which encourages a dichotomous worldview that includes a sharp delineation between members and non-members, can be undermined by processes facilitated by the Internet. Furthermore, the Internet can provide an alternative source of information to that disseminated by the movement's leaders, and enable this to be communicated through horizontal networks that can both operate within the normal confines of the movement and cut across the boundary between the movement and the rest of society.

It has not been claimed that the changes which have been described would not occur anyway. And it has certainly not been suggested that the Internet has been the only factor in promoting such processes. But it has been argued that the Internet can make a significant contribution to the undermining of a single, unquestionable means of control. At the same time, it has also been suggested that leaders can make effective use of the facilities offered by the Internet to strengthen their control over the membership – or that they may change the nature of the control so that it is more diffuse and, thus, less brittle.

One final comment might be added. In this study, the influence of the Internet has been observed in movements that were new before the arrival of the Internet – they had already faced the challenges of being a new, alternative movement without its presence. How *new* new religions will deal with this new electronic environment remains to be seen. What is, however, clear is that any student of religion – or, indeed, of contemporary society – will ignore this new variable at his or her peril.

Notes

1 I would like to express my gratitude to STICERD (the Suntory and Toyota International Centre for Economics and Related Disciplines) for assistance in funding some of the research on which this chapter was based.
2 Bulletin Board Systems.
3 Multi-User Domains or Dungeons.
4 They may, for example, have Judaeo/Christian, Hindu, Islamic, Buddhist, Shinto, pagan, or satanic roots or a mixture of these or various other traditions; they may be atheistic, philosophical, or psychological – or in touch with flying saucers and beings from outer space.
5 They may, for example, chant, pray, meditate, celebrate mass or indulge in ritual sacrifice via the Internet.
6 They may, for example, consist of a small commune run according to democratic principles, or be an international organization, possibly claiming to be a theocracy.
7 They may, for example, spend their lives witnessing as missionaries, or work as bankers in the city; they may be vegetarians and/or indulge in unusual sexual practices; they may offer courses to develop the god within, and/or they may run a hostel caring for AIDS sufferers – or they may eke out a living off the land, and refuse to pay taxes.
8 They may, for example, consider women an inferior species without a soul, or revere them as souls who are far more spiritual than men; they may believe children should be allowed to roam free, or that they should be chastised for any minor misdemeanour; they may be right-wing conservatives, or left-wing socialists – or they may eschew anything to do with the rest of the world, let alone politics.
9 Several movements will say that they are not new because they can trace their theological roots back through hundreds or even thousands of years. ISKCON, for example, traces its roots back to the sixteenth-century monk Lord Chaitanya. From a sociological perspective, however, it is a new organization that came into being when, in the 1960s, its founder, A. C. Bhaktivedanta Swami Prabhupada, travelled to the United States, attracted some Western hippies to a life of devotion to Krishna, and incorporated his new Society.
10 It should be stressed that, although the conditions and processes that are being described in this chapter are drawn from reality, they are, none the less, to some degree caricatures or ideal typical in the Weberian sense. The features of ideal

types rarely, if ever, exist in their 'ideal' form, but can be observed as being more or less present in any particular situation. The types serve as a model that is not more or less true, but more or less useful for recognizing some of the structures and processes that are to be found, to a greater or lesser degree, in certain kinds of organizations. Here, the exercise is to assist in the recognition of a number of ways in which some NRMs have sometimes operated in order to promote control over their membership by means of boundary preservation and vertical authority structures.

11 Jesus is reported as having said 'If any man come to me, and hate not his father, and mother, and wife, and children, and brethren, and sisters, yea, and his own life also, he cannot be my disciple' (Luke 14:26, see also Matthew 10:35–36).

12 To take but a few examples, the Vatican issues a list of books that Catholics are enjoined not to read; mainstream Protestants in the United States protect their children from drugs and Darwinism by educating them in home schools; Muslim women are frequently expected to refrain from contact with members of the opposite sex who are not close family members.

13 This may be the case, at least so far as the inner core of the membership is concerned, even in those NRMs that claim to promote the development of the individual – as with the Church of Scientology's Sea Org (Wallis 1976) and the group that was formed around Ma Anand Sheela at Rajneeshpuram (Milne 1986).

14 There have been reports of members (or their rebellious children) being placed in solitary confinement for varying periods of time – but this has usually been to protect other members from their influence rather than to protect the miscreants, and corrective procedures have been more likely to be of an 'educational' than a physical nature. For an example of extreme methods of controlling members in an isolated community see Robert Balch's (1985) description of life during one stage of the movement that was later to hit the headlines as 'the suicide cult', Heaven's Gate.

15 This was particularly the case when the practice of deprogramming was prevalent, but it is also justified in movements such as the Cooneyites and The Family International with reference to Jesus' sending out his disciples in pairs (Mark 6:7, Luke 10:1).

16 There is no space to explore the topic here, but a whole book could be written about the difference that the Internet has made to the recruiting practices of new religions; see Dawson and Hennebry (1999).

17 This used to happen during the residential workshops that the Unification Church ran in California in the 1970s.

18 As Stanley Milgram (1974) and others have illustrated, there are some people who are particularly prone to obey those in positions of authority, whatever the consequences might be – even, on occasion, when they are told to do something that involves threatening an innocent person's life.

19 It is, however, important to recognize that authority (that is, power which is accepted as legitimate) relies on a two-way relationship. Unless followers perceive and acknowledge their charisma, such leaders can achieve nothing (Barker 1993).

20 Both these methods were employed by the Unification Church in the 1970s.

21 This applies to the Brahma Kumaris, and in ISKCON sex is not meant to take place except for the procreation of children within a marriage, so couples who do not want children are expected not to consummate their marriage.

22 Synanon provided an example of the former, the Rajneeshees (later known as Osho lovers) of the latter.

23 This practice is reported to have occurred in Sahaja Yoga.

24 Again the Unification Church provided an example with the 'Matching Ceremonies' arranged by Sun Myung Moon in preparation for the Blessings or

mass weddings – a practice that has been replaced by more familiar forms of arranged marriages involving the parents of prospective couples.

25 See Palmer (1994) for some of the ways women are treated in NRMs and Palmer and Hardman (1999) for some of the ways children are raised in the movements.

26 Wright (1986: 149), in a small-scale study of the Unification Church, ISKON, and the Children of God, suggests the dyad may evoke a stronger commitment than the group.

27 One such challenge has been the arrival of social scientists researching the movements (Barker 1995b).

28 This is especially likely to occur with the arrival of second and subsequent generations who have been born into the movement (Barker 1995a).

29 No attempt is being made in this chapter to distinguish between the accuracy and inaccuracy of the content of any knowledge or information available to members. The relevant distinction for the present purpose is between knowledge or information that the leadership wants and that which it does not want the membership to receive. The distinction between knowledge and information is one of degree, information being more particular while knowledge extends to a general perspective or understanding of social reality.

30 Of course, religions vary in the number of sites (if any) that they maintain, and the degrees of sophistication of these sites, which differ in such details as how user-friendly they are and in their use of menus, graphics, their incorporation of sound, video, different languages, personal websites and so on. They also vary in the degree to which they cater for members and/or for non-members, the openness of their sites and extent and method of control of access by non-members. Some offer interactive learning; some offer online services, including ritual participation. Some can be picked up through numerous keywords on numerous search engines; others are hard to find if one does not know what one is looking for. Some of a religion's opponents may be successful in getting their own sites higher on a search engine's lists than the religion itself. Some feature in scholarly sites, others do not. Some respond to negative claims that are made about them on other websites; others treat their opponents with a lofty disdain.

31 That is, observing without making one's presence known.

32 There are ways in which this discussion might be approached along the lines of Marshall McLuhan's (1964) aphorism that the medium is the message, but I do not wish to go so far as to suggest that what is communicated is of less importance and of less power than the media themselves.

33 Of course, a movement exists only in so far as it consists of individuals, but a social group has properties that are not reducible to the properties of the constituent individuals, and it is such features of the social group in which the sociologist is interested.

34 Children, unlike converts, cannot be expelled if they question beliefs or practices.

35 There are, of course, various other ways in which one might see second-generation members as being more easily 'socialized' into the movement's worldview. That, however, is not the subject of this chapter.

36 It is by no means rare nowadays for social scientists to lurk in front of their computer screens as part of (or even all of) their 'field work'.

37 For example, one such periodical, *The Round Table*, circulated within the Unification Church for a short time, but although the actions of second-level leaders were questioned, I never read any criticism of Moon himself.

38 Stories about the Moon family and the sexual exploits of Moon himself have been discussed at length by Unificationists on both closed and open discussion groups – and there have been more graphic descriptions of the sexual practices of the late David Berg by former members of The Family International.

39 I have spoken to several members who have confessed that they had 'lurked' for a long time without revealing their presence on critical discussion groups, but continued to feel isolated from other members or their 'real' (as opposed to virtual) community – one such informant told me 'the computer was my only friend'.

40 This can be more successful in some situations than in others – all the Japanese participants dropped out of one group's restricted discussion group overnight, but members from the same movement in other countries continued to communicate on the list.

41 The belief being that praying for eight or so hours a day will enhance the spiritual atmosphere of the surrounding area.

42 Several movements have periodic 'purges' when questioning members are expelled or requested to move to a less involved level of membership. The International Churches of Christ have provided an example of the former, The Family International of the latter.

43 That is, will lose some of its sectarian characteristics of 'separateness' and exclusivity.

44 Although they have not always been accepted, letters (responding to accusations and disruptive questioning) distributed by its current leaders, Maria and Peter, to members of The Family International provide an example of such a move.

References

Asch, S.E. (1959) 'Effects of Group Pressure upon the Modification and Distortion of Judgements', in E.E. Maccoby, T.M. Newcomb, and E.L. Hartley (eds) *Readings in Social Psychology*, London: Methuen [Third edition].

Balch, R.W. (1985) '"When the Light Goes Out, Darkness Comes": A Study of Defection from a Totalistic Cult', in R. Stark (ed.) *Religious Movements: Genesis, Exodus, and Numbers*, New York: Paragon.

Barker, E. (1993) 'Charismatization: The Social Production of an Ethos Propitious to the Mobilization of Sentiments', in E. Barker, J.T. Beckford and K. Dobbelaere (eds) *Secularization, Rationalism and Sectarianism*, Oxford: Clarendon Press.

Barker, E. (1995a) 'Plus ça change . . .', in E. Barker and J.-F. Mayer (eds) *Twenty Years On: Changes in New Religious Movements*, London: Sage. Special Edition of *Social Compass*, 42 (2).

Barker, E. (1995b) 'The Scientific Study of Religion? You Must be Joking!', *Journal for the Scientific Study of Religion*, 34 (3), pp. 287–310. Also available at: http://www.cfh.lviv.ua/Barker.doc

Barker, E. (1995c) *New Religious Movements: A Practical Introduction*, London: HMSO [First published in 1989].

Barker, E. (1998) 'Standing at the Cross-Roads: The Politics of Marginality in "Subversive Organizations"', in D.G. Bromley (ed.) *The Politics of Religious Apostasy: The Role of Apostates in the Transformation of Religious Movements*, Westport, CT and London: Praeger.

Barker, E. (2002) 'Watching for Violence: A Comparative Analysis of the Roles of Five Cult-Watching Groups', in D.G. Bromley and J.G. Melton (eds) *Cults, Religion and Violence*, Cambridge: Cambridge University Press. Also available at: http://www.cesnur.org/2001/london2001/barker.htm.

Berger, P. (1969) *The Social Reality of Religion*, London: Faber and Faber [First published in 1967 as *The Sacred Canopy*].

Berger, P.L. and Luckmann, T. (1967) *The Social Construction of Reality: Everything that Passes for Knowledge in Society*, London: Allen Lane.

Dawson, L.L. and Hennebry , J. (1999) 'New Religions and the Internet: Recruiting in a New Public Space', *Journal of Contemporary Religion*, 14 (1), pp. 17–39.

Hadden, J.K. and Cowan, D.E. (eds) (2000) *Religion on the Internet: Research Prospects and Promises*, Amsterdam and London: JAI.

Hall, J.H. (1987) *Gone from the Promised Land: Jonestown in American Cultural History*, New Brunswick, NJ: Transaction.

Horsfall, S. (2000) 'How Religious Organizations Use the Internet: A Preliminary Inquiry', in J.K. Hadden and D.E. Cowan (eds) *Religion on the Internet: Research Prospects and Promises*, Amsterdam, London and New York: Elsevier Science, pp. 153–182.

Kollock, P. and Smith, M.A. (1999) 'Communities in Cyberspace', in M.A. Smith and P. Kollock (eds) *Communities in Cyberspace*, London: Routledge, pp. 3–25.

McLuhan, M.H. (1964) *Understanding Media*, London: Routledge and Kegan Paul.

Mayer, J.-F. (2000) 'Religious Movements and the Internet: The New Frontier of Cult Controversies', in J.K. Hadden and D.E. Cowan (eds) *Religion on the Internet: Research Prospects and Promises*, Amsterdam, London and New York: Elsevier Science, pp. 249–276.

Milgram, S. (1974) *Obedience to Authority*, New York: Harper and Row.

Milne, H. (1986) *Bhagwan: The God that Failed*, London: Caliban Books.

Palmer, S.J. (1994) *Moon Sisters, Krishna Mothers, Rajneesh Lovers: Women's Roles in New Religions*, Syracuse, NY: Syracuse University Press.

Palmer, S.J. and Hardman, C.E. (1999) 'Children in New Religions', New Brunswick: Rutgers University Press.

Wallis, R. (1976) *The Road to Total Freedom: A Sociological Analysis of Scientology*, London: Heinemann.

Wellman, B. and Gulia, M. (1999) 'Virtual Communities as Communities: Net Surfers Don't Ride Alone', in M.A. Smith and P. Kollock (eds) *Communities in Cyberspace*, London: Routledge, pp. 167–194.

Wilson, B.R. (1970) *Religious Sects: A Sociological Study*, London: Weidenfeld and Nicolson.

Wright, S. (1986) 'Dyadic Intimacy and Social Control in Three Cult Movements', *Sociological Analysis*, 44 (2), pp. 137–150.

Chapter 6

Seeking for truth

Plausibility alignment on a Baha'i email list

David Piff and Margit Warburg

Computer-mediated communication and web technologies have been exploited in many religious communities, both by leaders and the rank and file. The technologies allow instantaneous and interactive communication on a global scale, but these features are utilized in different ways, depending, among other things, on whether the websites are set up by the leadership or by the members at large. In the first case, the interactive process is typically a way of shaping and controlling the flow of information to a person visiting the website. In the second case, conversational communication on email discussion lists provides spaces where both ongoing and novel issues arising in the course of a community's life can be discussed and adjusted or understood anew. Some of these issues may provoke ideas and views that are neither mainstream nor clearly heretical, but reside in that grey area where a discussion needs to be unofficial.

In what follows, we consider the dynamics of online interaction among members of an independent (i.e. not officially sponsored) Baha'i-oriented discussion group, Talisman, by analysing a single discussion thread. The progress of this thread illustrates an interactive process of seeking truth (or at least shared understanding) and provides an instance of plausibility alignment carried out at the grass roots among a group of Baha'is. Talisman discussants undertook their discursive enterprise without a mandate from or supervision by a Baha'i institution. This factor, and the generally high educational level of participants, made Talisman atypical of Baha'i discussion lists, many of which enjoy sponsorship by agencies of the Baha'i community, and function with full-time moderators.

Plausibility alignment

The term 'plausibility alignment', adopted from Jill McMillan (1988), denotes a process by which a religious community – it could be any social group – maintains a correspondence between its worldview and information impinging on the group from the social context in which it resides. The process is crucial to the ongoing viability of a community whose members are beset by competing messages and truth claims from the broader social milieu. McMillan's piece was based on the work of Peter Berger. In *The Social Construction of Reality* (1966), Berger and his collaborator Thomas Luckmann described the critical importance of 'plausibility structures' – social bases and processes that support and maintain particular social worlds. These 'structures' need to be constantly reinforced through social processes, largely though not exclusively through conversations among members of the social group. In *The Sacred Canopy* (1967), Berger considered some implications of his findings for religious institutions. Among other points, he argued that 'secularization' created an unprecedented situation: religious legitimations of the world 'have lost their plausibility not only for a few intellectuals . . . but for broad masses of entire societies' (Berger 1967: 124). For Berger, secularization was critically linked to 'pluralism'. In pluralistic situations, religions have to compete not only with one another but also with the reality-defining agencies of society at large – government, the media, the scientific establishment, and so forth. Berger wrote, 'A "religious preference" can be abandoned as readily as it was first adopted' (1967: 134). 'As a result, the religious tradition, which previously could be authoritatively imposed, now has to be marketed. It must be "sold" to a clientele that is no longer constrained to "buy"' (1967: 138). To remain credible, religions are forced to re-evaluate continuously and adaptively and adjust themselves in light of what the public at large and their own adherents generally find believable. Though Berger does not use the term, the processes referred to as globalization have extended the parameters of pluralism and exacerbated this situation.

In her article, McMillan undertook a survey of literature which elucidated various aspects of the concept of plausibility alignment. She argued that 'the loss of plausibility presents a rhetorical problem to the religious institution' (McMillan 1988: 327), and illustrated this point through a case study of a major Christian denomination's wrestling with the issue of sexism. She focused on a formal position paper prepared by the Presbyterian Church of the United States. McMillan noted how the paper had been crafted to be acceptable to audiences both without and within the church (the latter audience being the more important) and, simultaneously, to break new ground by presenting, though in a very mild and tentative way, a new statement regarding sexist language. The exercise described by McMillan was carried out under the auspices of church authorities; examples of similar productions could be found to illustrate very similar processes across a wide range of religious groups, including the Baha'i religion.

The present chapter, on the other hand, considers an instance of plausibility alignment carried out by a group of Baha'is at the grass-roots level who were concerned about issues of 'credibility', but who carried no official mandate or sanction for their activity.

The globe-spanning interactive capability of the Internet is exceedingly well suited for facilitating plausibility alignment in a dispersed group. In the

Baha'i context, electronic discussion lists offer participants a way to bypass the religion's restrictions regarding publication of material that has not been institutionally reviewed (Warburg 2003). However, for the leadership of a religion, it is probably not possible to permit a grass-roots process of plausibility alignment to result directly in formal changes in religious doctrine or presentation. To do so would be to allow the process to intrude upon a core responsibility of the religious leadership, that of collectively acknowledged interpretation.

Baha'i online

The Baha'i religion has its origins in a Shi'ite millenarian movement, which rose in Iran in the middle of the nineteenth century. The movement was called Babism after its prophet-leader, Ali Muhammad Shirazi (1819–1850), known as the Bab. The Babi movement broke with Islam in 1848 and became engaged in a series of bloody conflicts with the Iranian government. The movement had been all but crushed by 1852, but Babism was revived and transformed into the Baha'i religion by Mirza Husayn Ali Nuri (1817–1892), known as Baha'u'llah. Baha'is believe that he was not only the prophet and founder of a religious community but was the 'promised one of all religions', whose mission was to establish the 'Most Great Peace,' the 'Kingdom of God on Earth'. Baha'u'llah's son, Abdu'l-Baha (1844–1921), later became the leader of the Baha'i religion, and he again was succeeded by his grandson, Shoghi Effendi (1897–1957). During the twentieth century, through systematic missionary efforts, the Baha'i religion spread all over the world. Today, the religion has a collective leadership of nine elected men who constitute the highest authoritative Baha'i body, the Universal House of Justice, situated in the Baha'i World Centre in Haifa, Israel. All Baha'i communities around the world refer to the Universal House of Justice in administrative and spiritual matters. The most sacred places on earth for the Baha'is are the shrines of Baha'u'llah and of the Bab, both situated in the Haifa area, and Haifa is therefore also a place of pilgrimage for Baha'is.

The official Baha'i website, The Baha'i World, is an apt illustration of Christopher Helland's characterization of an 'official' World Wide Web presence: 'Official web sites are often professionally designed; the information presented and the environments created are controlled spaces where nothing is left to chance. In this way the religious organization is attempting to continue their institutional control and structure on-line' (Helland 2002: 295). Www.bahai.org provides an attractive public gateway with links to brief introductory information about the religion and to texts and pictures illustrative of its view of itself as a global community. The site is professionally maintained and kept current with news of recent Baha'i events and accomplishments, and offers links to similar websites sponsored by some sixty national Baha'i communities throughout the world. This cluster of websites constitutes the principal formal presence of the religion in cyber-space.

At the other end of the information spectrum, websites sponsored by individuals and, more importantly, discussion groups organized to exchange views about the religion represent unofficial Baha'i cyber presences. These spaces, which are not reachable from The Baha'i World, allow relatively free-flowing and casual discussion of aspects of Baha'i life. To illustrate some of the dynamics of online interaction, and, importantly, an instance of plausibility alignment, we shall consider a Talisman discussion thread from April 1995. As we intend to explore the text of the thread more deeply than is usually done in sociological literature, we will have to content ourselves with consideration of a single thread. This thread is one of many hundreds that could have been selected from Talisman to illustrate the same processes.

Online plausibility negotiation – a Talisman thread

Talisman, which functioned from October 1994 until May 1996, was created to be an academically oriented forum for open and serious discussion of Baha'i history, theology, administration, and community life.[1] It was created and managed by an American Baha'i university professor and open to members of the religion as well as to non-members. A few basic rules governed the group: discussions were un-moderated, but were expected to be courteous and based on evidence; participants were to avoid abusive language, ad-hominem arguments and accusations of heresy.

Despite its open membership policies, the overwhelming majority of participants on Talisman were Baha'is (there were also a handful of former Baha'is). Most 'Talismanians' were Western-educated; the group was pre-dominantly male and included a number of Baha'i intellectuals, among them journalists, professors, graduate students, and published scholars in such fields as Middle East studies, religious studies, history, anthropology, sociology, the natural sciences, and engineering. A number of Talisman participants, while well educated, were not academics. What transpired through the numerous discussion threads that unfolded and ramified on the list was, generally, an ongoing interrogation of the community's received knowledge and current understandings in the light of prevailing academic attitudes and standards. It should be noted, however, that there were also a good many (intentionally) humorous postings to the list. Significantly, the undertaking was initiated by Baha'is who felt the need for a forum in which to discuss issues that were of concern to many of them. Though similar discussions had taken place at Baha'i study classes in various locales, the quantity, quality, and speed of dissemination of such discussions were unprecedented.

The thread to be analysed here ran from 11 to 17 April 1995; its subject was the so-called Mount Carmel Project at the Baha'i World Centre in Haifa.

This project involved the erection of three major buildings at a site Baha'is referred to as the 'Arc', and the construction of an adjacent set of terraces and gardens surrounding the Shrine of the Bab and stretching nearly one kilometre up and down the slope of Mount Carmel. Shoghi Effendi originally planned both parts of the project, and two other buildings of the Arc had been completed earlier. The project was at that time well under way (the terraces were officially inaugurated on 22 May 2001).

According to popular Baha'i belief, the completion of the Mount Carmel Project would coincide in time with the 'Lesser Peace', a worldwide political peace settlement spoken of in Baha'i scriptures. This expectation originated in letters written by Shoghi Effendi. Addressing the Baha'is of the world in 1954 about the projected construction of the 'International Baha'i Archives' on Mount Carmel (the first of the buildings of the Arc), and extolling the spiritual significance of the project, Shoghi Effendi (1958: 74–75) wrote that

> The raising of this Edifice will in turn herald the construction, in the course of successive epochs of the Formative Age of the Faith, of several other structures, which will serve as the administrative seats of such divinely appointed institutions as the Guardianship, the Hands of the Cause, and the Universal House of Justice . . .
>   This vast and irresistible process, unexampled in the spiritual history of mankind, and which will synchronize with two no less significant developments – the establishment of the Lesser Peace and the evolution of Baha'i national and local institutions – the one outside and the other within the Baha'i world – will attain its final consummation in the Golden Age of the Faith . . . the advent of the Kingdom of the Father repeatedly lauded and promised by Jesus Christ.

From statements in the writings of Abdu'l-Baha, many Baha'is had come to believe that the Lesser Peace would appear around the end of the twentieth century (Piff and Warburg 2003). This expectation became a matter of some urgency when the extensive building projects begun in the early 1990s were proceeding, since Shoghi Effendi had said that these developments and the Lesser Peace would 'synchronize'. It was therefore not entirely surprising that Baha'i World Centre workers were heard to comment, 'with every stone laid, forces are being released in the world', or that 'whenever we dig into God's holy mountain, another old world order institution collapses' (Piff 2000).

Magic or foresight?

Space prohibits our fully discussing every message posted to the 'Arc' thread, but enough will be quoted to delineate its dynamics and identify the most important ideas dealt with.[2] In particular, the participants struggled with the possible connection between the completion of the project and developments in world affairs. Such causality might be inferred from Shoghi Effendi's prediction, and some Talisman participants obviously had difficulties in reconciling it with their academic background and the Baha'i doctrine of the harmony of religion and science. On 11 April 1995, a Baha'i academic from New Zealand initiated the discussion on Talisman:

> A . . . fellow academic currently investigating the writings [has asked,] can the Baha'is prove a connection between the establishment of Lesser Peace and the completion of the Arc? If so, can we do it now or only in hindsight?[3]

Almost immediately, a Talisman participant, an American academic, responded:

> In my . . . opinion, there is no connection between the building of the Arc and the establishment of the Lesser Peace. Certainly it is true that building these building[s] will not and cannot bring about the Lesser Peace in some magical way. Baha'is just look ridiculous to thinking people when they talk that way.[4]

Another participant quickly took issue with this view:

> It's not magic . . . it's scientifically based (if you want me to go into proofs and derivations etc we would have to first prove existence of God, then of other spiritual worlds etc etc but we would get there . . .) and these 'thinking people' are not taking into account that there are other spiritual worlds that interact with this world . . .[5]

And another chimed in, agreeing,

> You have said it all! . . . These 'thinking people' are part of the problem! In fact, it is an essential aspect of Baha'i 'world view' – for the lack of a better term – that these two worlds (spiritual and material) are intimately interrelated and affect each other.[6]

However, another member, also an academic, responded forcefully:

> Actually, I thought [TL] said it all. The way Baha'is discuss the Arc is considered 'magical' thinking. The buildings going up on Mt. Carmel are viewed by these 'thinking people' that some dismiss with a wave of a magic wand, as 'power art,' an effort to show the power of the Baha'i Faith and its administration . . .
>
> Alas, the social and economic development plans seem to have lost out in the process of raising funds for these buildings. I fear that the fact

that they are sitting in Israel – a country almost universally scorned in the world – is going to backfire on the Faith terribly. I wish we were putting our resources into human development, rather than into marble.[7]

In the postings quoted thus far one can already observe one of the most important characteristics of Talisman – its tendency to expose ideological divisions in the community – in this case between those who, in direct if not trenchant language, questioned prevalent Baha'i understandings and those who sought to maintain or defend more mainstream views. Also evident in the thread, at least in the post quoted just above, is dissatisfaction with the decisions of Baha'i leadership – here expressed as regret that Baha'is use their funds to erect monumental administrative buildings rather than to address human needs and problems more directly. As the Universal House of Justice, as a matter of Baha'i belief, is viewed as infallible, such a comment was bound to provoke a reaction.

A follow-up post, directed to LW and copied to Talisman, set out to prove the validity of Shoghi Effendi's statement regarding synchronization, and the Universal House of Justice's decision to pursue the Mount Carmel project at this time:

I'll try and put it as scientifically as possible so as to not be considered too 'magical' . . .

Step one . . . through complex calculus and lots of being a thinking person one comes to the conclusion that there is a Creator, God, Supreme Being, Allah.

Step two . . . this 'God' must communicate with created beings so Manifestations are sent at periods of about every 1,000 years (again record of history, analogies of sun and mirrors etc etc can prove this).

Step three . . . at this time in history the Manifestation which has inaugurated a new Universal Cycle was Baha'u'llah (complex calculus, Kitab-i-Iqan, Bible proofs, Quran proofs, whatever it takes to prove this).

Step four . . . Baha'u'llah, . . . ordains that a body called the 'Universal House of Justice' should guide the community of the followers of Baha'u'llah (and in a certain sense the world in general). This body has 'conferred infallibility' and all who follow Baha'u'llah joyfully submit to the decisions of this Supreme Body.

Step five . . . This same Supreme Body, in following the instructions of Baha'u'llah, . . . the wishes of Abdul Baha and expositions of Shoghi Effendi, decide and communicate in a letter of August 31, 1987 that the remaining buildings on the Arc are to be completed at this time of history. Moreover, this Supreme Body decides that these buildings will be built in Israel . . . whatever the rest of the world may think about Israel . . .

Shoghi Effendi, whose authority can be derived . . . from the Will of Abdul Baha states . . . that there is a synchronization between the completion of the Arc, the maturation of LSA's and the establishment of the Lesser Peace . . .

Now . . . was there any magic in any of that? Is there any question about whether the Baha'i world should or should not be doing this?

Thinking people can think what they want . . . but based on the above . . . I think the A+ goes to the instructions of the Universal House of Justice and expositions of Shoghi Effendi rather than the doubts and criticisms of thinking people.[8]

The following day, the same participant, SP, posted two messages containing several pages of quotations from Shoghi Effendi's writings regarding the Arc and the Lesser Peace. His first message began, 'Assuming we all accept equations 1–5, perhaps looking directly at the texts could help our consultation on the Arc . . .'[9] SP included texts that most Talisman subscribers presumably knew well and considered authoritative, and interspersed them with his own comments in which he argued for a connection between the two 'variables'.[10] The message failed to elicit any direct reply.

Another poster, putting a positive spin on the notion of 'power art', stated, 'There is something powerful about marble – it exudes authority, reverence, strength, cleanliness, durability, refinement. It is metamorphic beyond its mere creation.' He continued, 'The Arc is God's metropolis for at least a thousand years – it is an extremely rare bounty to have a part in its birth.'[11] In a separate message, the same individual suggested that 'the completion of the buildings by itself is not what is going to bring about the Lesser Peace, it is the maturation that we must go through to achieve that goal which is significant'.[12] Another participant discounted the expressed concern about the location of the Baha'i World Centre in Israel. 'In fact,' he wrote, 'a Muslim threw [this] in my face once, accusing the Baha'is of supporting the Zionist state by sending money there.' He continued:

I asked him if he sent money to Mecca. He said he did not, that Saudi Arabia took care of the Holy Shrines there. I replied that the . . . money we send . . . does not go to the 'Zionist' government, but to take care of our properties.

In short, I say, let it be a teaching tool! We have absolutely nothing to be ashamed of regarding what we are doing on the Mountain of God!

O, and is that mountain magical??? Every pilgrim I've talked to thinks so.[13]

A great deal of the thread explored the issue of synchronization and causation. One poster argued that Shoghi Effendi had never intended to imply a causal connection between events when he wrote that the building of administrative edifices at the Baha'i World Centre would synchronize with the Lesser Peace.[14] Another wrote that though synchronicity is not understood as a causal connection, 'can one say . . . this means they are absolutely coincidental; that there is no connection between them, even a connection which might exist in the Mind of God?'[15] Another remarked, 'Synchronous events can occur quite naturally when the same underlying conditions that foster the occurrence of one also foster the occurrence of the other . . . [A condition of] relative international stability that could lead to the lesser peace would also encourage the building of the Arc.'[16] Another participant, a historian, explained in more detail:

> If one believes that a state of Lesser Peace will come in the short term of future history; and one believes that Baha'is will build edifices in Haifa in the same time frame; then there is nothing illogical in saying that these two developments will synchronize while not positing a connection between them.
>
> Because of the advent of weapons of mass destruction . . . large-scale world wars are no longer feasible as rational policy decisions. Thus, the Lesser Peace, the peace of Mutually Assured Destruction, is approaching . . . Shoghi Effendi was keenly aware of the significance of Hiroshima.
>
> One could on the other hand predict that in the short term (within 75 years), the Baha'i community would grow to the point where it would need to build the Arc; this could have been extrapolated from the 10-year World Crusade itself . . .
>
> There is no rational basis for asserting that the synchronicity of these developments has a causal character. Why should paying workmen to build buildings affect international diplomacy? Any connection can only be . . . in the minds of Baha'is.
>
> The building of the Arc is well underway, and clearly has some major advantages for the international administration of the Faith. But this effort . . . has been a major drain on local resources, leaving us with far fewer local [centres] than we need.
>
> It seems to me that it is legitimate for Baha'is to express a strong preference that, once this major building initiative is completed, a couple of decades of investment in local communities should be initiated.[17]

A final posting to the thread suggested another solution to the question of synchronization/causation:

> That processes are synchronous without being causally related (to each other or to a common 3rd) is possible [but] not most likely. That erecting some buildings in Haifa will cause the world's peoples to recognize their interdependence and help to make their politicians ready to effectuate

that interdependence is not entirely impossible – but very nearly. When the impossible has been eliminated, what remains, in this case, is that the synchronous processes are coordinated because the House of Justice, observing the accelerating rate of developments in the move towards a world polity, has put its foot on the accelerator to ensure our internal development keeps pace.[18]

Interactive seeking for truth

Though in its early stages this thread exposed significant divergences of opinion in the community, it was possible for a Baha'i to come away from reading through the entire series of postings satisfied that a problematic element of the Baha'i worldview had been put into rational perspective: There was nothing magical at work – Shoghi Effendi, an astute observer of history, knew the Lesser Peace could not be far off and exploited this insight to direct the course of the Baha'i community. The Universal House of Justice, in initiating the construction project on Mount Carmel, had acted in the same way. At the same time, nothing in the thread ruled out the possibility that spiritual and material reality were connected. Whatever the reason, the supreme spiritual authority of the Baha'i community had decided to initiate the construction work now, almost everyone thought it was a good thing, and world conditions appeared to foster the undertaking.

Internet threads are artefacts of verbal exchanges performed before largely silent audiences – Talisman had more than a hundred subscribers at this time who chose not to participate in the Arc discussion. Some messages in the thread were addressed to Talisman at large; others were addressed as responses to particular members and simultaneously copied to the group. We, of course, know nothing of messages that might have passed privately between list members but were not copied to the list. As with any electronic discussion group, reading Talisman was a process of following the course of several concurrent conversations, and the Arc thread was interspersed with a number of others that vied for participants' attention.[19]

Several of the posts considered here exhibit another noteworthy feature – formulaic expressions of humility (these have been edited out of the extracts presented above). For example, TL prefaced his post with the disclaimer, 'In my very humble, flawed, imperfect and frequently incorrect opinion . . .'[20] SP echoed this when commenting on texts from Shoghi Effendi's writings, warning readers that his (SP's) 'personal extremely potentially fallible inter-pretations' would be marked by asterisks.[21] SP also noted parenthetically that despite his frequent references to 'equations' and 'variables' he 'hate[d] math – can't you tell!'[22] The function of such rhetorical touches was appar-ently to emphasize the humanity of the poster and, perhaps, soften the force of an opinion, thus increasing the likelihood that the view put forward would be accepted. Instances of humour sprinkled throughout the thread probably served the same function. Such features are not unique to Talisman and contribute to the social ambience and community feeling of email discussion groups.

It is, of course, impossible to conclude that the actual participants in this thread came away convinced. For example, TL and LW, whose postings had initiated the discussion, posted only a single message each to the thread. We cannot infer from the postings what their motives were to remain silent; lack of interest, frustration, or other things to do (other threads to participate in) may have led them and others to abandon the discussion. Nor were all aspects covered to the extent that it could be said that a conclusion was reached. In particular, the suggestion that construction of monumental buildings was an inappropriate expenditure had not been fully discussed, though one participant suggested that, following completion of the Mount Carmel buildings, it would be appropriate for Baha'is to express a wish for an enhanced programme of local investment.

Taken together, however, the various postings constituted a well-rounded exploration of the issue and suggested a resolution that, while unofficial, was both logical and respectful of the religion's writings and institutions. In this, and in its brevity, the thread we have considered here is somewhat atypical. Many Talisman threads ran on much longer. For example, a thread on Baha'i teachings regarding the virgin birth of Jesus Christ, a very useful example of discursive plausibility alignment, ran for over a month (21 January to 28 February 1996) and, when printed, amounted to seventy-five single-spaced pages. Some recurring questions never reached resolution – notably, that, according to an ordinance of Baha'u'llah, only men and not women are eligible as members of the Universal House of Justice.

The availability of Baha'i email lists and the facility they provide for relatively free discussion of any topic has fostered important developments in the intellectual life of the Baha'i community. In addition, email has permitted creation of a substantial accessible record of the community's internal discourse. On Talisman (and, to a significant though lesser extent, on other Baha'i email lists) prevailing community understandings of Baha'i history, theology, community life, and administrative practice were evaluated and discussed more thoroughly and frankly at the grass-roots level than had previously been possible.

A case of plausibility alignment

We suggest that – speaking very broadly and generally – the 'purview' of Talisman – though never defined in these terms – can be interpreted as an ongoing group exercise in plausibility alignment. The process of plausibility alignment is continual, as external circumstances are constantly changing, and necessitates continual adjustment or revision of the group's ideology (as the members understand it) to correspond with developments in the world at large. It occurs in leadership circles as well as at the grass roots and helps assure that threats to the group's self-perception arising from such things as dramatic developments in the daily news, problematic aspects of its own ideology, or lapses in the conduct of its members can be managed or neutralized. More generally, the process provides a means by which the community can maintain its collective sense of itself.

Baha'i is a lay religion, governed by elected institutions, and the Baha'i leaders are elected or appointed from the ranks of the community; they are not academically trained theologians or religious scholars. Underlying Baha'i administration is a doctrine referred to as the Covenant, which specifies the leadership succession in the religion, and forbids Baha'is from organizing opposition to it, on penalty of expulsion from the community. Many postings to the thread prominently displayed avowals of loyalty and obedience to the senior Baha'i institutions. The reference to Baha'is 'joyfully submitting' to the decisions of the Universal House of Justice; suggestions that Baha'is, far from concerning themselves with the wisdom of locating the projects in Israel, use this fact as part of their teaching message; affirmations that Mount Carmel is a magical place; expressions of satisfaction at being able to participate in such a historic undertaking – all contrast sharply with one participant's expressed doubts about the project. Indeed, a number of the posts seem to be a sort of implicit shouting down of a member who had displayed sentiments considered inappropriate. Over the course of Talisman there were many instances of this, from both the 'heterodox' and 'orthodox' wings of the group.

Almost by definition, the activities on a mailing list such as Talisman are of a kind that the leadership of a religious community, as stewards of its public image, would wish to de-emphasize. The Universal House of Justice has expressed concerns regarding the reach and speed of email, and the risks it entails, in a number of communications. In a letter to an individual written on its behalf in 1996 the House of Justice commented,

> In the past, discussions among Baha'is would take place orally among groups of friends in private, or at summer schools and other Baha'i events, or in letters between individuals. Inevitably, many erroneous statements were made; not all comments were as temperate as they should have been; many statements were misunderstood by those who heard them . . . Now, the same kind of discussion is spread among a hundred or more people . . . is in a form more durable than speech, and can be disseminated to a vast readership at the touch of a button. Such discussions among Baha'is call for self-restraint and purity of motive as well as cordiality, frankness and openness.[23]

The quotation illustrates the dilemma for the Universal House of Justice when a mailing list such as Talisman becomes a prominent discussion forum unconnected to the Baha'i administration. On the one hand, it is a Baha'i principle that the individual has the right and duty independently to seek truth. On the other hand, a group of individuals who collectively seek truth in online discussions have initiated the kind of conversation that normally takes place inside the religious organization. As with any other leadership, the House of Justice could have chosen to endorse the website, and could have appointed high-ranking Baha'is to participate in the discussion. Had that been done, the discussion list would have soon lost its exploratory character, participants would have dropped away and a forum for independent plausibility alignment would have been lost to the community. The Universal House of Justice could also have chosen to ignore the discussion list completely, running the risk that its influence might increase beyond administrative control, or, perhaps more likely, that it would become a major source of intra-community contention. The House of Justice could have ordered that the discussion list be immediately shut down, or, a less drastic step, could have asked American Baha'i authorities to put pressure on individual posters to exercise restraint or self-censorship in expression of their views. This was apparently the course of action followed, and eventually led to the closing of the list (see Cole 1998).[24]

The propensity of email discussions to become contentious is well documented, and Talisman was no exception.[25] Put in terms of plausibility alignment, Talisman participants were unable, in the end, to find ways to adjust a number of critical disjunctures in community opinion, but continued to argue and explore these difficult issues even after most participants probably recognized that the discussions were no longer productive.

In its initial phase, Talisman seemed a successful exercise in bypass, in that free discussion of weighty community issues was facilitated by the Internet. Initially, the group functioned without interference from Baha'i institutions. However, the fact that it was closed demonstrates that groups such as Talisman are not just entities floating in cyberspace. They also represent a group of people who are under obligations elsewhere and whose decisions to contribute to the discussion must take into account the requirement that as members of the Baha'i religion they should not ignore serious advice or instructions from the Baha'i organization. This instance suggests that the much-heralded bypass opportunity of the Internet may be more of an ideal construction than a reality in many cases.

The query underlying the particular thread analysed – was it meaningful to establish a connection between completion of the Mount Carmel project and the advent of world peace? – brought into focus a number of community concerns, notably the ongoing desire among Baha'is to bring new converts into the community, and to reach 'people of capacity' with its message. Reaching thinking people with the Baha'i message is rendered problematic by Baha'i teachings that appear out of step with contemporary values and by an ambient supernaturalism that permeates both official and popular

Baha'i. A second important issue is the harmony between science and religion – that religious teachings are to accord with reason. Some Baha'is have troubled themselves to disentangle Baha'i teachings both from the extravagances of popular Baha'i culture and from literal understandings of Baha'i scriptures. The references to 'magical thinking', 'power art', and Baha'is looking 'ridiculous' reflect the vehemence of this effort. But a campaign to 'correct' popular understandings is evidently resented by other sections of the community as potentially dangerous and often arrogant. Several dismissive references to 'thinking people' illustrated a view that may be phrased as: Who are these people to question what Shoghi Effendi said or what the Universal House of Justice decided? One poster made a laboured attempt to demonstrate the logical derivation of his belief, apparently to prove that even spiritual realities have a scientific basis.

A third concern intertwined with the thread is actually a grass-roots version of the same need that brought about the creation of a professionally designed official Baha'i website – the imperative for a religious community to make a good appearance before the world. By hashing out troubling questions through the give and take of email discourse, participants on Talisman (and on other Baha'i associated email lists) sought to assure themselves that Baha'i teachings, properly understood, were not only valid spiritually but harmonious with rational traditions.

Notes

1 The history and influence of Talisman and its impact on the Baha'i community's relations with the Internet have been sketched elsewhere; see K. P. Johnson (1997), K. Bacquet (2001) and D. Piff (forthcoming).
2 The thread consisted of twenty-one messages posted by thirteen participants, four of whom were women. An edited print of the thread runs to sixteen single-spaced pages. ('Edited' means deletion of repeated material, as when an earlier message is appended to its reply, and deletion of computer routing data, etc., from email address blocks.)
3 Posting to Talisman by ML, 'science, religion, Arc' 11 April 1995.
4 Posting to Talisman by TL, 'Re: Arc' 12 April 1995.
5 Posting to Talisman by SP, 'Re: Arc' 12 April 1995.
6 Posting to Talisman by FS, 'Re: Arc – Buildings <-> Lesser Peace' 12 April 1995.
7 Posting to Talisman by LW, 'The Arc' 12 April 1995.
8 Posting to Talisman by SP, 'Re: The Arc' 12 April 1995.
9 Posting to Talisman by SP, 'Arc texts' 13 April 1995.
10 Posting to Talisman by SP, 'Lesser peace texts' 13 April 1995.
11 Posting to Talisman by SA, 'Re: The Arc' 13 April 1995.
12 Posting to Talisman by SA, 'Re: Arc' 12 April 1995.
13 Posting to Talisman by MH, 'Re: The Arc' 13 April 1995.
14 Postings to Talisman by AR, 'The Arc' and 'Re: The Arc,' 13 and 16 April 1995.
15 Posting to Talisman by CM, 'Re: The Arc' 16 April 1995.
16 Posting to Talisman by AJ, 'Re[2]: The Arc' 17 April 1995.

17 Posting to Talisman by JC, 'Re: The Arc' 16 April 1995. The '10-year World Crusade' refers to a global 'teaching plan', 1953–1963, during which the Baha'i religion enjoyed significant numeric and geographic expansion.
18 Posting to Talisman by SM, 'arc synchronization' 17 April 1995.
19 Among topics on Talisman during the period 11–17 April 1995 were threads on feminist theory, art, the Aqdas and Baha'i Sharia, Amnesty International, bigamy/polygyny, Covenant-breakers, and Baha'i cemeteries in Iran.
20 Posting to Talisman by TL, 'Re: Arc' 12 April 1995.
21 Posting to Talisman by SP, 'Arc texts' 13 April 1995.
22 Posting to Talisman by SP, 'Lesser peace texts' 13 April 1995.
23 Letter to an individual from the Department of the Secretariat, 16 February 1996, posted to Talisman on 20 February 1996. The Secretariat stated that in view of the 'far-reaching problems' to which such discussions can give rise, 'a new level of self-discipline . . . is needed by those who take part'.
24 Following the demise of Talisman there were several developments in Baha'i-oriented discussion lists. Bahai-Studies was created by a Baha'i sociologist at an American university for scholarly discussion of Baha'i academic and other issues. List rules explicitly forbade postings critical of the Baha'i administration. Talisman eventually evolved into Talisman9 for 'free and open discussion of issues in the Baha'i faith from an intellectual point of view', but welcomed criticism of Baha'i institutions. H-Bahai was initiated for academic discussion of Babi and Baha'i topics; membership was generally restricted to individuals with advanced degrees in fields relevant to Baha'i studies. Somewhat later, Bridges was created for similar discussions, but with membership by invitation and restricted to Baha'is.
25 An example, of many that could be provided, is the often-turbulent history of Nurel-L mailing list, founded by Irving Hexham. Though Nurel-L was moderated, and explicitly devoted to scholarly discussion of new religious movements among professionals and interested members of the general public, it was impossible for Hexham to keep discussions from degenerating into fractiousness (in his case, he had to outlaw discussion of Scientology); see Cowan (2000).

Bibliography

Bacquet, K. (2001) 'Enemies Within: Conflict and Control in the Baha'i Community', *Cultic Studies Journal*, 18, pp. 109–140.

Berger, P. (1967) *The Sacred Canopy: Elements of a Sociological Theory of Religion*, New York: Doubleday.

Berger, P. and Luckmann, T. (1966) *The Social Construction of Reality: A Treatise in the Sociology of Knowledge*, New York: Doubleday.

Cole, J. (1998) 'The Baha'i Faith in America as Panopticon, 1963–1997', *Journal for the Scientific Study of Religion*, 37 (2), pp. 234–238.

Cowan, D.E. (2000) 'Religion, Rhetoric and Scholarship: Managing Vested Interest in E-space', in J.K. Hadden and D.E. Cowan (eds) *Religion on the Internet: Research Prospects and Promises*, New York: Elsevier Science, pp. 101–126.

Helland, C. (2002) 'Surfing for Salvation', *Religion*, 32, pp. 293–302.

Johnson, K.P. (1997) 'Baha'i Leaders Vexed by On-line Critics', *Gnosis*, 42, pp. 9–10.

McMillan, J. (1988) 'Institutional Plausibility Alignment as Rhetorical Exercise: A Mainline Denomination's Struggle with the Exigence of Sexism', *Journal for the Scientific Study of Religion*, 27 (3), pp. 326–344.

Piff, D. (2000) *Baha'i Lore*, Oxford: George Ronald.

Piff, D. (forthcoming) 'The Globalization of Information: Baha'i Constructions of the Internet', in M. Warburg, M. Warmind, and A. Hvithamar (eds) *Baha'i and Globalisation*, Aarhus: Aarhus University Press.

Piff, D. and Warburg, M. (2003) 'Millennial Catastrophism in Popular Baha'i Lore', in M. Rothstein and R. Kranenborg (eds) *New Religions in a Post-modern World*, Aarhus: Aarhus University Press, pp. 123–136.

Shoghi Effendi (1958) *Messages to the Baha'i World*, Wilmette: Baha'i Publishing Trust.

Talisman, electronic discussion group postings 1994–1996 collected by D. Piff.

Warburg, M. (2003) 'Religious Groups and Globalisation: A Comparative Perspective', in J. Beckford and J. Richardson (eds) *Challenging Religion: Essays in Honour of Eileen Barker*, London: Routledge, pp. 47–55.

Chapter 7

A symbolic universe

Information terrorism and new religions in cyberspace[1]

Massimo Introvigne

The very notion of cyberspace is a somewhat obvious example of the social construction of a symbolic universe as described by Berger and Luckmann (1967: 76–79) through a threefold process of externalization, objectivation, and internalization. The term 'cyberspace' comes from fiction, and was originally defined by cyberpunk novelist William Gibson (1984: 67) as 'a consensual hallucination experienced together by billions of legitimate operators'. In his novel *Neuromancer*, Gibson invented the notion of cyberspace as a computer-accessible location where all the existing information in the world was collected. Later, John P. Barlow described the real world of connected computers using the same term as Gibson. Some claim, therefore, that cyberspace, as it exists today, should be called 'Barlovian cyberspace' in order to distinguish it from the fictional 'Gibsonian cyberspace' of cyberpunk literature (Jordan 1999: 20–21).

Interestingly enough, two of the most well-known social scientific textbooks on cyberspace, the first strictly sociological and the second social-psychological, divide their discussion of cyberspace into three parallel parts. Jordan (1999), who is primarily interested in power and social politics in cyberspace, sees three layers of virtual space: individual, social, and imaginary. Gackenbach (1998) also divided the textbook she edited on *Psychology and the Internet* into three parts devoted respectively to the intrapersonal (or personal), interpersonal, and transpersonal dimensions of cyberspace. The three dimensions in the two textbooks (personal-individual, interpersonal-social, and transpersonal-imaginary) are obviously parallel. To a certain extent, they also parallel Berger and Luckmann's social construction model:

- In the personal-individual stage, a myriad different, individual human actions create cyberspace as a new form of social institution. This process goes from the individuals to the new institution, and corresponds to Berger and Luckmann's 'externalization'. Each individual can still experience cyberspace alone, on his or her own computer, and the experience may remain psychologically 'intrapersonal'.

- When cyberspace appears, as a given 'objective' reality, it can be shared by a potentially infinite number of individuals. They will now have cyberspace as a mediated reality connecting each individual to all others, or each group to other groups: new forms of interpersonal-social relations develop. This corresponds to Berger and Luckmann's 'objectivation'.
- Subjective understanding of the objectified cyberspace gives rise to transpersonal-imaginary experiences, a virtual imaginary in which both 'visions of heaven' and 'fears of hell' develop (Jordan 1999: 185). This, in turn, corresponds to Berger and Luckmann's 'internalization'.

A significant amount of literature now exists on all three stages of this process. For our purposes, it is particularly important to note that the main social and psychological problem in cyberspace has been discussed under the name of 'information overload'.

Sociologists have explored the paradoxical notion of receiving too much information, more than even the most gifted individual is able to absorb. Shenk (1997: 15) states that information overload 'threatens our ability to educate ourselves, and leaves us more vulnerable as consumers and less cohesive as a society'. Kraut and Attewell (1997: 325), in their study of transnational corporations, noted that 'communication is a resource-consuming process . . . As a result, one would expect that as the volume of communication increases, so will the problems of feeling rushed and overloaded'. Jordan (1999: 117) points to the problem of having 'so much information that the ability to understand it is impaired: the important cannot be distinguished from the unimportant, and too large amounts of information simply cannot be absorbed'. He also mentions a related phenomenon, the 'spiral of technopower', generated when information overload is confronted by introducing new technological tools for information management (Jordan 1999: 128). If these tools are good enough, however, they in turn increase the amount of information available in cyberspace, and 'simply return users, after varying lengths of time, to the first step because new forms of information overload emerge'.

The whole concept of information overload is, in turn, politically negotiated and conditioned. Ultimately, the evaluation of the information overload is connected with the transpersonal-imaginary level of cyberspace, at which political evaluations are made about whether so much information is liberating or threatening. The political issue, here, is that the overload may threaten our normal ability to internalize an information hierarchy. When dealing with the printed media, we realize that *The New York Times* is not infallible, but is in any case more reliable than the *Weekly World News*. A similar information hierarchy is much more difficult to reconstruct in cyberspace, although it is slowly emerging in specialized areas such as financial information. Libertarians may celebrate the subversion of offline hierarchies as the greatest achievement of cyberspace, and some early scholarly studies agreed with them (see for instance Rheingold 1993).

It is true that any attempt to censor parts of cyberspace may sooner or later be bypassed. However, as Jordan (1999: 79) notes, claiming that subverting offline hierarchies automatically creates an anti-hierarchical, and truly democratic, communication may be an example of the logical fallacy known as technological determinism. The latter mistakenly implies that a certain technology necessarily determines a certain social outcome. 'Such pure or strong forms of technological determinism are always weak because they define causes of society through non-social systems, technologies, that appear social as soon as they are themselves investigated' (Jordan 1999: 79). Jordan suggests that cyber-political issues are much more complicated, and that 'offline hierarchies are subverted by cyberspace but are also reconstituted in cyberspace . . . The subversion of hierarchy does not mean that cyberspace is devoid of hierarchy. Rather, new and different hierarchies emerge' (Jordan 1999: 83). Arguing from a social psychological perspective, and studying newsgroups and other sub-Web online communities, Reid (1998: 33) concludes that 'virtual communities are not the *agora*; they are not a place of open and free public discourse. It is a mistake to think that the Internet is an inherently democratic institution, or that it will necessarily lead to increased personal freedoms and increased understanding between people.' The technology allows those who have the best equipment, or technical capabilities, to claim that their information is also inherently better, 'creating social hierarchies that can be every bit as restrictive and oppressive as some in the corporeal world'.

Terrorism via the Internet

Whereas in the early 1990s social science pessimism about the information overload regarded it as an entirely spontaneous phenomenon, in the second half of the decade a new scholarly literature emerged, suggesting that the over-load may be manipulated for the purpose of damaging specific organizations, governments or groups (Denning and Denning 1998; Denning 1999). Internet terrorism became an increasingly well-researched issue, but the term itself was variously defined. Terrorism, in itself, is a socially constructed notion that is continuously renegotiated at the political level. It is almost a truism that one person's terrorist is another person's freedom fighter. Terrorism is generally defined as the symbolic use of actual violence, for political reasons, against non-military targets. By symbolic use, scholars of terrorism suggest that terrorism is successful when its message reaches a large public, much larger than the circle of those actually harmed by it (Thornton 1964; Wilkinson 1975). Violence, in turn, is a controversial concept. In the area of religion-related terrorism particularly, the impact of verbal violence has been regarded as tantamount to terrorism (Sprinzak 1999: 316).

In turn, terrorism against transnational corporations has often been studied in the shape of 'information terrorism'. This is usually defined as the systematic spreading of information aimed at damaging or destroying the business of a corporation. Corporations have used various strategies in order to persuade law enforcement agencies and lawmakers that information terrorism is not necessarily more 'clean' than other forms of terrorism, and as such deserves no added indulgence. While it is true that information terrorism does not normally involve the loss of human life, it may inflict damage far greater than other non-lethal terrorist activities. An ecoterrorist group targeting a transnational corporation, for instance, may cause comparatively little damage by blowing up one or more warehouses. Additionally, after the first terrorist acts, security will inevitably be increased, as also the risk for the terrorists themselves. Successfully spreading 'information' that a key product of the same corporation causes cancer, or other lethal diseases, is much more effective. 'Internet terrorism', as used in the relevant literature, seems to cover different and not necessarily related activities. Cyber-terrorism, i.e. attack to systems and infrastructures, should be distinguished from information terrorism via the Internet. Here, the Internet is the privileged source used to spread information aimed at damaging or destroying a particular organization.

Legal literature discusses cases in which the target is a corporation ('Legal Wars on the Web: A Checklist' 1999). Categorizing these activities as 'terrorist' seems to be more appropriate when they are perpetrated in furtherance of a political (as opposed to a merely economic) aim. The Internet, in this sense, may be particularly attractive for information terrorism as a way of circumventing possible censorship by the mainline media, and of making legal counter-attacks more difficult. This has been particularly true of 'single-issue terrorism' in fields such as animal rights, environmentalism, and abortion (Smith 1998). In these fields, a preferred strategy, in which the Internet has played a key role, has been the publication of 'hit lists' of both individuals and corporations allegedly associated with extraordinary evil. Perhaps the most famous legal cases, evidencing the problems in defining the boundaries between verbal and non-verbal violence, concern the anti-abortion websites publishing the so-called Nuremberg Files. This list includes names and other personal information concerning a number of doctors who perform abortions, and qualifies them as 'baby butchers'.

Anti-cult extremism and the Internet

New religious movements and the Internet have an interesting, if controversial, relationship. Following the mass suicide of Heaven's Gate in March 1997, many commentaries reported on the movement's active propaganda via the Internet, and expressed the fear that naive Internet passers-by might easily be recruited into suicidal cults through well-crafted websites. Relevant scholarship suggests that, while not unheard of (Kellner 1996; O'Leary 1996), Internet conversions to new religious movements are rare, and do not contribute significantly to their growth (Dawson and Hennebry 1999; Mayer 2000). On the other hand, it has also been suggested that 'the so-called "anti-cult" groups [are] the main beneficiaries of the development of the Internet at this point' (Mayer 2000).

The development of these so-called anti-cult movements has been documented in scholarly literature on new religious movements since the early 1980s (see Shupe and Bromley 1980; Shupe, Bromley and Oliver 1984; Shupe and Bromley 1985; Beckford 1985). More recently, these studies have been both updated (see Melton 1999) and re-examined in a cross-cultural perspective (Shupe and Bromley 1994; Usarski 1999; Chryssides 1999). While the demise of the largest American anti-cult organization, the Cult Awareness Network, finally occurred because of its involvement in a violent and illegal activity, i.e. forcible deprogramming, mainline anti-cult groups in the United States have maintained throughout their history an interest in researching and arguing their position, and not only in political or direct action. Anti-cult movements in Europe have been less research-oriented and more pro-active from their very beginning. Following the Order of the Solar Temple suicides and homicides in 1994–1997 in particular, some European anti-cult movements experienced an unprecedented degree of public support and influenced national anti-cult legislation, particularly in France.

Although wars between new religious movements and their opponents have found a battleground on the Internet since at least the Web's early beginnings, very few groups have actually been accused of cyber-terrorism. Aum Shinri-kyo was accused by a Christian website in Japan of preparing a cyber-attack against national infrastructures, but no evidence for this charge has emerged. Cult wars are much more related to information terrorism via the Internet. Here, again, it should be stressed that information terrorism is a politically constructed category and what for one is verbal terrorism is for another free speech. Authoritative scholars of information terrorism via the Internet, such as Denning (1999: 101–129), include 'perception management' in their studies, in the form of 'offensive operations [which] reach the minds of a population by injecting content into the population's information space'. She lists systematic 'lies and distortions', fabrications, hoaxes, social engineering, 'denouncement' ('messages that discredit, defame, demonize, or dehumanize an opponent'), and – strictly related to the latter – 'conspiracy theories'. Denning (1999: 90–94) also includes harassment through hate mail or 'spamming', and even systematic copyright infringement. The latter, she argues, may in fact become part of terrorist 'offensive information warfare' when aimed at destroying an organization or corporation through the destruction of copyright as one of its most valuable assets. The whole notion of 'copyright terrorism' is a good example of how language in this field is politically negotiated. The Church of Scientology (which has obtained quite a few court orders against Internet opponents on the basis of copyright infringement) and its critics have liberally traded accusations of 'copyright terrorism'.

For the Church of Scientology, this is systematic copyright infringement, while for its opponents the real 'terrorism' lies in its use of the copyright law for the purpose of silencing its critics (Holeton 1998: 353).

Apart from copyright issues, other kinds of information terrorism and offensive information warfare listed by Denning are well represented in the cult wars on the Internet. Unlike in the United States, the largest anti-cult organizations in Europe have but a limited presence on the Internet. They probably see no reason for diverting resources from other successful strategies. On the other hand, fringe groups and (particularly) single individuals in the anti-cult camp operate large websites. What differentiates anti-cult information terrorism and offensive information warfare via the Internet from less extreme forms of anti-cult activity in cyberspace is the presence of one or more of the criteria outlined by Denning: 'messages that . . . demonize, or dehumanize an opponent', 'conspiracy theories', and the systematic 'publication of false statements'. A fourth element is the publication of 'hit lists' of individuals (other than the founders and leaders of the targeted movements), thus inviting – if not extreme measures, as in the tragic case of the Nuremberg Files – at least discrimination, and boycotts of 'cult-related' businesses. Although a few dozen similar anti-cult enterprises exist on the Web, I will examine just three specific examples, one related to the involvement of anti-cultists in post-September 11 controversies about Islam and the USA and two to new religious movements, before discussing reactions by the targeted new religions movements.

Internet wars after 11 September 2001: the case of the Association of Italian Muslims

A key feature of some of the most extreme anti-cult activities on the Internet has been an almost pathological anti-Americanism. It would be tempting, but well beyond the scope of this chapter, to discuss the relationship between the spread of extreme anti-Americanism in France (see Revel 2002) and the prevalence of extreme anti-cultism in that country, not only on the Web. The image of 'cults' as an 'American Trojan horse' aimed at de-secularizing secular France has become widespread even in otherwise respectable French media. After 11 September 2001, a number of prominent figures of the extreme anti-cult Internet milieu increased their attacks on the United States, and some of them went so far as to co-operate openly with Muslim fundamentalists. A case in point is the small network of Italian anti-cultists active on the Internet. Anti-cultism is not as popular in Italy as it is in other countries: online anti-cult crusades in Italy seldom generate serious offline consequences, although they may be quoted and used in other countries. There is, for instance, an entire website, Kelebek (operated by a former Italian leader of New Acropolis, Miguel Martinez), devoted to slandering scholars associated with CESNUR, the Center for Studies on New Religions (whose managing director is the author of this chapter) as 'cult apologists'. In this case, however, several hundreds of pages have been online for years without generating (as far as I know) a single line of comment in any of the mainline Italian media. On the other hand, the anti-CESNUR website (which includes many pages in languages other than Italian) has been quoted within the framework of local campaigns against 'cults' (and 'cult apologists') in France, Germany, and (more occasionally) in the USA.

The large anti-CESNUR section of this website has substantially not been updated since 11 September, as its sponsors seem to have focused on facets of anti-Americanism other than the struggle against 'American' cults and their alleged 'apologists'. With 'cults' almost forgotten, the energies of the Kelebek website have been devoted to criticizing President Bush, the Iraqi war, and the war against terrorism in general; not unexpectedly, the anti-American slogans used remain very much the same as when US-based 'multinational cults' were criticized. And the sympathy for Kelebek's previous crusade against 'cult apologists' has persuaded other activists in the small Italian anti-cult community to advertise and support Kelebek's new efforts, unrelated as they may be to the 'cult' issue.

A thorn in the side of both moderate and radical Islamic fundamentalists in Italy was a tiny group known as the Associazione Musulmani Italiani (Association of Italian Muslims), the result of the 1993 merger of two very small Muslim organizations in Rome. Although representing only a handful of followers, its leader Abdul Hadi Palazzi has emerged as one of the most vocal critics of the fundamentalist Islamic Brotherhood (or Society of Muslim Brothers), the Brotherhood-connected leadership of the largest Italian Muslim organization (UCOII), and the Brotherhood-related preachers, such as Qatar's charismatic Shaykh Yusuf al-Qaradawi, who come to Rome to participate in events of inter-religious dialogue sponsored by the Roman Catholic Church. Not only are Palazzi and his organization (now renamed Italian Muslim Assembly, after his separation from the Associazione Musulmani Italiani) pro-US; they are vehemently pro-Israel, and represent a unique 'Muslim-Zionist' position, constantly exposing the Islamic Brotherhood as having as one of its branches the terrorist movement Hamas in Palestine. In fact, outside observers suspect Palazzi to be connected with Israeli intelligence (see Allam 2002), and certainly he has been a guest at gatherings in Israel and elsewhere sponsored by intelligence-connected organizations. The very existence of Palazzi's organization, small and unrepresentative of the Italian Muslim community as it is, allows pro-Israeli and anti-Islamic Brotherhood political institutions in Italy, the USA and Israel to claim that at least 'a portion' of the Islamic world supports their positions (and to deny that UCOII is the 'sole' representative of the Italian Muslim community).

The strategy of focusing an entire website against a single objective (a speciality of extreme Internet anti-cultists) has been used against Palazzi and his organizations. Although an international anti-Palazzi website is signed by one Francesca Russo, and apparently a young scholar by this name is prepared to accept some responsibility for it, Palazzi claims that the same person who authored the anti-CESNUR website, Miguel Martinez, is behind the attack. Certainly, the style is strikingly similar, Martinez has advertised the anti-Palazzi initiative on Kelebek and vehemently attacked Palazzi himself, and his anti-American position is consistent with the tune of the criticism against Palazzi. Be this as it may, this bizarre incident is an interesting example of how, after 11 September, extreme anti-cultists who were at the same time anti-American activists 'recycled' themselves in extreme campaigns ultimately aimed at the American and Israeli administrations, and confirms how deep the connection between extreme anti-cultism and anti-Americanism is.

Sûkyô Mahikari and Scientology

Mayer (2000) has studied the impact of the web assault against Sûkyô Mahikari, a Japanese new religious movement, by Australian ex-member Garry A. Greenwood. Later self-published by the author (Greenwood 1997), his book *All the Emperor's Men* has been available via the Web since 1995 (see www.geocities.com/Tokyo/Shrine/5712/copy.htm). While Greenwood starts with facts well known among scholars of Sûkyô Mahikari (although perhaps not among its members), such as the founder's association in his early life with other Japanese new religious movements, the text – and the website – quickly degenerate. The founder of Mahikari, Kotama Okada (1901–1974), is first dehumanized by being associated with a number of war crimes committed by the Japanese Army, in which he was an officer, during the Second World War. Although Okada was undoubtedly a fervent nationalist, allegations of atrocities are unsubstantiated (see Introvigne 1999a). Secondly, the movement is dehumanized by being associated with Nazism and anti-Semitism. Again, as in other Japanese movements, an anti-Semitic element was present in Mahikari's early texts, but it is elevated to a completely different order of magnitude in Greenwood's allegations. Mahikari, he writes, is 'promoting the same notorious ideals as those enforced by Adolf Hitler' (Greenwood 1997: 76). Finally, Mahikari is further dehumanized through an association with Aum Shinri-kyo. Greenwood repeats the common Japanese anti-cult theme that the sins of Aum Shinri-kyo are the sins of new religious movements in general, but with a distinct conspiratorial emphasis. This conspiracy, Greenwood states, is called 'The Black Hand', and the fingers are Aum Shinri-kyo, Sûkyô Mahikari, the Unification Church, Agonshu, and Soka Gakkai. 'Now that one of the hand's fingers (Aum Shinri-kyo) has been severed, the remaining four must now strive even harder until it can regrow, or be replaced with something different, presumably under a different disguise' (Greenwood 1997: 91). Ultimately, within the framework of a 'yellow danger' rhetoric, Japan itself becomes demonized as the 'author' of a national conspiracy aimed at enforcing a 'global theocracy' under the Japanese emperor, through cults no matter how criminal, international terrorism, and violence. Anti-cultism, therefore, ultimately becomes a form of racism. Greenwood's web page is an example of how some actual (and actually objectionable) features of new religious movements, or the careers of their leaders, are so distorted through gross exaggeration that the rhetoric of controversy mutates into character assassination, demonization, and racism.

The Church of Scientology is the subject of the largest number of such assaults. Again, it is almost a truism that Scientology is surrounded by controversy, and has been particularly unpopular among web libertarians since its use of vigorous legal strategies against copyright infringement and defamation. On the other hand, the demonization of Scientology in some websites goes far beyond normal controversy. The most typical – and one of the largest – web pages demonizing Scientology is the Tilman Hausherr home page in Berlin, Germany (see www.snafu.de/~tilman). Although it includes links to pages against a variety of other 'cults', from Jehovah's Witnesses to Opus Dei, most of this large-scale website is devoted purely to disparaging Scientology. Among hundreds of pages, one can hardly find any reconstruction of Scientology's beliefs, or a philosophical, or theological, criticism of its worldview. Hausherr offers instead a lengthy list of anti-Scientology articles already published in a wide range of newspapers and magazines, decisions unfavourable to Scientology in courts of law, personal recollections by apostate ex-members, and governmental reports against Scientology.

The first welcome in this web page is a quote from an early parliamentary report in Australia that 'Scientology is evil; its techniques evil; its practice a serious danger to the community, medically, morally and socially; and its adherents are sadly deluded and often mentally ill'. Hausherr's page is, to some extent, redeemed by a sense of humour normally lacking among the extreme fringes of anti-cultism. However, as Hexham and Poewe (1999: 212–213, 219) have noted, although 'attacks on respectable German politicians by members of Scientology' calling them 'Nazis' were both 'tasteless' and 'counterproductive', it is indeed true that 'some members of the German anti-cult movement threaten the noble cause of preserving democracy' they claim to serve. 'Although phrased somewhat differently, the rhetoric used by the German anti-cult movement to discredit Scientology mirrors the rhetoric used by National Socialists to attack Jews.' It is difficult to be amused when reading Hausherr's web page laundry lists of individual Scientologists and of 'companies and organizations owned or managed by people listed as Scientologists'. Some are well-known Scientologists such as Kristie Alley or John Travolta. Most, however, are private individuals unknown to the general public. Companies 'owned or managed by people listed as Scientologists' (an ambiguous concept) range from law firms to architects, computer businesses, and to Elvis Presley Enterprises (Priscilla Presley is a Scientologist).

Finally, there is a list of 'miscellaneous support for Scientology', including both academics and other scholarly 'cult apologists' (Hausherr maintains an encyclopaedia of cult apologists in the form of a Frequently Asked Questions section, and posts it regularly to Usenet groups), as well as others accused of being 'soft' on Scientology. The latter include CNN (accused of having 'a long record of supporting Scientology'), the Internal Revenue Service (IRS) (because of the 1993 settlement), the Los Angeles Police Department, and even a lawyer who actually fought *against* Scientology but settled in terms Hausherr did not approve of. It is unlikely that CNN or Elvis Presley Enterprises will really suffer from being listed in Hausherr's web page. A doctor, dentist, or architect in a small town, or a small business, on the other hand, may be easily discriminated against. If 'Scientology is evil', nobody should associate with an 'evil' business. And who would want a Scientologist as a doctor or architect if Scientologists are 'often mentally ill'? Although no actual violence is advocated, the list, a main feature of Hausherr's site, becomes in fact a 'hit list'.

There are other websites devoted to attacking Scientology in Europe, most of them subsequent national versions in the local languages of Hausherr's enterprise, although also including domestic articles and court decisions. The general message is very much the same.

Reactions

Scientology reacts quite forcefully in the legal arena. There are, also, pro-Scientology websites mostly devoted to personal attacks against the most active online and offline opponents (such as www.parishioners.org). There have also been more technical cyber-attacks, minor forms of cyber-terrorism, used against Scientology critics. The most famous was, perhaps, the so-called 'attack of the robotic poets' (Poulsen 1999). A 'poetry machine' is able to send thousands of unsolicited messages to Usenet groups reusing headers of frequent contributors. News groups are thus flooded by a deluge of riddles reminiscent of the cut-up experiments of the Beat generation poets (such as: 'Why is another horseman either cytoplasm enchantingly?'). Although other news groups were also targeted, the 'most consistent target' (Poulsen 1999) was alt.religion.scientology, a news group in which some Scientologists are also active, but which in fact is dominated by Scientology critics. Tilman Hausherr, a daily contributor to alt.religion.scientology, coined the word 'sporgeries' (spam-forgeries), and promoted software to kill the unwelcome messages. Hausherr also claimed that anonymous friends of Scientology perpetrated other cyber-attacks against the hostile news group.

Robotic poets notwithstanding, alt.religion.scientology is a well-known and successful group on the Usenet. The fight between the Church of Scientology and alt.religion.scientology might be one of the best-known Usenet sagas. On the other hand, the news group is far from being user-friendly for the outsider, since what may be classified as real information is submerged by endless tirades, occasional flame wars (the Usenet name for fighting with an increasingly loud tone), and simple four-letter word sequences. Although some Scientologists do participate in the news group, most participants are rabid opponents of Scientology. One 'Bernie', who claims to be a moderate critic of Scientologists, manages an impressive website collecting examples of flames, insults, and racist remarks against Scientology that, in his opinion, have now far exceeded the measure of what is tolerable (www.bernie. cncfamily.com/ars.htm).

On the other hand, notwithstanding the concerns of 'Bernie', or the Church of Scientology, and the folk hero status of the anti-cult cyber-warriors among the Internet libertarian community, they are mostly preaching to the converted. The overwhelming majority of messages in alt.religion.scientology are posted by fellow anti-cultists. The impact on Scientology and its statistics by both Usenet and Internet has been minimal in terms of loss of membership, although the media and government agencies hostile to Scientology have found the Web anti-cultism to be a useful resource. In general, Scientologists fully expect to be attacked and criticized; their worldview allows ample room for enemies (generally perceived as criminally motivated) and the Internet attack has easily been explained as just another confirmation that Scientology, by being 'right' and successful in what it does, raises the wrath of powerful (if criminal) opponents. The vigorous legal reaction by the leadership is generally both expected and supported by Scientologists.

Contrary to the case of Scientology, the damage inflicted by Greenwood on Sûkyô Mahikari has been very extensive in Europe and Australia (but less so in Japan and also in Africa, a remarkably unwired continent where the movement has an important constituency). Members and ex-members interviewed for this study have reported that, for months and even years, copies of Greenwood's and other anti-Mahikari web pages were passed within the movement by one member to another causing considerable damage. The leadership's reaction was from weak to non-existent. Members raising questions were largely told that (1) the movement has a general policy discouraging the use of the Internet; and (2) the fact that the member raised the question was evidence that the member was weak and had personal problems in need of a spiritual solution (a strong member would not entertain doubts in the first place). It is unclear whether these were reactions by local European and Australian leaders, or were approved by the headquarters in Japan. The latter were perhaps slow in evaluating the extent of the damage, partially because of their general attitude towards the Internet, and also because the damage was less apparent in Japan. They were also unfamiliar with some of the issues raised by the opponents (for instance, Greenwood's accusation that Mahikari's founder extensively used the infamous anti-Semitic text known as the *Protocols of the Elders of Zion* was false, but the Sûkyô Mahikari leadership was so unfamiliar with the *Protocols* that it was initially unable to prepare a clear reply). Last but not least, the leaders had a theological reason for their lack of reaction. Unlike Scientology, Sûkyô Mahikari believes that opponents are not simply criminals but that their activities correspond to a cosmic play between the divinities of justice (now returning to their ruling role in the world) and the divinities of indulgence; the latter may cause injustice, yet their action is somewhat necessary for the cosmic balance to be preserved. The result of this cosmic play is a cleansing activity of the world, and the Internet assaults, mirroring cosmic events, were cleansing the organization of its weak members. Hence the partially voluntary lack of legal and other reaction against attacks which may have lost Sûkyô Mahikari almost half of its membership in certain Western countries.

Scientology and Sûkyô Mahikari represent two extremes in how new religious movements deal with extreme Internet anti-cultism. Most ignore it on the surface, yet deal quietly with it through internal counter-propaganda campaigns, often successful enough to avoid major damage. The cases of Scientology and Sûkyô Mahikari evidence the important element that the reaction, or lack thereof, to these campaigns is also based on theological presuppositions not immediately apparent to the outsider.

Conclusion

The symbolic universe of cyberspace seems to be a new arena where 'cults' and their enemies cross swords. So far, this Internet arena has exhibited a better potential for destruction than for construction when it comes to marginal religious movements. The Web is not the best place for recruiting; it is an excellent place for spreading rumours, slander, and defamation against a given target. It is quicker and less expensive than other media, and enjoys a unique legal situation. In several countries, anti-defamation laws specifically tailored to the Internet have yet to be written. Even when a website is closed down in one country, it can move to another country in a matter of a few hours; the possibilities for compelling the defamed party to litigate in a jurisdiction more favourable to the slanderer (what lawyers call 'forum shopping') are almost limitless. The case of Scientology, however, shows that systematic legal reaction may achieve some results, although there are also risks associated with over-reacting.

A first theoretical problem is whether the use of the Internet for systematic defamation, taking advantage of the legal loopholes, may be legitimately defined as a form of 'information terrorism'. Extreme anti-cultists react quite strongly when called 'Internet terrorists'. Certainly, the category of 'terrorism' is in turn politically negotiated and socially constructed. The question is only partially equivalent to whether it is possible and relevant to extend the meaning of the word 'terrorism' to cover 'verbal violence'. Publishing 'hit lists', names and addresses of private individuals, destroying the possibility of enforcing copyrights, and systematically breaching privacy laws on websites whose legal domicile is outside any jurisdiction where privacy laws may be enforced, represent more than 'verbal violence' and are better described as a form of violence positioned in a grey area between verbal and physical.

Another problem is whether, in view of possible abuses by extremists (whether called 'Internet terrorists' or otherwise), the early emphasis on the Internet as an eminently liberating device was not inherently misleading. While celebrations of the Internet as a new and more democratic approach to information were probably premature, dystopic perspectives of manipulated Internet hierarchies subverting offline hierarchies, destroying responsibility and accountability in the process, need not necessarily prevail. Students educated in the use of the Internet since primary school (Garner and Gillingham 1996), religious leaders, reporters, and perhaps in the long run even anti-cult government officials, will learn to distinguish between the Web equivalents of tabloids and *The New York Times*. Gackenbach and Ellerman (1998) invite us to avoid the easy comparison with television, and 'take a lesson from radio' instead. Before the 1920s, and in some countries up to the Second World War, radio was dominated by thousands of small, independent local stations. Almost everybody was able to air literally anything from radio stations, originally with little or no control, and widespread fears were expressed that people would believe anything coming from them (perhaps originating from foreign spies and other subversives). 'The exponential growth of the Internet', Gackenbach and Ellerman (1998: 11) note, 'has happened before', with radio.

Although some secret services did use radio stations for prewar propaganda, ultimately the worst doom scenarios were never realized. Slowly but surely, it was not only technological evolution and governmental regulation that limited the number of stations and created more accountability (a development we may, or may not, see on the Internet in the near future), but the ordinary citizen was now able to reconstruct and internalize a new hierarchy of information sources, including radio. It is true that, after a few years, information hierarchy frames had to be reconstructed and re-internalized in order to include television, and today we face the Internet. Technologies, however, are also social, and technological determinism has been largely debunked as a positivistic fallacy. While vigilance against information terrorism via the Internet is in order, the best weapon against any form of information terrorism will ultimately be the integration of new sources into the already existing and internalized hierarchy of information sources. Education, social science, and courts of law (reconstructing new meanings to cater for concepts such as copyright or defamation as applied to cyberspace) will each have a major role to play in this eminently human enterprise.

Note

1   Earlier, partial versions of this paper have been published by Intovigne (1999b, 2000, and 2001).

References

Allam, M. (2002) *Bin Laden in Italia. Viaggio nell'Islam radicale*, Milan: Mondadori.

Beckford, J.A. (1985) *Cult Controversies: The Social Response to New Religious Movements*, London: Tavistock Publications.

Berger, P. and Luckmann, T. (1967) *The Social Construction of Reality*, Harmondsworth: Penguin Books.

Chryssides, G.D. (1999) 'Britain's Anti-Cult Movement', in B. Wilson and J. Cresswell (eds) *New Religious Movements: Challenge and Response*, London and New York: Routledge, pp. 257–273.

Dawson, L.L. and Hennebry, J. (1999) 'New Religions and the Internet: Recruiting in New Public Space', *Journal of Contemporary Religion*, 14 (1), pp. 17–39.

Denning, D.E. (1999) *Information Warfare and Security*, Reading (Massachusetts): Addison-Wesley.

Denning, D.E. and Denning, P.J. (eds) (1998) *Internet Besieged: Countering Cyberspace Scofflaws*, New York: ACM Press.

Gackenbach, J. (ed.) (1998) *Psychology and the Internet: Intrapersonal, Interpersonal, and Transpersonal Implications*, San Diego (California) and London: Academic Press.

Gackenbach, J. and Ellerman, E. (1998) 'Introduction to Psychological Aspects of Internet Use', in J. Gackenbach (ed.) *Psychology and the Internet: Intrapersonal, Interpersonal, and Transpersonal Implications*, San Diego (California) and London: Academic Press, pp. 1–26.

Garner, R. and Gillingham, M.G. (1996) *Internet Communication in Six Classrooms: Conversations Across Time, Space, and Culture*, Mahwah (New Jersey): Lawrence Erlbaum Associates.

Gibson, W. (1984) *Neuromancer*, London: Grafton Books.

Greenwood, G.A. (1997) *All the Emperor's Men*, Alstonville (New South Wales, Australia): The Author [First published in 1995].

Hadden, J. and Cowan, D.E. (eds) (2000) *Religion on the Internet: Research Prospects and Promises*, Amsterdam, London and New York: JAI Press.

Hexham, I. and Poewe, K. (1999) '"Verfassungsfeindlich": Church, State, and New Religions in Germany', *Nova Religio: The Journal of Alternative and Emergent Religions*, 2 (2), pp. 208–227.

Holeton, R. (1998) *Composing Cyberspace: Identity, Community, and Knowledge in the Electronic Age*, Boston: McGraw-Hill.

Introvigne, M. (1999a) *Sûkyô Mahikari*, Leumann (Turin): Elle Di Ci.

Introvigne, M. (1999b) 'So Many Evil Things: Anti-Cult Terrorism via the Internet', paper presented at the annual conference of the Association of Sociology of Religion, Chicago, 5 August 1999. Available from: http://www.cesnur.org.

Introvigne, M. (2000) 'So Many Evil Things: Anti-Cult Terrorism via the Internet', in J.K. Hadden, and D.E. Cowan (eds) *Religion on the Internet: Research Prospects and Promises*, Amsterdam, London, and New York: Elsevier Science, pp. 277–306.

Introvigne, M. (2001) 'Nyreligiøse bevægelser og kultmodstandere på nettet', in M.J. Jensen, M.K. Pedersen, and A.C.B. Talbro (eds) *Når nettet ændrer verden*, Copenhagen: Børsens Forlag, pp. 224–236.

Jordan, T. (1999) *Cyberpower: The Culture and Politics of Cyberspace in the Internet*, London and New York: Routledge.

Kellner, M.A. (1996) *God on the Internet*, Foster City (California): IDG Books Worldwide.

Kiesler, S. (ed.) (1997) *Culture of the Internet*, Mahwah (New Jersey): Lawrence Erlbaum Associates.

Kraut, R.E. and Attewell, P. (1997) 'Media Use in a Global Corporation: Electronic Mail and Organizational Knowledge', in S. Kiesler (ed.) *Culture of the Internet*, Mahwah (New Jersey): Lawrence Erlbaum Associates, pp. 323–342.

'Legal Wars on the Web: A Checklist' (1999) *Horizon*, 5, pp. 1–3.

Mayer, J.-F. (2000) 'Religious Movements and the Internet: The New Frontier of Cult Controversies', in J.K. Hadden and D.E. Cowan (eds) *Religion on the Internet: Research Prospects and Promises*, Amsterdam, London and New York: Elsevier Science, pp. 249–276.

Melton, J.G. (1999) 'Anti-Cultists in the United States: An Historical Perspective', in B. Wilson and J. Cresswell (eds) *New Religious Movements: Challenge and Response*, London and New York: Routledge, pp. 213–233.

O'Leary, S.D. (1996) 'Cyberspace as Sacred Space: Communicating Religion on Computer Networks', *Journal of the American Academy of Religion*, 64(4), pp. 781–808.

Poulsen, K. (1999) 'Attack of the Robotic Poets'. Available: http://www.techtv.com/cybercrime/features/story/0,23008,2254578,00.html [Accessed January 2003].

Reid, E. (1998) 'The Self and the Internet: Variations on the Illusion of One Self', in J. Gackenbach (ed.) *Psychology and the Internet: Intrapersonal, Interpersonal, and Transpersonal Implications*, San Diego (California) and London: Academic Press, pp. 29–42.

Revel, J.-F. (2002) *L'Obsession anti-américaine: son fonctionnement, ses causes, ses inconséquences*, Paris: Plon.

Rheingold, H. (1993) *The Virtual Community: Homesteading on the Electronic Frontier*, New York: Addison-Wesley.

Shenk, D. (1997) *Data Smog: Surviving the Information Age*, San Francisco: Harper SanFrancisco.

Shupe, A.D., Jr, and Bromley, D.G. (1980) *The New Vigilantes: Deprogrammers, Anti-Cultists, and the New Religions*, Beverly Hills (California): Sage Publications.

Shupe, A.D., Jr, and Bromley, D.G. (1985) *A Documentary History of the Anti-Cult Movement*, Arlington (Texas): Center for Social Research, University of Texas.

Shupe, A.D., Jr, and Bromley, D.G. (eds) (1994) *Anti-Cult Movements in Cross-Cultural Perspective*, New York: Garland.

Shupe, A.D., Jr, Bromley, D.G., and Oliver, D.L. (1984) *The Anti-Cult Movement in America: A Bibliography and Historical Survey*, New York: Garland.

Smith, G.D. (1998). 'Single Issue Terrorism', *Commentary of Canadian Security Intelligence Service*, 74, Ottawa: Canadian Security Intelligence Service.

Sprinzak, E. (1999) *Brother against Brother: Violence and Extremism in Israeli Politics from Altalena to the Rabin Assassination*, New York: The Free Press.

Thornton, T.P. (1964) 'Terror as a Weapon of Political Agitation', in H. Eckstein (ed.) *Internal War*, New York: Collier and Macmillan, pp. 22–42.

Usarski, F. (1999) 'The Response to New Religious Movements in East Germany after Reunification', in B. Wilson and J. Cresswell (eds) *New Religious Movements: Challenge and Response*, London and New York: Routledge, pp. 237–254.

Wilkinson, P. (1975) *Political Terrorism*, London: Macmillan.

Wilson, Bryan, and Jamie Cresswell (eds) (1999) *New Religious Movements: Challenge and Response*, London and New York: Routledge.

Part III

Constructing religious identities and communities online

Chapter 8

Constructing religious identity on the Internet

Mia Lövheim and Alf G. Linderman

Most of us have probably come across the famous comic strip depicting a dog sitting in front of a computer screen reassuring his friend that 'on the Internet no one knows that you're a dog' (*The New Yorker Magazine*, July 1993). This modern metaphor of life in an increasingly computer-mediated society highlights an important dilemma in the area of research on the impact of computer-mediated communication on issues of identity construction. Sherry Turkle's well-known book *Life on the Screen* (1995) can be seen as an example of how much attention during the first phase of research was focused on exploring the possibilities of the Internet as a space for experimental, playful identity construction free from the restrictions of the 'real' world. The supposedly flexible, partial, and fluid identities constructed online were seen as the ultimate expression of postmodern theories about the deconstruction of the coherent self of modern and premodern society (Turkle 1995: 180).

More recent research (Smith and Kollock 1999; Slevin 2000) within the field has, however, increasingly come to emphasize the need to recognize that even in a 'body-less' context like the Internet, identity construction still seems to be a *social* process – a process taking place in relation to other individuals. The aim of this chapter is therefore to explore the issue of identity construction on the Internet as a process of social interaction – even though the arenas on which this interaction takes place have become mediated through different applications of computer technique. Approaching identity construction on the Internet as an issue of social interaction further implies that we need to relate to previous theories about changing conditions for social interaction and identity construction in late modern society. These changes imply new and often ambiguous conditions for the formation of individual as well as social identity. The chapter will therefore start off with a discussion of changing conditions for the construction of identity in late modern society, focusing on the development of trust and commitment in the relation between the individual and various forms of social collectives.[1] The second section of the article will introduce the tension between resources and restrictions for social interactions and the construction of identity implied by the Internet. This introduction will be followed by a discussion of how identity is constructed online in relation to empirical examples from online arenas focusing on religion. Finally, we will relate these empirical examples to the discussion of the construction of identity in late modernity.

Before starting out we will need to clarify our use of the concept 'identity'. In this chapter we are primarily focusing on the process whereby the individual relates himself or herself to a certain collective. This process can be described as the basis for developing the social dimension of an individual's identity, i.e. the repertoire of internalized ways of acting in and making meaning of social interaction and of events and information that the individual encounters during his or her life (Goffman 1959). When we study issues of social interaction and identity construction in a new arena such as the Internet, we necessarily start out from preconceived understandings of how these processes work. As will be discussed further in the next section, religious beliefs and practices as we traditionally know them have provided a location for the individual's sense of belonging to a larger social community as well as for the social order, values, and norms of this community. We want to explore similarities and differences between traditional settings for social interaction and computer-mediated interaction.

Social interaction and social capital in late modern society

Anthony Giddens (1991) points to social trust as a basic category relevant to the process of identity construction. From early childhood, the individual experiences interaction with parents and others, an interaction through which the individual can develop her/his conception of the self. Trust in the continuity and the coherence of the external social reality is essential to this process. Through a development based on trust in the social context in which individuals find themselves, they gradually find out who they are. Individuals experience that they are part of a social context that implies commitment and moral obligations. As people interact on the basis of social trust, and as they co-operate with and relate to one another, this interaction generates what is commonly referred to as *social capital*. To define the level of social capital in a certain context is a way of measuring and expressing the degree of social interaction in this particular social context. The more people engage in social interaction with one another, the higher is the level of social capital established through this interaction.

Social trust is the foundation for the development of individual identity. The process of individual identity construction is an ongoing reflexive process between the individual and the social context. The process of identity construction therefore is part of the social interaction that constitutes social capital. Thus, there is an inherent relation between the reflexive process of identity construction and social capital.

If we look at religion as a social phenomenon, it is obvious that it is one significant arena for the development of social capital. Social capital has throughout history been developed in religious communities through processes of establishing, maintaining, and conveying systems of beliefs and practices. Shared religious beliefs and practices have provided support and legitimacy for individual as well as collective processes of constructing identity and meaning (Durkheim 1965). As we examine the reflexive processes of religious identity construction, we are thus at the core of the study of social capital as it comes into play in the area of religion.

The traditional way through which an individual adopts religion as a model of meaning making is through socialization into a religious community. Through interaction with others, the individual internalizes norms and values and integrates them in his or her self-identity (Berger and Luckmann 1979). As scholars such as Anthony Giddens (1991) and Manuel Castells (1997) have pointed out, the local face-to-face setting can however no longer be seen as the sole context for social interaction. In late modern society, work, relationships, and social activities are increasingly being organized across local time and space. As a consequence of this development, it has been suggested that today's Western world has lost much of the social glue that has allowed societies to cohere. Giddens points to the ongoing disembedding of social institutions. He specifically uses the term 'disembedding' to distinguish this concept from the more commonly used concept 'differentiation'. He wants to emphasize not only that what he refers to is a process where social relations are differentiated, but that social relations are lifted out of the social local context. As social relations are lifted out from local contexts, various kinds of abstract systems come into play that separate social interaction from the particularities of the local context (Giddens 1991: 18ff). Whereas knowledge in the time of the Enlightenment was thought of as a secure foundation for human existence, knowledge in modern society becomes relative. Social institutions drawing on and conveying knowledge by necessity become involved in an ongoing global reflexive process. This development as a whole introduces a new kind of risk and insecurity to the individual. While the individual has the option to choose from a variety of sources for information and a variety of social contexts to relate to, the meaning of this information and these contexts also becomes relative and uncertain. There is always the possibility that that which the individual has chosen becomes obsolete or irrelevant. Knowledge can change, and there is diversity and inconsistency in terms of values. This makes identity construction a more uncertain project, and social capital becomes a more complex entity.

Robert Putnam (2000: 22) makes an important distinction between *bonding* and *bridging* social capital:

> Some forms of social capital are, by choice or necessity, inward looking
> and tend to reinforce exclusive identities and homogeneous groups [i.e.
> bonding social capital] . . . Other networks are outward looking and
> encompass people across diverse social cleavages [i.e. bridging social
> capital].

Religious communities typically represent both bonding and bridging social
capital. People from different social contexts come together (bridging social
capital) to establish a relatively homogeneous religious identity (bonding
social capital). Bonding social capital alone can nurture exclusion of others
while bridging social capital generates broader social relations. As we look
at specific processes of identity construction, it is of significance to recognize
to what extent these processes relate to social capital in general, and to
bonding and bridging social capital in particular.

Putnam eloquently points to many signs of the obliteration of social capital
in American society. Through the analysis of political, civic, and religious
participation, together with many other measures of the degree to which
people engage in social interaction, Putnam comes to the conclusion that
American society faces serious challenges if it is to remain strong in terms
of social capital. The reduction of social capital in general and bridging
social capital in particular endangers social stability and security. Although
there is obvious support for Putnam's thesis, others have observed that his
argument perhaps overlooks the latent capacity of social institutions. With
reference to the aftermath of 11 September 2001 when the Twin Towers were
demolished, Nancy Ammerman (2002) points to the apparent revitalization
of social institutions at a moment when social support and a sense of unity
were needed. The latent capacity of social institutions must be taken into
account, according to Ammerman.

Putnam also points to some tendencies that go against the collapse of
American community. Besides pointing to some social movements, he also
refers to the Internet as one arena where new ways of social interaction are
developed. The question is whether computer-mediated communication is
an expression of social interaction in a genuine sense, or if it only represents
yet another force driving the breakdown of social relations and social capital.
With reference to the many bad predictions about the social consequences
of the telephone made by those who experienced that era of communication
development, Putnam concludes that we are in need of much more scholarly
scrutiny in the area of computer-mediated communication and its potential to be a significant site for social interaction and the building of social
capital.

Given the discussion above, one important area to study is, of course,
how computer-mediated communication comes into play in the process of
identity construction. As has been shown above, the study of religious identity
construction is at the core of the study of social capital in late modern society.

Therefore, we shall now turn to the discussion of identity construction with reference to resources and restrictions of computer-mediated communication, particularly the Internet.

Constructing identity on the Internet: resources and restrictions

Previous research has to a great extent discussed the question of how the new forms of social interaction made possible through computer-mediated communication relate to the forms of social interaction we traditionally know of (see for example Smith and Kollock 1999; Jones 1995; Lövheim 2002). As pointed out in the introduction, this chapter will focus on the possible resources and restrictions implied by the Internet for the individual process of relating to a potential collective of individuals sharing the same, in this case religious, beliefs and practices as a basis for identity construction. James Slevin (2000) as well as Donna Haraway (1999) approaches computer-mediated communication as introducing a new dialectic of power and powerlessness in relation to how individuals and groups handle the challenges of late modern society. The Internet may enrich the process of identity construction through providing new possibilities of creating and acquiring the tools, skills and knowledge needed for handling the increased insecurity and ambivalence of late modern society. Thus the Internet might expand the possibilities of the individual in his or her project of constructing a meaningful, integrated self-identity that might also be communicated in social interaction (Slevin 2000: 24, 114). Furthermore, the Internet, through its capacity to transcend borders of time and space, makes possible the forging of relations between individuals from a diversity of cultural and social settings (Slevin 2000: 178; Haraway, 1999: 289; Højsgaard 2002: 111–112).

The specific conditions for interaction on the Internet also imply certain restrictions as to the resources that are possible to acquire. It is important not to forget that access to information, and the tools for creative constructions of identities and alliances, are still restricted in terms of income, gender, and race (Slevin 2000: 41f). Susan Herring's research on gender and participation in chat rooms is one of many indications that the Internet reflects, or even might reinforce, certain inequalities in society (Herring 1999; see also Burkhalter 1999). Although the Internet offers opportunities to acquire new skills and new knowledge, different Internet arenas also *require* certain technical, social, and cultural skills that different individuals may be more or less endowed with.

As discussed in the previous section, the development of social trust between individuals in social relations might foster certain resources for handling the process of constructing individual and collective identity in late modern society, i.e. social capital. The construction of social capital, however, also involves entering into social relations that imply certain demands on the individuals involved. These demands might be more or less compatible with the values and needs of these individuals.

Goffman points out (1959) that a key factor in social interaction is the construction and maintenance of a single definition of the situation in which the interaction is set. The development of a shared understanding of the aim and the rules of the interaction is significant if meaningful social interaction is to take place. Previous studies of for example the interaction in an 'electronic bar' for lesbians have indicated that the development of a common framework for meaning making as well as supportive relationships is possible through computer-mediated communication (Correll 1995). Relationships on the Internet are, however, in another way than in a local context constructed according to the choices made by individual members in terms of time and commitment. Thus the partiality, temporality, and contingency of social relations in late modern society can often be exaggerated by the particular characteristics of computer-mediated communication. This situation makes these relationships more vulnerable to the impact of individual users who through their participation may uphold, transform, or challenge the essential common setting (Correll 1995; Pargman 2000).

Constructing religious identity on the Internet: empirical examples

The Internet greatly increases the possibility for an individual seeker to find information about established as well as alternative religious organizations. The relatively low cost and effort of setting up a web page have furthermore inspired millions of people representing different religious groups or various personal beliefs to spread their message to an ever widening audience. Through browsing on the Internet, young and old people alike can explore religious beliefs and practices very different from their own without ever leaving the comfort and safety of their homes, and without the risk of being harassed by importunate representatives. This popular image of what religion on the Internet is all about is, however, in great need of being specified and differentiated (Dawson 2000). As a contribution to this important task, we have chosen to discuss briefly some empirical examples drawn from the studies that have been carried out within the scope of a Swedish research project initiated in 1998.[2] On the basis of these studies, it is possible broadly to identify three different ways in which the Internet may provide tools for individuals in the process of connecting to some form of religious collective. These can be summarized as follows:

- Information: finding and spreading information about diverse beliefs and practices
- Interactivity: responding to and getting responses from people of different contexts

- Interdependence: constructing and upholding networks across time and space.

In the following part of this section we will explore the issue of *how* what we have previously defined as social capital might be constructed through these computer-based social relations, and also *what kind* of social capital develops in these encounters. This will be done through focusing on the *resources* that relations maintained over the Internet might provide for individuals and groups, and what kind of *commitments and demands* develop in such relations. It is important at the outset of the presentation to point out that the separation of these different tools or ways of using the Internet is based on analytical rather than empirical reasons. As will be obvious in the upcoming examples, different 'tools' often merge in actual practice. Furthermore, the examples will emphasize that different individuals in different contexts might use the possibilities of the Internet in different ways. There are various ways of specifying the categories among which these variations occur. In the studies referred to in this chapter we have been focusing on gender, religious context and type of interactive arena on the Internet.[3] The examples in the following sections thus refer to the use of web pages and to two different forms of asynchronous communication over the Internet: email discussion lists, and discussion groups accessible through a web page on the Internet. All the examples in the coming sections refer to Swedish adults between 18 and 24 years old.

Information

The examples of Alruna and David indicate how the possibilities opened up by the Internet to find and spread information about religious beliefs and practices can provide resources to the process of constructing individual and collective identities. These examples both involve some kind of religious beliefs and practices that more or less diverge from mainline religion, in this case primarily the Evangelical-Lutheran Church of Sweden. Previous research has indicated that the possibilities of the Internet greatly expand the possibilities of finding and spreading information for this kind of religious movement (Dawson and Hennebry 1999).

Alruna is a 19-year-old student with former sporadic contacts with the Church of Sweden. Since the age of 17, she has identified herself as a witch. As is the case with many of her fellow believers, Alruna found information about Wicca and Witchcraft solely on the Internet:

> The problem is that it has been very difficult to find people who share my thoughts, and who are interested in this as strongly as I am.
> . . . I don't know what or where I would have been today if I hadn't had the Internet, actually. Because it helped me so incredibly in getting

contacts and knowing where to find this and that. It wouldn't have worked otherwise.

When Alruna found out that there actually were people out there who called themselves witches, she started to expand her knowledge through contacting by mail Wiccans living in other parts of the country, and by downloading information from various sources on the Internet. Alruna, however, used the Internet not only as a place to *find* information, but also as an opportunity to *communicate* her belief through initiating and moderating an email discussion list and through the construction of a personal home page. In 2002, Alruna's home page had become one of the most frequently quoted sources of information about Wicca and Witchcraft in Sweden.[4] Alruna herself every day received several questions by email from young practitioners as well as from worried parents wanting advice and more information about this new religious form of expression.

Alruna's story indicates how the Internet might be used by the individual believer as a tool for making sense of experiences that diverge from the beliefs and practices offered by local religious institutions. The need to write down questions, thoughts, and arguments as contributions to her home page and to the list seems to create a unique opportunity for her to reflect on, develop, and express her religious identity:

> If you study Wicca by yourself as I have had to do, you find yourself in situations when you think it is incredibly tough and incredibly hard and so on, and then you'll need something that sort of pushes you to go on, read on, and I had my home page and I thought 'oh, it would really be interesting to write about that', and then I had to learn about it. So I learn myself at the same time as I write, because then I have to formulate it in my own way and think the whole thing through.

Thus computer-mediated communication might provide the opportunities and promote the skills needed to be religious in a situation of heightened reflexivity where the individual has to face the task of constantly accounting for his or her choices and motives.

The experiences of David, a 23-year-old operator at a computer company, are a parallel to Alruna's story. David is one of the webmasters of a web page that is one of several loosely knit websites primarily attracting young men who are drawn towards a conservative evangelical tradition. This tradition does not exist solely online, but also as a somewhat oppositional minority tradition in the Church of Sweden. The opportunities for taking part in a local community are however concentrated in certain areas of Sweden. For David and several other young Christians, the need for information and interaction with other like-minded people is to a large extent maintained by the contacts and discussion groups provided by these websites.

I come from a Christian context where . . . there is no interest in these kinds of discussions and debates. Now I'm that kind of person who brings it up anyway, right or wrong, but you don't get much of a response in a context where people are not interested. I think the Internet can be a forum for people who do not find room for this kind of discussions in their congregations, for example.

Alruna's and David's use of the Internet as a tool in a continuing process of constructing a religious self-identity indicates that skills learned through and by the Internet can become resources not only on a personal but also on a social level. Through Alruna's home page, and through the interaction on the list that she moderates, several other people have become involved in a collective project of religious identity construction. The web page moderated by David and his friends provides another example of how small, temporary and somewhat overlapping networks on the Internet seem to provide plausibility structures for cognitive minorities (Berger 1969: 31f) needed in the construction of alternative religious identities in the Swedish context. Furthermore, Alruna's and David's experiences can be seen as one example of the way in which the Internet makes possible a reacquisition of knowledge and power over religious beliefs and practices long held by religious institutions. As the case of Alruna in particular shows, the Internet might offer someone without the formal religious knowledge or position required in offline contexts a possibility to become an authority in a certain religious field.

Interactivity

The ability of the Internet to make (religious) identity construction a more individual project should not be overemphasized. One of the most prominent things that distinguish the Internet from previous communication media is the possibility of *interactivity* (Slevin 2000: 70, 78f). On the Internet, a message sent from one person could, depending on the design of the Internet arena in question, stimulate responses from one or several persons, in real time or somewhat delayed. The possibility of interactivity calls attention to the social character of interaction on the Internet. Looking back at the examples in the previous section, interaction through a web page or in a discussion group might provide opportunities for confirmation and support. For David and Alruna, interaction in their respective contexts provides opportunities to find legitimacy for a religious identity based on a minority tradition in the Swedish religious context. As Alruna puts it: 'Many times I have said that Internet has been my salvation, because for the first time I understood that I was not alone.'

In order to understand such findings more thoroughly, a closer study of the specific patterns of interactivity developing in a certain context is needed.

Alruna and David are both members of websites which they themselves have initiated, and where they belong to the group of participants who – on the basis of their previous record of activity – are in a certain position of dominance. The experiences of three young women who are members of a Swedish web community (Lövheim 2000b) might be useful in revealing the possible resources but also restrictions that a certain Internet arena may supply. This web community, which brings together several hundred thousand Swedish teenagers, has a wide variety of discussion groups which are largely unmoderated. An analysis of the exchange structure in the groups related to religious issues reveals that even though they offer a variety of diverging opinions, the interaction in several of them is to a large extent dominated by certain groups of participants. Ulrika is one of the young women in the web community who, after spending some time there, chose not to take part in the discussion groups on religion any more. The fact that the same issues and conflicts were raised over and over again among the regulars of the group made her bored. The character of the interaction also gave her a feeling of being excluded – a feeling that was exaggerated by the lack of respect for other people's opinions and true commitment of belief that she experienced in the discussions:

> It's often quite boring, I think. I don't know, but I feel like no one in that group is emotionally engaged in their faith . . . it's more like: I've been studying comparative religion and now I'm gonna show off for a while. No but . . . it seems like a lot of people have a lot of OPINIONS but like they don't really have any . . . it's something they have been studying, it's just this academic display of opinions.

Maria, however, a Christian young woman who is a member of the same web community, takes an active part in the discussions in the Christian groups. In contrast to Ulrika, she does not feel put off by the character of the discussion groups. For her, the divergent opinions and the display of wit give her the opportunity to challenge and develop her own beliefs in a way different from that she uses in the local context:

> It's like in reality you agree about everything and you read the Bible and . . . but there you can have more heated discussions and talk to people who are . . . who really hate Christians and are Satanists and so on. It's like more fun in some ways and you can be tougher because it's anonymous . . .
> *Do you feel like you're becoming more convinced in your faith or do you feel challenged by these discussions?*
> No I'm so convinced that I am right so I don't feel that way, it's actually . . . fun and you really get to deepen your faith and find arguments . . .

Sometimes I am afraid that I will not find any argument that holds and then I'm like 'don't ask any difficult questions now because I have to be able to answer them!' I feel sort of responsible to defend Christianity, that I must show them that it's true and so on.

Hanna is another young Christian woman who does not use the discussion groups for much the same reasons as Ulrika. Hanna is, however, an active user of the possibility offered at the web community of sending personal messages to other members. Hanna's explanation of why she uses this mode of interaction indicates a different way of handling a challenging situation where divergent opinions on religious beliefs intersect. The choice of using a system for private communication furthermore represents a strategy for developing alternative ways of interacting outside of the public character of the discussion groups. As Hanna explains below, the system for personal messages provides a possibility to develop the more relational, supporting, and tolerant exchange structure sought after by several of the girls in the study:

> *Do you think that many girls do like you do, write personal messages instead of contributions to the groups?*
> Yes I REALLY think so, it's much more like that because . . . girls are more like that on the whole, like . . . more of this personal, relations and so on and not so much . . . just this thing that girls hang out in pairs and guys in gangs. Guys are more like 'I want people to see me and now I want to say what I think to EVERYBODY'. Girls are more like 'I want to help HER because she is not feeling well' or something like that. So you use the situation like in different ways.

These three young women represent different ways of handling a certain arena for interaction on the Internet. Their varying experiences indicate that in order to specify how the Internet can provide resources as well as restrictions in the process of constructing religious identities, we need further studies of the complex interplay between the conditions of a specific arena and the individual's repertoire of skills and resources in terms of gender and religious background. The experiences of Ulrika, Maria, and Hanna indicate that such aspects as the patterns of social interaction developing in a certain context, as well as the understandings of religion and gender that come to dominate interactions, structure an individual's possibilities to make use of the resources offered at a particular Internet arena. Clearly, interaction on the Internet can challenge as well as strengthen an individual's previous understandings of religious and gendered identities (for a fuller discussion of such indications, see Lövheim 2004a, 2004b).

Interdependence

As indicated above, the Internet greatly increases the amount of possible traditions to which an individual seeker might connect. The examples above also point to the fact that connecting to a religious tradition involves a relation not only to certain beliefs and practices but also to the people sharing these. This issue relates to the possibilities of forming relationships online (see also Lövheim 2002) and how these apply to the individual project of handling the existential dilemmas of late modernity. As discussed above, all forms of social relations in late modern society have to face the dilemma of how to maintain relations of commitment and mutuality, in a situation where the values and needs of the individual participants become increasingly temporal, subjective, and contingent.

The examples discussed above show that the Internet in many ways expands the possibilities of constructing networks of people sharing all sorts of ideas. The email discussion list aimed at issues of New Age and neo-paganism, founded by the young woman Alruna presented earlier, represents one of the oldest and largest of these networks in the Swedish context. The list was founded in 1998 and has around a hundred members. The group of members is, however, highly variable as people tend to join or leave the list almost daily. Also, the activity of the list varies considerably.[5] These loosely connected networks thus in several ways diverge from previous forms of religious communities. Above all, they lack a stable group of people gathering in a certain time and place that forms the basis of collective representations (Durkheim 1965). Despite their lack of such characteristics, networks such as this list might not only be seen as a product of the temporality, diversity, and partiality of interaction on the Internet. Such networks can also be tools for handling the late modern situation. A key aspect of this possibility is the accessibility of such networks to people who in the local context cannot find like-minded persons with whom they might share their religious beliefs and practices.

On the Internet, the place and time of the gathering can furthermore be more flexible. Thus, even if the activity on the list at times drops considerably, an accessible 'site' for collective construction of religious identity is always possible. The plurality of perspectives that the participants of the list represent makes discussions typically partial and fugitive. This seemingly heterogeneous and contingent character of the opinions and experiences voiced in the postings to the list seems to be an important part of the process of forming collective values and norms on the list. Through advocating tolerance and plurality *in practice*, the list seems to become a place for developing a collective religious identity that gives legitimacy to the right of every member to follow his or her own heart. Rather than a homogeneous body of shared beliefs, it is the experience of being different or 'strange' in the eyes of mainstream religions, and consequently the values of tolerance and individual freedom of belief, that seems to form the basis of the collective identity.

Observations of this email discussion list, along with observations made in the discussion groups on Wicca and neo-paganism at the web community presented earlier, indicate that the accessibility and diversity that give possibilities for constructing a religious identity based on heterogeneity also imply certain problematic aspects. These problems concern the previously discussed question of how individuals and groups should handle the uncertainty and contingency of religious identity and meaning in late modern society. All forms of identity construction can be said to involve processes of differentiation in order to establish similarity and difference. In the groups observed, this process of differentiation mainly concerns not 'believers' and 'non-believers' in neo-paganism and Wicca, but rather the relation between more experienced members and 'wannabes'. This refers to the constant flow of younger practitioners entering the groups asking for 'fast-food versions' of Wiccan spells and ritual. The 'wannabes' can sometimes be welcomed as new members of the group, but many times they rather seem to give rise to a discussion about the essence of Wicca and the threat of pop culture versions of alternative religions. These discussions can be seen as reactions towards diversity and temporality *within* the developing collective. A high degree of plurality implied by the accessibility of these groups can thus give rise to a feeling of relativism and contingency that threatens the authenticity and legitimacy of the tentatively defined collective identity, as indicated in this contribution by Flora:

> There are approximately one hundred different groups on magic that are occupied by self-appointed witches inspired by popular magazines. Why do they have to take part in ALL groups? Is it not possible for us other practising persons to have a group of our own? Perhaps one should start a group that one keeps secret from the general public by leaving it as soon as one has made it? It will still remain at the Site . . . Then one could give out the name of the group to those that have something interesting to say? . . . *pondering* In that case, notify your interest.

This process may imply two related tendencies that have consequences for the relationships within these networks. Firstly, the awareness of the fragility of the common identity that seems to give benefits of legitimacy and belonging may lead certain individuals, like Flora, into developing a larger responsibility towards maintaining common values and norms. These people thus form the core of a computer-mediated network and might often take on positions of authority in relation to beliefs and practices. Secondly, the process of reflecting upon and articulating certain values and norms as parts of a collective religious identity initiates a process towards hierarchy and rules that may not be compatible with the values of pluralism and individual freedom cherished in these religious traditions.

These tendencies come even more to the fore in online groups discussing Christianity. Christianity is by tradition the dominant religion in Sweden (Skog 2001). The existence of a basic common knowledge of religious symbols, norms, and values among all the participants tends to make discussions in these groups more focused. In online groups that are open to people of many different opinions, discussions however also tend to become polarized between 'believers' and 'non-believers'. This polarization is so strong that individual Christians wanting to raise alternative views tend to refrain from this out of fear of letting the 'non-believers' get the upper hand in the discussion. Here, some possible consequences of the processes of consolidation discussed above might be found. Firstly, there is a risk that the possibility of fruitful diversity might be overpowered by the need for a shared, social identity. During the course of the studies within the project the groups that to a large extent are characterized by these processes seem to attract fewer people than groups that maintain a certain degree of diversity. Some of the young people, like Lugh below from the Wicca website, also express concern over the fact that processes of developing hierarchy and rules that for many of them are seen as the main obstacle to joining a religious community offline now also seem to be happening online:

> I become a bit irritated if someone enters and thinks that 'you are not proper Wiccans because you do not follow our tradition', like that. It feels like . . . people become elitist and so on . . . there's no possibility for people to, well, become Wiccans unless they start off by themselves so . . . // . . . it's doesn't really fit . . . like . . . the foundation of this religion . . .

Concluding discussion

In this chapter we have been exploring identity construction on the Internet as a process of social interaction. This explorative effort has had the specific intention of developing previous scholarly approaches to the study of (religious) identity construction and the Internet. In the introduction, we pointed to the need of relating to previous theories about changing conditions for social interaction and identity construction in late modern society. Our starting point in this chapter has been theories of social interaction and social capital and how they might be applied to issues of identity construction in the area of religion. As the empirical examples discussed above indicate, the application of this intersection between theories of social capital and theories of religion to the emerging field of identity construction on the Internet has indicated several interesting findings.

Firstly, the application of the theories of social capital to individual and collective experiences of using the Internet might open up new possibilities to deepen our understanding of the ambivalent tendencies in the construction of interdependence and of collective identities pointed out in the last examples above. The empirical examples support previous research in suggesting that the specific conditions of interaction on the Internet provide certain resources that can be beneficial for individual seekers as well as for developing religious collectives. The different experiences of the young women referred to in the second example, as well as the processes of consolidation in online groups referred to in the last example, however, indicate that these conditions may also generate processes that restrict these potential benefits. Certain patterns of interaction developed in order to build a strong in-group identity may simply result in the exclusion of individuals who do not comply with these norms and values. In a certain time and context, the possibility of using the Internet to build new alliances, characterized by plurality and fruitful ways of handling the dilemmas of accessibility and partiality faced by late modern communities, seems to develop into processes of differentiation and homogenization. In order to further our understanding of *how* trust and commitment are being developed in social relations constructed on the Internet, as well as *what kind* of relations are developed, the distinction suggested by Putnam between *bridging* and *bonding* social capital might be a useful tool.

Secondly, the empirical examples also indicate how the intersection between what happens in social interactions on the Internet, and theories of social capital, might in a fruitful way develop our conception of social trust, community, and religion. The question of how to make sense of the transformations of the collective dimension of religion in a seemingly increasingly individualistic society is among the most crucial in the present sociology of religion (Bar-Haim 1997). Lorne Dawson in his chapter in this volume furthermore raises the question of what the constructed and arbitrary character of online religion means for the dimension of belonging, and the sharing of a set of beliefs and practices as fundamental to religion as we know it.

The empirical examples discussed in this chapter can be seen as indications of new forms of relations between the individual and the collective developing in late modern society. These forms of relationships may not resemble what we traditionally (idealistically?) associate with 'religious community'. On the other hand, they may not be too different from the way religious identities and religious community are expressed in 'real life' in late modern society. It is obvious that these relationships between the individual and the religious collective are more temporal, flexible, and formed according to a plurality of individual needs. However, the examples discussed here indicate that individuals are taking on responsibilities and commitments outside the traditional forms of religious leadership. The possibility of maintaining a heterogeneous, temporal 'site' for the collective constructing of religious identity furthermore indicates that these kinds of networks in some aspects 'work' better as a connection between the individual and the larger community in the present situation than 'traditional' communities organized around homogeneity and stability (Wellman and Gulia 1999).

More longitudinal studies will be needed in order to answer questions as to how these new forms of communities on the Internet will manage the delicate balance between congeniality and plurality, and the degree to which the Internet can become a trusted context for individual as well as social projects of constructing religious identity.

Notes

1   This discussion represents an elaboration of the issues discussed in Linderman and Lövheim (2003).
2   Further information about these studies can be found in Linderman and Lövheim (1997) and Lövheim (2000a; 2000b; 2002; 2004b).
3   The data of the study were collected using a combination of online questionnaires, online observations and offline interviews.
4   This assumption is based on empirical fieldwork within the research project.
5   This information is founded on ongoing observations of the list as well as on interviews with the moderator of the list.

References

Ammerman, N. (2002) 'Grieving Together: September 11 as a Measure of Social Capital', in Markham, I.S. and Abu-Rabi, I.M. (eds) *September 11: Religious Perspectives on the Causes and Consequences*, Oxford: Oneworld Publications.
Bar-Haim, G. (1997) 'The Dispersed Sacred. Anomie and the Crisis of Ritual', in Hoover, S.M. and Lundby, K. (eds) *Rethinking Media, Religion, and Culture*, Thousand Oaks, CA: Sage Publications.
Berger, P.L. (1969) *A Rumour of Angles*, London: Allen Lane/Penguin Press.
Berger, P.L. and Luckmann, T. (1979) *Kunskapssociologi. Hur individen uppfattar och formar sin sociala verklighet*, Stockholm: Wahlström and Widstrand [Originally published in 1967].
Burkhalter, B. (1999) 'Reading Race On-line. Discovering Racial Identity in Usenet Discussions', in Smith, M.A. and Kollock, P. (eds) *Communities in Cyberspace*, London and New York: Routledge.
Castells, M. (1997) *The Information Age. Economy, Society and Culture. Volume II: The Power of Identity*, Oxford: Blackwell.
Correll, S. (1995) 'The Ethnography of an Electronic Bar', *Journal of Contemporary Ethnography*, 24 (3), pp. 270–298.
Dawson, L.L. (2000) 'Researching Religion in Cyberspace. Issues and Strategies', in Hadden, J.K. and Cowan, D.E. (eds) *Religion on the Internet. Research Prospects and Promises*, Amsterdam, London, and New York: Elsevier Science.
Dawson, L.L. and Hennebry, J. (1999) 'New Religions and the Internet. Recruiting in a New Public Space', *Journal of Contemporary Religion*, 14 (1), pp. 17–39.
Durkheim, E. (1965) *The Elementary Forms of Religious Life*, New York: Free Press.

Giddens, A. (1991) *Modernity and Self-identity. Self and Society in the Late Modern Age*, Cambridge: Polity Press.

Goffman, E. (1959) *The Presentation of Self in Everyday Life*, London: Penguin Books.

Haraway, D. (1999) 'A Cyborg Manifesto', in During, S. (ed.) *The Cultural Studies Reader*, London and New York: Routledge [Originally published in 1991].

Herring, S. (1999) 'The Rhetorical Dynamics of Gender Harassment On-Line', *The Information Society*, 3 (15), pp. 151–169.

Hoover, S.M. and Lundby, K. (eds) (1997) *Rethinking Religion, Media and Culture*, Thousand Oaks, CA: Sage Publications.

Højsgaard, M.T. (2002) 'Kulturmøder i cyberspace', *Religionsvidenskabeligt Tidsskrift*, 40, pp. 99–115.

Jones, S.G. (ed.) (1995) *Cybersociety. Computer-Mediated Communication and Community*, Thousand Oaks, CA: Sage Publications.

Linderman, A.G. and Lövheim, M. (1997) *IT, Gemenskap och Identitet. En forskningsansats med religion som typfall*, Uppsala: Teologiska institutionen.

Linderman, A.G. and Lövheim, M. (2003) 'Internet, Religion and the Attribution of Social Trust', in Mitchell, J. and Marriage, S. (eds) *Studies in Media, Religion and Culture*, Edinburgh, London and New York: T&T Clark/Continuum.

Lövheim, M. (2000a) 'Ungdomar, religion och Internet', *Locus*, 1, pp. 23–32.

Lövheim, M. (2000b) 'Brave New Girls? Gender, Religious Context and the Use of CMC', paper presented to The Annual Meeting of the Society for the Scientific Study of Religion and the Religious Research Association, Houston, USA, 19–22 October 2000.

Lövheim, M. (2002) 'Nätet – en plats för nya former av gemenskap?', in Dahlgren, P. (ed.) *Internet, Medier och Kommunikation*, Lund: Studentlitteratur.

Lövheim, M. (2004a) 'Intersecting Identities: Young People, Religion, and Interaction on the Internet', Ph.D. thesis, Uppsala: Uppsala University, Department of Theology.

Lövheim, M. (2004b) 'Young People, Religious Identity, and the Internet', in Dawson, L.L. and D.E. Cowan (eds) *Religion Online: Finding Faith on the Internet*, New York: Routledge, pp. 59–74.

Pargman, D. (2000) *Code Begets Community. On Social and Technical Aspects of Managing a Virtual Community*, Linköping: Linköping Studies in Art and Science 224.

Putnam, R.D. (2000) *Bowling Alone. The Collapse and Revival of American Community*, New York: Simon and Schuster.

Skog, M. (ed.) (2001) *Det religiösa Sverige*, Örebro: Libris.

Slevin, J. (2000) *The Internet and Society*, Cambridge: Polity Press.

Smith, K.A. and Kollock, P. (eds) (1999) *Communities in Cyberspace*, London and New York: Routledge.

Turkle, S. (1995) *Life on the Screen. Identity in the Age of the Internet*, New York: Simon and Schuster.

Wellman, B. and Gulia, M. (1999) 'Virtual Communities as Communities. Netsurfers Don't Ride Alone', in Smith, M.A. and Kollock, P. (eds) *Communities in Cyberspace*, London and New York: Routledge.

Chapter 9

Online Buddhist Community

An alternative religious organization in the information age

Mun-Cho Kim

Passing the turn of the millennium, human society is undergoing a very dynamic process induced by an array of historical events such as technological revolution, global economy, the decline of Marxism-Leninism, the diffusion of postmodern lifestyle, and new forms of relationships between state, economy, and civil society. Unlike the previous transition of industrialization driven by labour-saving mechanical technology, information technology is playing such a significant role in the current social transformation that 'information society' has become a catchword of our time. There exist a large number of social-scientific studies dealing with the societal transformation attributable to new information technology (see, for instance, Castells 1996; Kling 1996; Lyon 1988; and Webster 1995). Among a large body of specialized research studies, only a few authors, however, have attempted a broad historical sweep and bold theorizing. To my knowledge, Manuel Castells seems to be the most remarkable.

In his trilogy *The Information Age: Economy, Society and Culture* Castells concludes a decade of research by presenting an empirically grounded, cross-cultural account of major social, economic, and political transformations which have reshaped the landscapes of human knowledge and experience across the globe. The basic model underlying his trilogy is a dialectical inter-action of social relations and technology, or, in Castells's terminology, 'modes of production' and 'modes of development'. Admitting that the evolution of the capitalist mode of production is driven by private capital's competitive pressure to maximize profits, Castells makes it clear that modes of development evolve according to their own logic. He defines the evolution-ary logic of the current 'informational modes of development' according to the 'information technology paradigm'. The characteristics of the 'infor-mation technology paradigm' described by Castells are: (1) Information is the raw material as well as the outcome. The new technologies act on information rather than on matter. (2) Because information is an integral part of all human activity, these technologies are pervasive. (3) Information technologies foster a networking logic, because they allow one to deal with complexity and unpredictability, which are themselves increased by these technologies. (4) The networking logic is based on flexibility. (5) Specific technologies converge into highly integrated systems (Castells 1996: 60–65).

Social transformation driven by advanced information technologies never occurs in a gradual and continuous fashion. It is widely open to sectional, functional, and temporal variations. Taking all those variations into account, I construct a progressive model of social informatization (see fig. 9.1). The initial phase called 'computerization stage' is a state characterized by the construction of technological infrastructure including the installation of computer hardware. The effect of computerization lies in automating repetitive tasks and reducing working time and expenditure of energy. The information technology at this stage remains instrumental in so far as it involves the enhancement of job efficiency without influencing other aspects of human activities. Next follows the 'networking stage' where computing and telecommunication functions are incorporated. At this stage, the fusion of computing and telecommunication technologies constitutes an extensive 'informational grid' linking people, homes, schools, factories, offices, shops, banks, hospitals, etc. In the third 'flexibility stage', 'borderlessness' emerges as the most prevalent phenomenon. Until the modern industrial era, divisions between groups, organizations, sectors, regions, nations were rather clear-cut

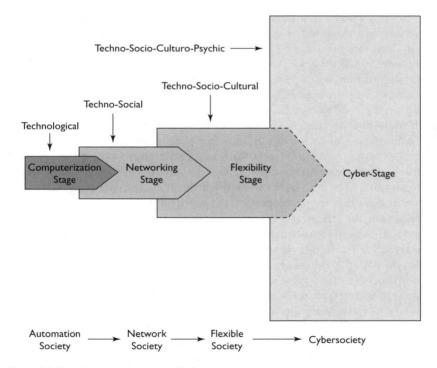

Figure 9.1 Developmental model of information society.

and often legally protected. But an extraordinary increase in the social networking tends to dissolve those divisions. Massive exchange of information beyond the time-space limitation dissociates those boundaries.

The pinnacle of the informatization process as far as I see it is 'cyber-stage', an outcome of the fusion of advanced information technology and multimedia technology. Compared to the previous three stages – computerization, networking, and flexibility – the last cyber-stage looks far more epochal, since cyberspace can be perceived as a timeless, boundless space of a high degree of freedom (Kim 1999: 77–82). Cyberspace, the constitutive element of cyber society, is defined as a conceptual space of interaction where people using computer-mediated communication technology interact. Cyberspace is the place of anonymous encounter as well. It is characterized by a multilateral-multiplicative structure of hyperlinks. Further, cyberspace is *a*temporal and *a*spatial in the sense that it is not bound up with time or space. But the most distinguishable trait of cyberspace may be its virtual property (Loader 1997). That is why the term *cyberspace* is often used interchangeably with *virtual reality*.

Religion in the information age

Sociologists who have studied the relationship between religion and modern society have articulated at least three functions of religion. These three sets of religious functions can be characterized as interpretative, interactive, and integrative functions respectively. The interpretative function has to do with the ability of religion to provide meaningful answers to ultimate and eternal questions about human existence. Basically, people in modern society are living under conditions of uncertainty and insecurity, and the capacity of each individual to control the conditions of his or her life is very limited. Being perplexed in such a situation, some people feel the necessity of some sort of explanation, and in some such cases religion may offer the prospect or hope of spiritual intercession (O'Dea 1966). Also, religion can function to legitimate, that is to provide justification for, an existing social order. Religion does this by reinterpreting the realities of everyday life as part of a greater cosmic scheme. By placing everyone's daily existence in the context of a broader system of order, religion makes the status quo seem difficult or impossible to change (Berger 1967). The interactive function of religion has to do with the ability of religious organizations to provide opportunities for some people to associate with others with whom they can exchange ideas, benefits, lifestyles, tastes, and so forth. On the basis of study of Western converts to Eastern religions, H. Cox (1977) argues that what people are looking for is friendship, companionship, acceptance, and recognition, and, for some people in modern society, membership of a religious organization provides a sense of community making it easier to cope with either loneliness or isolation. In addition to the interpretative and the interactive aspects of religious life, religion does also have an integrative function; it is a form of social 'cement' integrating believers by regularly bringing them together to enact various rituals and by providing them with shared values and beliefs that bind them together into a unified moral community (Durkheim 1947: 47).

On the basis of this tripartite classification scheme, it may be possible as well to differentiate types of religious communities into 'Belief Community', 'Relational Community', and 'Affective Community' in which 'need for otherness', 'need for affiliation', and 'need for collective identity' respectively prevail. Religion, in sum, can be seen as a means of making communion, and, to the extent that most religious expressions take the form of communication, they have been accompanied by relevant means of communication as well.

In any case, during history, religious individuals, groups, and institutions have quickly encompassed almost every new communication technology. The Christian Bible may be one of the noticeable products. Thanks to Gutenberg's printing press, fifteenth-century Europeans were able to get access to the religious documents that were formerly available only to the wealthy. Radio and television had a remarkable impact upon religion as well. With the advent of those mass broadcasting technologies, people started to think of themselves as audience or customers rather than participants. Consequently, their expectations of the quality of the worship event increased (Brasher 2001: 15–16). The popularity of mega-churches soared; religious programmes were broadcast in many cities; televised worship drew on local and national television audiences; cable television and its satellite distribution provided even greater scope for evangelical use. Needless to say, the Internet is playing a powerful role in religious communications as well.

The Internet provides immediate access to a wide range of religious information, usually more quickly than do the traditional channels of distribution. The Internet also provides means for candid discussions that are relatively free from the influence of pre-existing religious authorities. In addition, owing to its virtual character, the Internet contains interactive environments that facilitate the unfolding of religious experiences and ideas of various kinds. But more than anything else, as indicated in table 9.1, only within cyberspace do we have at once highly private, focused, and multi-way communications. Accordingly, the Internet could be expected to be the imagined locale where people can find alternative spiritual sanctuaries with few speech restrictions.

Studying online religious communication in Korea

To date, only a small number of studies have been reported concerning the issue of online religious communication in Korea (e.g., Park 2000, Kim 2000). Unfortunately, these studies have been either very preliminary case

Table 9.1 Media characteristics with regard to the attributes of communication

Medium	Attribute			
	Privacy	*Audience*	*Direction*	*Temporality*
Internet	High	Focused	Multi-way	Variable
Phone	High	Focused	2-way	Immediate
Mail	High	Focused	2-way	Delayed
Radio	Low	Broad	1-way	Immediate
TV	Low	Broad	1-way	Immediate
Print	Low	Broad	1-way	Delayed

Source: Revised version of Boehlefeld (1996: 147).

descriptions or illusive conceptual discussions. The present study may be the first and only analysis of online Buddhist communication in Korea that seeks to combine empirical and theoretical approaches.

With the rapid expansion of the information highway in Korea driven by ambitious National Information Infrastructure policy, the commercial telecommunication network began to flourish in the early 1990s. Four major information service providers – Chollian, Hitel, Nownuri, and Unitel – appeared thereafter in Korea. With regard to the present study twenty-four online religious communities were initially found in these major information service providers. The distribution with respect to religious denomination of the twenty-four online religious communities is summarized in table 9.2.

Korean Buddhist communities on the Internet in 1997 included BUD (abbreviation of Buddhism), BOSAL (Korean for the Buddhist term 'Bodhisattva'), and Won BUD in Chollian as well as BUD in Hitel, BUD in Nownuri, and BUD in Unitel. The Chollian, Hitel, Nownuri and Unitel portals remained major information service providers in Korea until 1997, just before the massive diffusion of the Internet.

Table 9.2 Number of religious communities within major Korean information service providers in 1997

Religion	Chollian	Hitel	Nownuri	Unitel	Total
Protestant	3	1	3	2	9
Catholic	1	1	1	1	4
Buddhism	2	1	1	1	5
Won Buddhism	1	0	0	0	1
Unification Church	0	1	0	0	1
Other	1	1	1	1	4
Total	8	5	6	5	24

Source: Summarized version of Park (1997: 4–5).

In terms of methodology, a triangulation strategy, combining methods of content analysis, participatory observation, and interview, was adopted for the present study, focusing primarily on the Chollian Buddhist Community (C-BUD). Content analysis of the information exchange in this community was conducted in order to figure out basic communication patterns. Participatory observations were carried out to discover what was going on in chat rooms and various offline meetings. Interviews with past and current executive members were also included for more valid interpretations. The data were collected between September 1996 and August 1997. It was the time when most online communities based on independent information service providers were incorporated into huge search engines or portal sites. More recent web-based online communications are not included in this study.

Chollian Buddhist Community

The Chollian Buddhist Community (C-BUD) was formed on 6 September 1991. C-BUD, consisting of more than three hundred subcommunities, was regarded as one of the most successful online religious communities in Korea until the late 1990s when web-based online communities began to emerge. The three main menus of C-BUD as well as a supporting menu and the submenus belonging to them are listed in table 9.3.

Nowadays, most online communities are located via search engines or portal sites. Complying with this new trend, C-BUD members decided to transform their online community into a web-based one and launched their own website on the Internet on 30 August 2001 (see www.buddhasite.net). Although many religious communities have their own sites, most online religious communities in the early 1990s were registered only in a specific search engine or portal site. However, C-BUD had its own service solution with an independent domain. That is apparently one of the reasons why C-BUD has been most successful in soliciting loyalty from its members and maintaining a solid group identity. Thus, contrary to café-type religious

Table 9.3 Menus and submenus in the Chollian Buddhist Community (C-BUD)

Main menu			Supporting menu
Learning sector	*Relieving sector*	*Sharing sector*	*Office sector*
LS1: Beginner	RS1: Café	SS1: Sermon	OS1: Newsletter
LS2: Counselling	RS2: Inner Circle	SS2: Meditation	OS2: Newcomer
LS3: Holy Texts	RS3: Personal Affairs	SS3: Buddhist Culture	OS3: Membership
LS4: Debate	RS4: Guesthouse	SS4: Event	OS4: Management
	RS5: Open Letter	SS5: Library	OS5: Voting
	RS6: Chat Room		

Source: Rearranged version of Park (1997: 46).

communities simply providing scriptures, liturgies, and news, C-BUD has developed into a multi-pattern, alternative religious organization with interpretative and integrative as well as interactive functions.

Not far from the general patterns of Internet users around 1997, male users in their twenties and thirties turned out to be the majority of the C-BUD members: 71.8 percent of all members of the club who took part in the survey were males. Age distributions of the 1,146 members who registered at C-BUD between April and October 1997 are summarized in table 9.4. Besides, among the 530 members of the C-BUD whose occupations were identifiable, college students occupied the highest proportion (32.1 per cent) and next followed white-collar workers (23.2 per cent), professionals (8.7 per cent) and middle/high school students (7.7 per cent) in sequence. The monthly connection time amounted to 903 hours and 33 minutes in March 1996 and 1819 hours and 37 minutes in September 1997. The average connection time was 51 hours and 46 minutes in March 1996 and 58 hours and 32 minutes in September 1997. The fact that busy daily workers were actively committed to online religious communications may be evidence that implies the constitution of alternative religious organizations in cyberspace.

The explicit purposes of the major online menus of the C-BUD tend to bifurcate into either 'intimacy' or 'information'. For instance, menus such as 'Café', 'Open Letter', and 'Personal Affairs' apparently were designed to facilitate intimacy, while 'Sermon', 'Meditation', 'Beginner', and 'Bible Study' seemingly were intended to increase the level of religious information transmission or exchange. On the other hand, 'Chat Room' aimed at dual functions of intimacy and information, while 'Debate' seemed to encompass both information exchange and some sort of religious practice.

Besides those online communication activities, there were also several offline activities in the C-BUD such as 'Cohort Meeting', 'Abrupt Meeting', 'Regional Meeting', 'Community Service', and 'Regular Communion'. Apparently, 'Cohort Meeting' and 'Abrupt Meeting' aimed at increasing intimacy, while 'Community Service' was intended for enhancing or giving opportunities of conducting religious practice. Two other offline activities, 'Regional Meeting' and 'Short-term Retreat', were supposed to meet a triple purpose – intimacy, information, and religious practice. The major online communications and offline activities with respect to their expected purpose are illustrated in fig. 9.2.

Table 9.4 Age composition of membership of the Chollian Buddhist Community in 1997

Age	−19	20–29	30–39	40–49	50 +	Total
%	8.0	56.7	26.7	7.5	1.1	100.0

Source: Park (1997: 24). N = 1146.

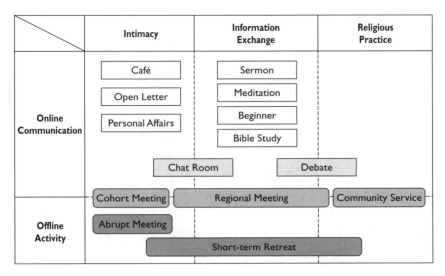

Figure 9.2 Intended purposes of major online/offline activities in the Chollian Buddhist Community (C-BUD).

Past studies of virtual communities propose that: (1) the development of virtual communities can be explained as an indication of declining traditional community, (2) community ties are to be consolidated when people meet on a regular basis in cyberspace, (3) the members of a virtual community meet online to do just about everything that other people do in face-to-face interactions (Jones 1995; Smith and Kollock 1999). This case study of an online Buddhist community has been carried out in order to investigate those propositions. Users' characteristics, formal structure, and verbal/behavioral activities were examined. In general, strong empirical evidence supporting the propositions was obtained.

Then, online communications and activities of the Chollian Buddhist Community were analysed in terms of the three basic functions of religion discussed above. By and large, three main menus that comprise the substantive part of the Chollian Buddhist Community, 'Learning Sector', 'Relieving Sector', and 'Sharing Sector', seemed to exactly match the three basic functions of religion that were designated earlier, that is the interpretative, the interactive, and the integrative function respectively. Simultaneously, five submenus of the supporting menu – from 'Office Sector' 1 to 5 – could be deployed into these three basic functions of religion (see fig. 9.3). However, when we further investigate the contents of actual online communications performed within each submenu, we can draw the conclusion that not all the submenu activities are equivalent to what their top menus originally designated. What is going on in 'Inner Circle' and 'Personal Affairs' in actual

Function & Community Type	Formal Menu	Activity
Interpretative Function – Belief Community (BC)	Learning Sector (LS)	LS1: Beginner LS2: Counselling LS3: Bible Study LS4: Debate
Interactive Function – Relational Community (RC)	Relieving Sector (RS)	RS1: Café RS2: Inner Circle RS3: Personal Affairs RS4: Guest House RS5: Open Letter RS6: Chat Room
Integrative Function – Affective Community (AC)	Sharing Sector (SS)	SS1: Sermon SS2: Meditation SS3: Buddhist Culture SS4: Event SS5: Library
Instrumental Function – Utilitarian Community (UC)		
System Operation	Office Sector (OS)	OS1: Newsletter OS2: Newcomer OS3: Membership OS4: Management OS5: Voting

Figure 9.3 Functions and functional relocation of the Chollian Buddhist Community (C-BUD).

practice does belong to the category of integrative function, and so do the activities of 'Sermon' and 'Meditation' to the category of interpretative function. Noticeably, part of the activities of 'Buddhist Culture', 'Event', 'Newsletter', 'Newcomer', and 'Membership' seem to have an instrumental function rather than an integrative or system-operating function, in as much as these activities focus quite a lot on the possibilities of giving monetary contributions and practical assistance to the club (see fig. 9.3).

While more than 80 per cent of the whole population in Korea is concentrated in cities, most Buddhist churches (temples) are still scattered in rural mountainous areas. Therefore, for busy full-time workers, it is difficult to visit a temple on a regular basis, and that is why Korean Buddhism is said to suffer from an 'elder/female excess phenomenon'. In this situation, the Chollian Buddhist Community (C-BUD) seems to have gained the interest of many people who regard offline meetings as too demanding. To a certain extent C-BUD even seems to constitute a possible alternative to some pre-existing religious organizations. Particularly, the openness and anonymity of most online communications promote active participation by members who might feel reluctant to participate in formalized offline patterns of worship. To its members, the online religious co-experiences of the C-BUD with like-minded individuals seem to have a great influence on their everyday lives (Kim and Park 1998).

Conclusion

In all, the findings of the present study suggest that the Chollian Buddhist Community from 1996 to 1997 performed multiple functions: (1) as a 'Belief Community' providing a system of Buddhist beliefs and practices, (2) as a 'Relational Community' that helps to satisfy the need for belonging for some people, (3) as an 'Affective Community' that provides a kind of group identity for those who seek it, and (4) as a 'Utilitarian Community' providing a means of resource mobilization. The results of the study make a plea for the development of a new ideal-typical construct that takes into account the diverse functions of contemporary religious organizations – interpretative, interactive, integrative, *and* instrumental.

Seemingly, online religious organizations are shifting gradually towards a locale of spiritual community of like-minded individuals. A shift from digital media to life-world can be detected in the development of online religion. Accordingly, a 'sanctuary model' instead of a 'tool model' appears to be more appropriate when it comes to understanding the current development of religious organization in the modern world. More than an additional *locale* for religious practice, online religious community seems to develop into an alternative religious organization that satisfies the multi-pattern needs of contemporary individuals who are trying to pursue a 'biographical solution to systemic contradictions in the individualized world' (Beck and Beck 2002: xvi).

References

Beck, U. and Beck, E. (2002) *Individualization*, London: Sage.
Berger, P. (1967) *The Sacred Canopy: Elements of a Sociological Theory of Religion*, Garden City, NY: Doubleday.
Boehlefeld, S.P. (1996) 'Doing the Right Thing: Ethical Cyberspace Research', *The Information Society*, 12, pp. 141–152.
Brasher, B. (2001) *Give Me That Online Religion*, San Francisco: Jossey-Bass.
Castells, M. (1996) *The Rise of the Network Society*, Oxford: Blackwell. First volume of the trilogy *The Information Age: Economy, Society and Culture*.
Cox, H. (1977) *Turning East: The Promise and Peril of the New Orientalism*, New York: Simon and Schuster.
Durkheim, E. (1947) *The Elementary Forms of Religious Life*, Glencoe, Ill.: Free Press.
Jones, S. (ed.) (1995) *Cybersociety: Computer-Mediated Communication and Community*, Thousand Oaks, Calif.: Sage.

Kim, E. (2000) 'Religious Practices and Missionary Activities on Internet', paper presented at the Second Symposium of the Korean Society for Buddhist Studies, Chonnam National University, 14 October 2000.

Kim, M. (1999) *Science Technology and the Future of Korea: On the Socialization of Information Technology*, Seoul: Korea University Press.

Kim, M. and Park, S. (1998) 'Analysis of Online Religious Activities: A Case Study of Chollian Buddhist Club', *Journal of Education*, 28, pp. 157–180.

Kling, R. (1996) *Computerization and Controversy: Value Conflicts and Social Choices*, San Diego: Academic Press [Second edition].

Loader, B.D. (ed.) (1997) *The Governance of Cyberspace: Politics, Technology and Global Restructuring*, London: Routledge.

Lyon, D. (1988) *The Information Society: Issues and Illusions*, Cambridge: Polity.

O'Dea, T. (1966) *The Sociology of Religion*, Englewood Cliffs, NJ: Prentice-Hall.

Park, S. (1997) 'Religious Activities in Cyberspace: A Case Study of Chollian Buddhist Club', MA Thesis, Korea University.

Park, S. (2000) 'Buddhist Religious Life in Cyberspace', *The Buddhist Review*, 2, pp. 299–319.

Smith, M.A. and Kollock, P. (eds) (1999) *Communities in Cyberspace*, New York: Routledge.

Webster, F. (1995) *Theories of the Information Society*, New York: Routledge.

Chapter 10

Virtual as contextual

A Net news theology

Debbie Herring

In this chapter I will explore the confluence of two emerging fields of academic interest, online ethnography and contextual theology. Ethnographic research in Net news groups is a growing and fashionable area of research, for a number of reasons. Social behaviour in virtual environments is a new phenomenon. The present generation of researchers has a unique opportunity to observe and document the way that people are adapting and adopting patterns of behaviour in response to the different conditions which obtain in a social group which depends for its existence on computer-mediated communication (CMC) technology. Net news groups may be singled out because they have advantages for the researcher: they are widely and publicly available and publicly archived, which simplifies the ethical considerations about the use of news group posts in a project; and many use only text as the medium for communication, which makes storage and retrieval of information relatively uncomplicated.

At the same time, in my own discipline, theology, there is an increasing interest in contextual theology: theology, that is, which takes as its starting point not statements about God but the *context* where people are engaging with God, and the religious thinking that occurs as a result of the particular characteristics of the context. It is reasonable to suggest that, at one level, all theology is contextual. Theology is something that people do, in particular places at particular times and in particular circumstances, and so any particular theology is likely to be situated in a context of sorts. Systematic and natural theologies, for example, are the products of scholarly reflection and belong to the academy and the church: that is the context in which they operate, and scholars and theologians are the 'practitioners', in that they engage with such theologies and work with them.

What distinguishes contextual theology[1] in the more specific sense in which it will be used here is that it deliberately and consciously starts with the people with whom it is concerned, and the context in which they share. Contextual theology is situated, specific, and self-conscious, and the process, reflection, and action that occur arise from the people and their particular circumstances. That context for theology may be small, local, or constrained, such as the community theology of an individual church, or it may be global but focused on the concerns of people bound together by a common cause, as is the case with black theology or urban theology, for example.

One particular aspect of contextual theology which distinguishes it from other forms of theology is its concern with theological *practice* – not only how people act on their beliefs but how they *act out* their beliefs. This kind of enacted theology is referred to as *praxis*. Traditional forms of theology have more often been concerned with belief (*doxa*) and how to believe correctly – hence the term orthodoxy. Correct practice (orthopraxy) also has a place in traditional forms of theology, but the concept of praxis as a normative value in a system of theology is unique to contextual theology. From a sociological point of view, the privileged value of praxis in contextual theology corresponds to the importance placed on phenomenology as an interpretative instrument in ethnographic and anthropological endeavour.

If a Net news group is in some sense a community, it seemed likely that such a group, especially one with an overtly Christian focus, would have an identifiable contextual theology of its own, and this project was designed partly to test this hypothesis. I was particularly interested in discovering whether it would be possible to identify and evaluate praxis in a text-based medium. The issue of whether or not a group of people who use CMC is a community or not is still the subject of some debate,[2] but, for the purposes of this project, it was deemed sufficient that the people being studied considered themselves to be a community.

The process

I make no apologies for going into considerable detail in describing the way this project was conducted. Although there is a growing body of literature describing the general principles of ethnographic research into computer-mediated communities,[3] there is nothing which describes the process of determining and evaluating the contextual theology of such a community – and very little for any other sort of community. The texts I have found most informative in this task are Schreiter's *Constructing Local Theologies* (1985) and Bevans's *Models of Contextual Theology* (1993 and 2002), but the method I have used is not substantially derived from either writer, since they are both concerned with physical, rather than virtual, communities. The process itself has been an exploratory, experimental one, and I lay it out here for information and for critique.

Because contextual theologies are by their very nature situated, it was necessary to identify clearly the situation in which the study was to be carried out. There are many Net news groups dedicated to discussion about Christianity: my own news group service carries forty-six with the word 'Christian' in the title. I was already familiar with the Net news group uk.religion.christian as a regular contributor, and it had a number of advantages which made it an appropriate group for this study. As a known contributor, my presence as a researcher was less likely to disrupt or constrain the discussion on the group. The group is moderated against a charter but not on content. This limits the amount of superfluous material – spam, commercial posts, and abuse – but allows free discussion of topics relevant to Christians and Christianity in the United Kingdom. It has no doctrinal or denominational affiliation or restrictions which might bias the theological insights to be found. It has what seemed at the time to be a manageable number of posts per day – although I admit now to overestimating the limits of 'manageable' – and the United Kingdom focus helped to limit the scope and nature of the discussions to a cultural context with which I was already familiar.

I explained in a post that I was undertaking research into the group by participant observation, and continued to remind the group that I was engaged in this research. The few responses I had were positive and encouraging. Shortly after the beginning of the project, and before the data collection phase began, the moderator decided that he wished to relinquish his position, and knowing that I was engaged in a research project, asked me to consider taking over as moderator. This gave me the advantage of easy access to the posting logs and insight into technical aspects of the group's life. Moderation of the group is managed by a combination of moderation software operating a green-list with human intervention for non-standard or deviant posts. However, it was important that, as the effective gatekeeper, I should not use the moderator's authority to manipulate the discourse to fit in with the aims of my research. It was decided to continue to use clear, and as far as possible, objective criteria for moderation of posts, and to use my university email address for moderation purposes to remind posters of my academic affiliation.

Data collection was by a combination of participant observation and a questionnaire. The data collection phase of this research project was divided into two overlapping parts. The first part was to archive the entire corpus of contributions to the news group uk.religion.christian over a two-year period. The resulting archive – some hundred thousand posts – was analysed to search for clues to the way the group thinks and acts theologically: its *doxa* and its praxis. At the time of writing, this analysis is not yet complete, so comments related to it in what follows are necessarily provisional.

The second phase consisted of a questionnaire which members of the group were invited to complete. Over a period of three months, the final three months of phase one, a fortnightly post to the group invited people to visit a web page questionnaire, which was also available by email, telephone, fax or hard copy.[4] The questionnaire was (contra the good advice in Glastonbury and MacKean 1991: 237) fairly long, and trials showed that it took at least half an hour to complete. The main reason for this was a decision to collect the maximum amount of information from some members of the group, recognizing that the length and complexity of the exercise might well deter some members from completing it.

It was important to consider whether the potential benefit of a lengthy and detailed survey might be offset by the fact that the response rate to long questionnaires is assumed to be poor (Newell 1993: 108). After some consideration, it was decided to take a calculated risk: response rates for online surveys are generally considered to be so low[5] anyway that the best that could be expected was a minimal response rate of 10 per cent. If that 10 per cent offered detailed data, there was some benefit to be gained. The worst possible outcome would be that no useful data might be forthcoming, in which case this would provide grounds for reflection on the way the group responds to this kind of research. In the event, a remarkably high response rate of 61 per cent was achieved from the first wave of questionnaire responses, and the additional responses in the following weeks indicate a final response rate somewhat higher even than this. In all, 114 responses were received over the three-month period, more than half of which were received during the first fortnight.

The questionnaire included questions for which the responses could be analysed using simple qualitative methods, and a number of open questions which provided scope for qualitative analysis. The reason for this mixture of methods was to make the best use of what was expected to be a minimum amount of data to produce a thick description[6] of how the respondents evaluate their participation in the group. The high response rate was a mixed blessing. The large amount of data it supplied means that conclusions can be drawn with some confidence, but tabulating and collating it proved time-consuming and much more complicated than had been anticipated.

The data

The data gathered during this project – posts to the group and questionnaire results – will be stored as a resource for others who wish to use them. A study such as this may be considered a baseline for other projects to use for comparison, and it is important therefore that the data are open to critical re-examination.

Preliminary examination of the data collected from the questionnaire phase of the project confirmed that the group does indeed identify itself as a community. Ninety-one of the 114 respondents to the questionnaire (80 per cent) answered 'Yes' to the question 'Would you describe uk.religion.christian as a community in some way?', even though another question designed to elicit what they meant by 'community' showed considerable diversity.

In an important essay 'Virtual Communities as Communities', Wellman and Gulia (1999: 170–171) define a number of key questions which need to be asked when describing virtual communities:

1. Are relationships on the Net narrow and specialised or are they broadly based? . . .
2. How does the Net affect people's ability to sustain weaker, less intimate relationships and to develop new relationships? . . .
3. Is support given on the Net reciprocated? . . .
4. To what extent are strong, intimate relationships possible on the Net? . . .
5. What is high involvement in virtual community doing to other forms of 'real-life' community involvement? . . .
6. To what extent does participation on the Net increase the diversity of community ties? To what extent do such diverse ties help to integrate heterogeneous groups? . . .
7. How does the architecture of the Net affect the nature of virtual community? . . .

Analysis of posts to the group and responses to the questionnaire within this framework shows that uk.religion.christian has a clearly identifiable community culture which encompasses both narrow and broadly based relationships (1 above) and that it enhances people's ability to sustain and develop weak and strong relationships (2 above). Questions designed to discover the extent to which posters made and maintained friendships through the group showed that 27 per cent had made new friends with whom they communicate by email, and 12 per cent had made new friends whom they met face to face. Support given is reciprocated (3 above) – indeed, questionnaire responses indicated that when it comes to prayer, a clear indicator of support within a Christian context, there was more willingness to give than to ask for support (69 per cent said that they pray for others who ask for prayer, but only 52 per cent would ask for prayer themselves). Questionnaire responses also seem to indicate that some strong intimate relationships do form in the group, and these may be carried over into real-life friendships, and in one case, marriage (4 above). The experience of high involvement in uk.religion.christian is integrated into people's real-life community involvement, with over 70 per cent discussing their uk.religion.christian activity with family and friends. Given that significant numbers have been led to change their views by their involvement on the group (70 per cent), change their behaviour (12 per cent) and/or change the way they worship (5 per cent), this would suggest a dynamic relationship between the virtual and the real in the lives of participants (5 above).

When it comes to the diversity of community ties (item 6 above), questionnaire responses especially reveal a remarkable pattern of diversification. The group has members of at least twenty-one different denominations plus atheists and pagans, and an overwhelming majority of the respondents to the questionnaire (89 per cent) claimed that uk.religion.christian had helped them to understand how other people think about religion. This understanding is carried into their real lives and church communities, at the very least when they discuss uk.religion.christian with family and friends, and of course, they bring their real-life experiences from their very diverse life situations into the group. There appears to be a good deal, therefore, of cross-fertilization between real life and life online.

Finally, the architecture of Usenet in general, and uk.religion.christian in particular, including the moderation mechanism, are also significant factors in the life of the community (7 above). Two examples will suffice to illustrate this. Firstly, the asynchronous patterns of posting which is a feature of Usenet means that people participate during times that are convenient to them. This allows people to have the sense of being fully part of an ongoing discussion even though the individual contributions to the discussion may happen over a period of hours or days. Secondly, and of particular note, a number of respondents to the questionnaire identified themselves as 'lurkers' (19 per cent), but they still clearly considered themselves to be community members: indeed four claimed that it had become part of their lives, and two even claimed that it had become an important part of their lives! The fact that people who never post to the group took the time to complete a lengthy questionnaire about the group and their involvement in it is some indication of their level of personal commitment. The ability to be both a committed member of a group and at the same time invisible for all practical purposes is a distinctive feature of Usenet which results from its architecture.

Contextual theology and uk.religion.christian

Through an analysis of existing theologies which are described as contextual (liberation theologies, black theologies, feminist and womanist theologies, local theologies and urban theologies) it is possible to compile a list of characteristics which are typical of contextual theologies. A contextual theology (1) is situated, specific, and self-conscious, (2) reads in, and appropriates to its own context, the traditions, history, and texts of the church, (3) places its own culture and traditions into the context of the traditions, history, and texts of the church, (4) engages these elements in dialectic within their own context,[7] (5) is expressed in, and leads to, action inspired and initiated by the theological activity (praxis), and privileges praxis over *doxa*[8] as the defining characteristic of a theology, (6) is grounded in the concerns of the people in their own context, (7) is developed by the people in their own context with reference to the wider church, (8) is received, owned, and acted upon by the people in their own context, (9) is expressed in the vernacular of the context, (10) is open to development as the context changes, (11) is concerned with challenging the oppression and injustices of the context.

The activity of uk.religion.christian is quite clearly situated within clear boundaries, although these boundaries may be less easy to define accurately than those in more conventional contexts. It occupies a particular 'area' of cyberspace, and has distinct modes of access and participation. A contextual theology in a Usenet group is quite specific to this situation. That what happens in the group is self-consciously 'theology' is indicated by the fact that 57 per cent of the respondents to the questionnaire, when asked 'Which of the following do you think uk.religion.christian represents?' picked out 'a place where theology takes place'.

The group certainly wrestles with the traditions, histories, and texts of the church. I would venture to suggest that it is precisely this wrestling which constitutes 'reading in, and appropriating to its own context', 'placing its own culture and traditions into the context of the traditions, history, and texts of the church', and 'engaging these elements in dialectic within their own context' (items 2, 3, and 4 above). Because of the very wide spectrum of belief represented, and because of the discursive nature of the medium, the adoption of such things as live issues for discussion is a very engaged form of appropriation. It is very unlikely that the group will ever read a single text or historical tradition in a single way as a corporate expression of engagement, as one would expect in a more conventional arena of contextual theology, though.

I shall expand a little on item 5 below. If my analysis of these first four points is correct, it follows that items 6, 7, and 8 above are the outcome of the appropriation process, and analysis of the discourse of the group is revealing ways that this might be illustrated. Item 9, the fact that a contextual theology is expressed in the vernacular of the context, is of particular interest, because this is another area where the process is authentically contextual, but the outcome is different from that in more conventional exercises in contextual theology.

The vernacular of any group is not made up only of its language and the imagery it uses. The theological process itself also has a vernacular quality. Thus the vernacular of the academy is debate and dialectic, and that of the church might be described as one of exegesis and corporate commitment to agreed beliefs. The process on uk.religion.christian is one of often unresolved discussion (I hesitate to call it debate, since in many cases two people holding very different views prefer merely to express them without any attempt to engage with the other, and what results may be heated polemic), mutually exploratory deconstruction of interpretative models, ludic comment, and angry apologetic. I suggest that what makes all this distinctively a contextual theology is that those engaged in these activities continue to post to the group and preserve this way of 'doing theology', displaying a commitment to the process and a determination to maintain it.

Item 10 above is difficult to determine in the context of uk.religion. christian. The group was created in 1995, so has had little enough time to show evidence of development as the context changes. In the framework of this study, which covered a period of just two years, any changes would be very small and difficult to evaluate, and any conclusions drawn from this limited data would be subject to alternative interpretation, so I have chosen not to address this particular aspect of contextual theology with reference to this group. I suspect that a study which set out to look for development over the entire period of the group's existence would indeed find it, but I have no data to offer that might support this assumption.

Item 11 above is problematic with respect to uk.religion.christian, and I shall return to it towards the end of this chapter.

The contextual theology of uk.religion.christian

In the rest of this chapter I will concentrate on describing specific aspects of the contextual theology of uk.religion.christian. Such an endeavour is necessarily provisional for two reasons. Firstly, because analysis of the data gathered is incomplete at the time of writing, the conclusions are open to revision. Secondly, contextual theologies tend by nature to be in a constant process of evolution: as the context evolves, so too will the theology expressed therein. It is important to remember that conclusions drawn on the basis of a two-year study may not reflect the position of the community outside the period of data collection. The best that this project can offer is a snapshot of the contextual theology of uk.religion.christian as it was during the period May 1999 to May 2001, and some general observations about aspects of the group's behaviour and discussion which appear to be persistent enough to be considered characteristics.

In the light of my comments above, it should be noted at the outset that a group composed of people of many different denominations is unlikely to coalesce around key doctrines and theological methods of exegesis and hermeneutics. An analysis of posts to the group confirms that this is the case. There are regular unresolved disputes between people who distinguish themselves by terms which describe their religious tradition (for example as 'conservative', 'evangelical', or 'liberal') over issues such as the status of scripture, roles of women in church and society, and devotion to saints. A study of the contextual theology of this group would not show any clear shared view on such matters, and so part of the task was to explore what, if any, of the shared values could be considered 'doctrine' in this context.

The questionnaire asked respondents to indicate which activities (from a list of eight), uk.religion.christian represents, and 57 per cent answered positively to 'a place where theology takes place'. This was second only to 'ecumenical dialogue' (69 per cent). It would appear therefore that the majority of group members see themselves as 'doing theology' when they participate in uk.religion.christian. They were not asked to specify what they meant by the terms in this context, and the open question 'Please describe uk.religion.christian in your own words' elicited replies that covered the whole spectrum of verbal interaction in a virtual environment, in positive and negative terms. In the same way, as mentioned above, the huge majority who said that the group was a community appeared to have divergent views about the nature of community, so it would seem that the same process is operating: there is convergence on a mutually valued ideal in each case ('being community', 'doing theology'), a convergence which depends at least partly on the fact that there is no single corporate definition which includes or excludes individual interpretations. The effect is one of orientation towards, rather than inclusion in or exclusion from, the corporate thought world of the group. This in itself is a theological model, which is not dissimilar to that described by Dave Andrews in *Christi-anarchy* (1999).

Theology emerges in the activity of the group in three ways. Since it is by definition a group concerned with Christianity, the content of posts is often theological: individuals discuss the meaning of Bible texts and the interpretation of the traditions and teachings of the churches, and explore contemporary issues in the light of Christianity.[9] In terms of the group, this is theology at a superficial level: although the discussions may be profound and subtle, they are, in the end, merely exchanges of opinion which may or may not influence the participants. At this level, there is very little consensus. Many posters hold the views taught by their church or religious body, or views and attitudes that they have adopted in their own lives. There is in general a willingness to exchange views amicably, and to explain and explore beliefs in public on the group for mutual edification. The questionnaire responses indicate that it is common for people to change their views as a result of their activity on the group (59 per cent), but this would appear to be the incidental outcome of discussions rather than the result of any formal programme of evangelism by specific individuals. It would seem to be more a case of numerous individual realignments than individual or mass conversion.

In a less obvious way, the group expresses its theology in a set of explicit and implicit rules and norms of behaviour which show the shared vision of the group as a whole and which are promoted and protected by the majority of group members. Many of these rules and norms may be interpreted in terms of conventional Christian values and with reference to the Bible and Christian tradition, although the group is not always explicit in making such a connection. Part of the role of theologians in the process of contextual theology is to evaluate their activity in the light of Biblical and traditional models which the untrained members might not immediately consider,[10] and offer these to the community for their own appropriation. But whether these values are *expressed* in terms drawn explicitly from the Bible and tradition or not, they are clearly evident from both the questionnaire and the discussion within the group. I would suggest that it is here that a concept of shared doctrine is most likely to be discovered, in the sense that a doctrine is an essential belief which the community uses to interpret and direct its corporate life.

The charter for uk.religion.christian (1996) is a source for the group's behavioural norms, and one of the foundations of the group's identity, but it cannot be considered to be an *expression* of the self-identity or theology of the group except in so far as it is accepted and adhered to by posters. It was drawn up and approved in 1995 by uk.net.news.config, the regulatory body for uk.* hierarchy news groups, with participation from uk.religion. christian members, and amended in the same forum in 1996 to incorporate moderation.[11] It would, however, be fair to say that it constituted an expression of the group's identity at the time that it was amended, because the desire for a change to moderated status arose from a wish to preserve the distinctive atmosphere of the group in the face of a flurry of disruptive posts from outside the United Kingdom.

It is significant that 78 per cent of the respondents to the questionnaire in spring 2001 had read the charter. Since the vast majority of posters remain within the charter at all times, it is reasonable to suggest that it plays a part in defining the values that people align themselves with when they post to the group. Moderation by a combination of software and human works only with the consent and co-operation of posters: if there were a general unwillingness to co-operate, the system would fail under the pressure of work that the human moderator would be required to do to maintain the charter and the group would almost certainly contract. It is notable that most groups which are moderated exclusively by a human moderator have low traffic and little activity.[12] The willingness shown by posters to abide by the charter and respect decisions from the moderator is pragmatic, in that it results in the free flow of discussion. In terms of the theological activity of the group, it also reflects a view of authority that is consonant with Romans 13: 1–2: 'Let every person be subject to the governing authorities; for there is no authority except from God, and those authorities that exist have been instituted by God. Therefore whoever resists authority resists what God has appointed, and those who resist will incur judgement.' This passage from the Christian Bible is a key text in debates about Christian political and social responsibility. It is often seen as problematic in contextual theologies which have to deal with oppressive regimes, where debate centres on the legitimacy of specific 'governing authorities'. The tacit acceptance of the moderator as a 'governing authority' by posters to the group suggests that they see the moderation system as legitimate and unproblematic.[13]

This does not mean that the moderator is not subject to criticism or that moderation decisions are always uncontested. If the moderator is thought to have deviated from the strictest fairness in interpreting the charter, posters express their disapproval both on the group and in private email to the moderator. In this group, the response to 'Who watches the watchers?' is 'The watched'!

In common with many Usenet groups, uk.religion.christian also has a document which addresses regular questions, normally called a FAQ

(Frequently Asked Questions), but on uk.religion.christian, this document has a wider scope, and so is called the metaFAQ (uk.religion.christian 1997). This was drawn up in April 1997 by a core member of the group and included the 'Guidelines for Use' which had been formulated a little earlier than the charter, in consultation with active posters to the group at that time. The metaFAQ therefore has a better claim to be considered an expression of the group's identity at the time it was assembled. It describes in detail how the moderation of the group operates, and includes pointers to information on 'netiquette', the widely accepted conventions of Internet communication. The metaFAQ is updated irregularly, but the 'Guidelines' section has remained unchanged since it was first written, although it has only unofficial status since the writing of the charter; 61 per cent of respondents to the questionnaire claimed to have read the metaFAQ.

The theology, such as it is, that emerges from these two documents is a theology composed of attitudes and purposes rather than of doctrines, and is entirely in keeping with the model for contextual theology discussed above. This is explicitly described in the metaFAQ:

> The guidelines, on the other hand, are not intended to be rules or lead to disputes about whose method of argument is correct. They are intended to be helpful reminders of the traps and pitfalls that exist. Their ethos is centred on one Bible verse, which is in Paul's instruction on a debate on food that rocked the Roman church: 'Let us therefore make every effort to do what leads to peace and to mutual edification' (Romans 14:19, New International Version).

Although the charter and the metaFAQ lay out the rules and document the attitudes which the group seeks to encourage, they are probably much less significant as indicators of uk.religion.christian's values than the un-written norms of the group. The ability of groups to regulate themselves is discussed by McLaughlin, Osborne, and Smith (1995),[14] who observe that the unwritten rules of a group are upheld by popular consent within the group, and that deviant behaviour is managed by expression of disapproval and exclusion. On uk.religion.christian, self-regulation is generally effective, and deviant behaviour rarely needs to be handled by the formal processes of the moderation system.[15] The group has evolved a number of unwritten rules and a community memory which feed this self-regulation process. Some of these rules are specific to the group: new posters, however inept or abrasive, are usually treated kindly and gently corrected, whereas in other groups such behaviour would invite immediate ridicule.[16] Other rules are part of the informal code of conduct that is widely accepted for news group participa-tion: that it is wise to read the group for long enough to become familiar with its style of communication before posting, for example.

What seems to be emerging at this level is something that approximates to the *doxa* of the community: the doctrines by which they live and by which they evaluate the lives and actions of others. On the rare occasions this level of theology is explicitly discussed, references to scripture are few and often oblique. Intemperate postings occasionally draw references to 'the fruits of the Spirit' (cf. Galatians 5:22), but, for the most part, people refer more generally to the 'Christian' ethos of the group.

The third level of theological activity is to be found in the behaviour of the group members towards one another, and especially in the way the group *as a group* identifies and regulates deviant behaviour. The term 'behaviour' in this sense refers to posting styles, the activity indicated by posting in a particular way, and the way that the content of posts may have a material effect on other posters.

Certain forms of behaviour are outlawed by the charter: posting personal abuse is not permitted, for example. Since the moderation system operates a green-list, whereby messages from trusted posters are automatically approved, it occasionally happens that a regular poster is able to contravene the charter and make a post which is personally abusive or irrelevant commercial advertising. Such an action is almost always identified by other members of the group, who may draw it to the attention of the moderator, and a clear charter violation almost inevitably leads to a fixed period of manual moderation. Other forms of abuse are permitted by the charter, but the posters usually express their objection to what they perceive as unacceptable, and it is reactions to such posts that highlight the theological praxis of the group. In my opinion, this is one of the most important findings of my research, so it is appropriate to give some specific examples.

Three examples

A message which is deemed to be non-discursive and inflammatory is normally treated as not worthy of reply, and one or more people may post an ASCII art sign saying 'Do not feed the trolls'.[17] This indicates that the group values productive and peaceable exchanges of views, and this was confirmed by responses to the questionnaire which rated ecumenical dialogue as the most important aspect of the group. If someone is identified as a 'troll', his or her post receives few if any responses, and what responses there are may be dismissive or very negative in tone. For the same reason, posts which are abusive of any particular group or denomination provoke strong expressions of disapproval, since such a post runs counter to the group's view of itself as a locus of ecumenical dialogue. When, as occasionally happens, a poster attacks Roman Catholics, for example, regulars of many denominations and none join the chorus of protest.

One regular poster's views were extreme, aggressive, and unpleasant, and were not shared by other group members, but he was tolerated with (mostly) good humour as the 'village idiot'. When he became repeatedly abusive of individual group members, he was punished in the manner prescribed by the charter, but, even after repeated offences, the group was divided over whether or not he should be banned from the group, with the majority arguing for tolerance even of views they did not share. However, as soon as this poster sent a message that was personally abusive of the moderator *as moderator*, the balance changed, and a significant majority supported a permanent ban from posting. This would indicate that whilst deviance from the norms may be tolerated to quite high levels, there are certain behaviours that are not permitted by the group.[18]

Another behaviour that is not tolerated is the misrepresentation of another poster. Inaccurate snipping[19] of a post occasionally results in a misattribution, and in one case, a poster deliberately edited the words of another without clearly indicating that this was the case. The resulting furore showed the tension between the doctrine of the group and its praxis. Mr A posted a message that implied that all Roman Catholics were simple-minded and superstitious in contrast to Protestants. This disparaging of fellow Christians is contrary to the norms of the group, although it is not outlawed by the charter, and Mrs B replied by copying the post verbatim, but replacing 'Roman Catholic' with 'black' and 'Protestant' with 'white'. As a way of highlighting the prejudice expressed by Mr A this was a very effective strategy. Mrs B's mistake was to begin the post with the words 'Mr A said . . .', which was untrue. Responses from other posters showed that although many agreed that Mr A's comments were not in tune with the group's norm, which prefers to show respect to the traditions of others, Mrs B had committed an unacceptable act against Mr A by misrepresenting him. Since Usenet posts are normally archived (then at http://www.deja.com, now at www.groups.google.com) this misattribution could remain on record to affect Mr A's reputation by effectively labelling him as racist.[20] In any case, representing his views this way was clearly defamatory. As far as the group was concerned, bad praxis was far more unacceptable than bad doctrine.

Of all the characteristics of contextual theology identified above, this heightened concern with praxis over doctrine is in character with contextual theologies in other areas, as discussed above.

An unresolved issue

There is, however, one aspect of current contextual theologies that the group does not and cannot participate in. All other contextual theologies to date address the concerns of people who in some way suffer because of the context in which they find themselves with respect to the rest of society. This is usually identified as poverty and oppression, and a key doctrine of most contextual theologies today is a concern for the outworking of God's justice *in the face of oppression* and a *'preferential option for the poor'*.[21] Obviously, those who have the means to make regular use of computer-mediated communication are not poor. The demographic profile of uk.religion.christian, as uncovered by the questionnaire, shows a community that is predominantly well educated, in employment, and socially integrated, so oppression is not a feature of this constituency. There are discussions about issues of economics and social justice, and individuals often express a concern for, and a personal commitment to, God's justice, but a contextual theology for the group cannot speak from a position of oppression with the voice of the oppressed, or from a position of poverty with the voice of the poor.

Whilst it is possible to argue that a contextual theology is as appropriate to the comfortably off as to the poor, to the socially acceptable as to the outcasts, and to the autonomous as to the oppressed, it is important to recognize that this is at present an unresolved aspect of the evaluation of the contextual theology of uk.religion.christian. It may be that this is an unresolved issue for contextual theology as a discipline: if a context has to embody a degree of oppression or poverty in order to be considered a suitable environment for a distinctive contextual theology, this would imply that there is no role for localized approaches to theology in communities which are powerful, comfortable, and content. However, the heightened concern with oppression that is common to current contextual theologies may prove to be less important, as other areas of human living are considered from a contextual perspective. It has been suggested, for example, that suburban contextual theologies should be explored (Vincent 2000: 26), which would not be predominantly concerned with issues of oppression and social exclusion.

In summary, it would seem from the preliminary results of this research project that the net new group uk.religion.christian does indeed have a distinctive theological method, distinctive doctrines and a distinctive form of praxis which it works out and expresses in the vernacular of computer-mediated communication in general and of the group in particular. It appears to share all but one of the characteristics of other contextual theologies, but has developed in, and is unique to, this particular community which exists only in a virtual environment.

Notes

1 Numerous theologies can be described as 'contextual': local, urban, liberation, and feminist theologies, for example. The generic term 'contextual theology' is used here in preference to 'contextual theologies' to highlight the common features which transcend the individual characteristics of specific contextual theologies.
2 See, for example, Baym (1998), Smith and Kollock (1999), and Watson (1997).
3 I have listed some of these on my website at www.cybertheology.net.
4 All respondents replied using the web interface or by email. No one requested fax, phone, or paper versions.
5 See Witmer *et al.* (1999: 147): 'although a 50 percent response rate is typically considered minimally adequate for much traditional survey research . . . response rates around 20 percent are not uncommon for unsolicited surveys . . . and response rates to online surveys may be 10 percent or lower'.
6 The term 'thick description' was coined by Gilbert Ryle (1968). The term 'thick

description' is explained as the difference between the observed versus the experienced. It was adopted and developed in social ethnography by Clifford Geertz in an essay entitled 'Thick Description: Toward an Interpretive Theory of Culture' to describe 'the kind of intellectual effort' (1973: 6) 'made toward grasping what anthropological analysis amounts to as a form of knowledge' (1973: 5) which involves using compounded data and interpretative insight to search for meaning in ethnographic data.

7　Items 2, 3 and 4 constitute the *doxa* of a community.

8　This is a reversal of the two aspects of theology as they exist in the more traditional contexts of systematic, dogmatic, and other scholastic and ecclesiastical approaches to theological endeavour, where praxis is intended to follow, and is derived from, doctrinal positions.

9　But not exclusively: they also discuss computers, politics, and television, exchange bad jokes, and play word games – these could be described as the leisure activities of the group.

10　For some discussion of this see Bevans (1992: 12–13). Mesters (1993: 9–10) highlights some of the pitfalls of this approach.

11　Moderation was introduced specifically to address the damaging effect on the group of a small number of posters from outside the United Kingdom, whose purpose in posting to the group appeared to be intentionally to disrupt and prevent any reasonable discussion.

12　Examples of this are the christnet.* groups.

13　This does not stop some individual posters from protesting loudly if their own behaviour on the group attracts the moderator's attention!

14　See also MacKinnon (1997).

15　A green-list poster who violates the charter is placed on manual moderation for two weeks, partly as a public punishment (to deter others) and partly to allow the moderator to review whether the poster is willing to abide by the charter of the group. A side-effect is that manually moderated posts are slower to appear than automatically moderated ones, so that an angry poster or a heated exchange has the opportunity to cool off when the freedom to post speedy and ill-thought-out replies is withdrawn. People who repeatedly violate the charter are technically liable to a ban from the group, but this has been invoked on only one, rather exceptional, occasion.

16　The Usenet group alt.folklore.urban is notorious for its cruel treatment of inept 'newbies' who do not observe the highly complicated rituals of posting etiquette for the group.

17　For a discussion of the meaning of the term 'troll' in this context see www.tuxedo.org/~esr/jargon/html/entry/troll.html.

18　This was an unusual instance of what is normally a moderation decision being taken by the group. The reason for this was that the target of some of the poster's abuse was the moderator while posting in a personal capacity. As moderator, I considered that imposing sanctions in these circumstances might be seen as settling personal scores, and invited the group to decide on the appropriate course of action.

19　Replies to posts are interleaved with the original posts, and superfluous material is deleted from the reply, a process generally referred to as 'snipping'. Material which has been removed in this way may be indicated by marking <snip> in the appropriate place.

20　In fact, this exchange is no longer archived, because Mrs B and Mr A either had their posts removed from the archive or chose to insert a 'no archive' header in their messages. I have the messages in my own archive of the group, but it is no

longer available in Google (www.groups.google.com), although there is a clear
reference to it in message id <tgti5ssgpqu2h70tc4o2ibkgjgqj2a1blk@4ax.com>
(17 December 1999) and part of the offending text is quoted in message id
<385e4a0e.1292096@bobble.good-stuff.co.uk> (18 December 1999).
21 Second Latin American Bishops' Conference, Medellin, Colombia, 1968,
Paragraph 42.1.

References

Andrews, D. (1999) *Christi-anarchy*, Oxford: Lion.
Baym, N. (1998) 'The Emergence of Online Community', in S.G. Jones (ed.)
Cybersociety 2.0, London: Sage, pp. 35–68.
Bevans, S.B. (1992) *Models of Contextual Theology*, Maryknoll, NY: Orbis.
Bevans, S.B. (2002) *Models of Contextual Theology*, Maryknoll, NY: Orbis [Revised
and Expanded Edition].
Geertz, C. (1973) 'Thick Description: Toward an Interpretive Theory of Culture', in
C. Geertz (ed.) *The Interpretation of Cultures*, New York: Basic Books, pp. 8–30.
Glastonbury, B. and MacKean, J. (1991) 'Survey Methods', in A. Graham and
C. Skinner (eds) *Handbook for Research Students in the Social Sciences*, London:
The Falmer Press, pp. 225–247.
MacKinnon, R.C. (1997) 'Punishing the Persona: Correctional Strategies for the
Virtual Offender', in S.G. Jones (ed.) *Virtual Culture*, London: Sage Publications,
pp. 206–235.
McLaughlin, M.L., Osborne, K.K., and Smith, C.B. (1995) 'Standards of Conduct
on Usenet', in S.G. Jones (ed.) *Cybersociety*, London: Sage Publications,
pp. 90–111.
Mesters, C. (1993) 'The Use of the Bible in Christian Communities of the Common
People', in N.K. Gottwald and R.A. Horsley (eds) *The Bible and Liberation*,
London: SPCK, pp. 3–16.
Newell, R. (1993) 'Questionnaires', in Michael Gilbert (ed.) *Researching Social Life*,
London: Sage Publications, pp. 94–115.
Ryle, G. (1949) *The Concept of Mind*, New York: Barnes and Noble.
Schreiter, R.J. (1985) *Constructing Local Theologies*, Maryknoll, NY: Orbis.
Smith, M.A. and Kollock, P. (eds) (1999) *Communities in Cyberspace*, London:
Routledge.
uk.religion.christian (1996) 'Charter for uk.religion.christian'. Available: http://www.
usenet.org.uk/uk.religion.christian.html [Accessed 31 July 2002].
uk.religion.christian (1997) 'MetaFAQ'. Available: http://www.anweald.co.uk/uk.
religion.christian.metaFAQ.html [Accessed 31 July 2002].
Vincent, J. (2000) 'Developing Contextual Theologies', in I.K. Duffield, C. Jones, and
J. Vincent, *Crucibles: Creating Theology at UTU*, Sheffield: Urban Theology Unit,
pp. 23–32.
Watson, N. (1997) 'Why We Argue About Virtual Community: A Case Study of the
Phish.Net Fan Community', in S.G. Jones (ed.) *Virtual Culture*, London: Sage
Publications, pp. 102–132.
Wellman, B. and Gulia, M. (1999) 'Virtual Communities as Communities: Net Surfers
Don't Ride Alone', in M.A. Smith and P. Kollock (eds) *Communities in Cyberspace*,
London: Routledge, pp. 167–194.

Witmer, D.F., Colman, R., and Katzman, S.L. (1999) 'From Paper-and-Pencil to Screen-and-Keyboard: Toward a Methodology for Survey Research on the Internet', in S.G. Jones (ed.) *Doing Internet Research: Critical Issues and Methods for Examining the Net*, Thousand Oaks, Calif., London and New Delhi: Sage Publications, pp. 145–162.

Chapter 11

Christian Web usage
Motives and desires

Michael J. Laney

The Internet has provided both a new context and an innovative instrument for scholars to carry out studies on the motivations and gratifications of users of religious communication in contemporary society. Religious websites in general offer a wealth of topics for exploration, from religious radio and television sites on the Web to sites for denominational headquarters, churches and ministry organizations and personal homepages. In order to investigate what the users think about these sites and what they get out of visiting them, a rather comprehensive research design needs to be set up. This chapter provides a thorough description of how such a study of the motivations and gratifications of religious website users can be carried out in practice. The empirical focus of the survey is the Christian web audience of the late twentieth century. Building on classic works on the religious usage of various mass media (cf. Abelman and Neuendorf 1985; Buddenbaum 1981; Christians 1985), this chapter also includes examples of how survey results from the new digital environments can be compared with and linked to existing research traditions.

Studies of uses and gratifications

In its simplest form, the uses and gratifications model in media research posits that audience members have certain needs or drives that are satisfied by using media sources. In the uses and gratifications paradigm the audience do not just passively consume the mediated images being broadcast into free space. Audiences tend to use those media that serve a purpose in their lives (Blumler 1979: 11–12). The actual needs satisfied by the media are called media gratifications. Our knowledge of these uses and gratifications typically comes from surveys in which a large number of people have been asked questions about how they use the media. Often, the various uses and gratifications have been classified into systems of categories (Dominick 1996: 47).

An example of such a category is 'cognition'. Cognition is the act of coming to know something. When a person uses a mass medium to obtain information about something, then he or she is using the medium in a cognitive way

(Dominick 1996: 47). To illustrate, the Abelman surveys found that many people give the following reasons for using television: '(a) I want to understand what is going on in the world, (b) I want to know what religious leaders are doing and, (c) I want to know what political leaders are doing' (Abelman 1988: 116). These reasons constitute the current-events type of cognitive gratifications. At the same time, many people, according to the Hamilton and Rubin's (1992: 674) surveys also report the following reasons for using television: 'So I can learn how to do things I haven't done before. Because it helps me learn things about myself and others. So I can learn about what could happen to me.' These statements illustrate a second type of cognition: using the media to satisfy a desire for general knowledge.

There are other common motives for using the media. Some people report that they use the media, particularly television and radio, but also the Internet, as a means to overcome loneliness (Murphy 1998a). Radio keeps people company in their cars. People who might otherwise be deprived of social relationships find companionship in media content and media personalities. In fact, some viewers might go so far as to develop feelings of kinship and friendship with mediated religious figures. As indicated above, humans occasionally also need to escape from certain activities, and for this reason they use media such as the Internet not only for relaxation but also for purposes best described as withdrawal uses. At times, people use the mass media to create a barrier between themselves and other people or other activities.

In their study of users of religious television, Hamilton and Rubin categorized this factor as avoidance: 'I watch religious programming to avoid programs that are heavy in violence. I watch religious programming to avoid shows with lots of sex' (Hamilton and Rubin 1992: 674). Hamilton and Rubin's (1992) seminal work on uses and gratifications among religious users of television further details how religiosity affects Christian churchgoers' motives for using television and their selection of programme content. Religious uses and gratifications thus seem to be consistent with uses and gratifications as a psychological communication perspective. This may in turn also explain media choices and consequences among users of religious websites.

Abelman (1988) studied religious television viewers' motivations for watching the religious talk show *The 700 Club* hosted by televangelist Pat Robertson. From that study emerged certain measures of gratifications such as 'reaction, entertainment, faith, habit, information, and escape' (Abelman 1988: 117). Additionally, studies point to the need for further study of the gratifications Internet users are seeking (Beinhoff 1997; Kaye 1996; King 1998; Lin 1997; and Murphy 1998b). However, these above-mentioned studies did not address the motivations for religious Web use.

Methodology

The survey instrument that was used in order to measure motivations for religious website usage as part of the present study of Christian website users was an electronic questionnaire. Application of the online surveying methodology continues to grow in the fields of both applied research (Kehoe, Pitkow, and Morton 1998) and academic research (King 1998; McMillan 1998; Murphy 1998a; and Sheehan and Hoy 1998). The questionnaire or survey format as well as portions of the methodological design for the data analysis conceptualization were modified from Murphy (1998b) and King (1998).

Uses and gratifications research traditionally employs a Likert-type scale to measure the respondent's degree of agreement or disagreement with the item, typically ranging from one to five. For this study the conventional one-to-five interval described in uses and gratifications literature was deemed appropriate with a value of one indicating strong agreement and five representing strong disagreement.

An issue for online studies is the difficulty of generalizing the results to the population. Since online studies by their very design operate in a dynamic environment of self-selection on the part of the respondent, the survey researcher seeks to make the sample as representative as possible. On the basis of research traditions employing exploratory studies (Kaye 1996; King 1998; McMillan and Downes 1998; McMillan 1998; Murphy 1998b; and Sheehan and Hoy 1998), a minimum target of 450 completed surveys was deemed necessary for purposes of analysis and further study of this topic.

The targeted user of this study is the visitor to Christian church (or ministry) websites. In an effort to reach this niche target audience, it was decided to solicit participation in the survey through church websites. While this definition may initially appear at first glance to eliminate many categories, such was not the case. An issue with such self-reporting is the inability for the researcher to determine whether the site is a bona-fide church or ministry. For example, many Christian television and radio stations identify themselves as a ministry, a church, or both. Additionally, some large churches also own and operate media ministries as extensions of their ministries. For the purposes of this study, targeted sites that were listed as Christian church or ministries in online directories, such as GOSHEN (Global Online Service Helping Evangelize the Nations) Net (Goshen 1998) or media publications, were utilized. In an effort to make the sample representative, as many Christian denominations as possible were selected. Additionally, every fourth site was selected in an effort to provide a balanced target listing from three independent sources, online directories and two religious media directories.

King (1998) and Murphy (1998b) in their Web studies found that in order to gather a minimum of 450 completed surveys, over 900 solicitations to webmasters requesting posting of the survey on their websites were necessary.

In an effort to maximize respondent exposure to the survey, King (1998) and Murphy (1998b) placed notices within television and radio trade publications. In this study, advertising in trade publications was not employed because a single Christian church trade publication does not exist. While trade publications exist for Christian music and television, church webmasters are not the target audience for these publications. Instead efforts were taken to maximize exposure to the survey by increasing the number of solicitations and attempting to include as many Christian denominations as possible.

An initial sample of 1101 sites was drawn from online Christian Web directories and Web addresses listed in Christian media directories, such as *Charisma and Ministries Today* and *National Religious Broadcasters*. As such, these 1101 Christian church and ministry sites were contacted; forty solicitations were returned due to 'failed mail' or 'incorrect addresses'. Eventually, Christian webmasters from 1061 churches in the United States, Canada, and New Zealand (the New Zealand website belongs to a Canadian-based ministry) which matched the target users listed in *GOSHEN Net* and representing forty-five Christian denominations received an invitation to host the survey on their websites. After the webmasters acknowledged their desire to participate in the study, the online survey was forwarded by email and they were contacted by email to ensure that they had received the file and that the link was activated. Of the 1061 sites contacted, eighty-five web-masters initially agreed to participate in the study. While a failure to respond or reply may imply a refusal, it must also be understood that many webmasters do not check their sites frequently, particularly those of smaller churches. In some cases the webmasters responded favourably, but failed to install the link due to a 'lack of time' or 'technical inability'. Ultimately, forty Christian websites were linked to the survey.

Forty Christian websites associated primarily with local churches linked visitors to the survey, and a small percentage found the survey through search engines or other methods. The total number of valid responses in the survey period from 14 June 1998 to 18 July 1998 was 912, with responses coming from forty-nine states, Puerto Rico, Guam, and the District of Columbia, as well as twenty-one countries. The respondents represented forty-five Christian denominations, with over 96 per cent claiming to have experienced spiritual or religious conversion. The participating websites were selected in order to compare with the target Christian Web users in size, ethnicity, economics, and religious practices. Before the actual survey period began two focus groups were conducted and the online survey instrument was pre-tested online in a laboratory.

As a self-selected online survey attempting to target users of Christian websites, the sample represented in this study was validated to the degree that it reached the intended users. The Graphic, Visualization, and Usability Centre's (GVU) studies conducted by Georgia Tech University are the most widely known self-selected surveys on the Internet, with response rates in excess of ten thousand from around the globe. The Eighth GVU World Wide Web Survey was utilized as a basis for comparison and contrast with the religious Web survey.

The twenty-seven items used in the survey were modifications of those used by Abelman (1987, 1988) and Hamilton and Rubin (1992). The items pertaining to Web use resemble those used by King (1998) and Murphy (1998a), and were varied slightly to embrace religious applications on the Web. In addition to the structured responses to the twenty-seven items, the respondents were allowed to add comments to each of the items.

Results

Table 11.1 shows a list of the twenty-seven uses and gratifications items used in the study, ranked by means. The standard deviations calculated are nominative since the distribution is invariably much skewed for those items with mean values between four and five. The values for standard deviation are therefore only indicative of the spread of responses.

The principal factor method was used to extract the factors, and this was followed by a varimax rotation to differentiate underlying factors. A varimax rotation is a common procedure to identify commonality in factors. Normally, factors with eigen-values greater than 1.0 are retained. However, caution is advised to ensure that the factors that are retained are of practical value. The screening results suggested four meaningful factors, so only these factors were initially retained for rotation. Three additional factors associated with television viewing (voyeurism, escape, and habit) were not retained owing to their low eigen-values.

The four extracted factors possessed eigen-values of at least 1.0, and they accounted for 35 per cent of the total variance. This is a rather low degree of variance; however, it suggests that an interaction is occurring, and serves as a reasonable point of departure for further research (see table 11.2). Nine items were subsequently found to load on the first factor, which was then labelled 'Religious entertainment and information items' (see table 11.4). Three items loaded on the second factor, and this factor was then labelled 'Reaction items'. Five items loaded on the third factor, which was labelled 'Faith items'. Six items loaded on the fourth factor, which was labelled 'Alternative items'.

A primary loading above 0.45 or below −0.45 was considered significant and was checked for reliability using Cronbach's Alpha (see table 11.3). These criteria were also employed by Kaye (1996) in his study of Web uses and gratifications. In light of these considerations, assignment of factors was based on two major criteria: (1) primary and secondary loadings numerically above 0.45, and (2) conceptual matching predicated upon the literature, context of the question, and personal judgement. This action reduced the

Table 11.1 Ranked means of religious uses and gratifications item agreement

Religious uses and gratifications items	Mean	Std. dev.	Valid N
Because this website offers messages that are positive and uplifting	1.9	0.894	912
Because this (conversion) experience is still important to me in everyday life	2.1	0.539	860
Because this website agrees with my religious preference/denomination	2.2	0.971	912
Because this website provides reinforcement and strengthens my spiritual beliefs	2.2	1.052	912
Because this website has links to other websites I like	2.2	0.996	912
For research information	2.3	0.996	912
I am a spiritual person	2.3	0.639	907
For sacred verses and texts	2.3	0.978	912
Because this website is entertaining	2.3	0.923	912
For information about religious community events	2.4	1.070	912
I am familiar with this website's ministry/ organization	2.6	1.224	912
For prayer requests	2.6	1.082	912
I desire spiritual/religious training	2.6	0.953	895
I desire friendship with others who are spiritually minded	2.6	0.971	895
Inspirational music and graphics	2.7	1.087	912
Alternative family oriented activities	2.8	0.998	912
I am attempting to explore my faith	2.9	1.063	898
I am interested in receiving free information	3.4	1.255	894
I am interested in making a purchase from this website's ministry	3.7	0.929	912
I am interested in making a monetary contribution to this website's ministry	3.9	0.838	912
I am doing research (academic, professional, personal, etc.)	3.9	1.464	811
I desire personal spiritual or religious conversion	4.0	1.488	782
I am searching this site for a church, synagogue, temple or mosque to affiliate	4.2	0.863	912
I am searching for an alternative to traditional religious services	4.2	1.367	891
I am interested in making a purchase	4.4	1.220	884
I allow my spiritual/religious beliefs to influence my selection of programme content	4.6	1.327	894
I am interested in making a monetary contribution	4.8	0.941	875

Note:
Response means are for agreement with statements 'I am motivated to visit a religious website because . . .' 1 – Strongly agree, 2 – agree, 3 – somewhat agree, 4 – disagree, 5 – strongly disagree.

Table 11.2 Four factor extractions for uses and gratifications of Christian website users

Factor	Eigen-value	Percentage variance
1 Religious entertainment and information items	3.87	15.3
2 Reaction items	2.18	12.8
3 Faith items	1.91	3.7
4 Alternative items	1.67	3.6

Table 11.3 Reliability analysis for scales of uses and gratifications among religious website users

Factor	Alpha[1]	Valid N
1 Religious entertainment and information items	0.83	912
2 Reaction	0.82	912
3 Faith items	0.81	895
4 Alternatives	0.79	884

1   Reliability coefficient for Cronbach's Alpha

total number of religious uses and gratification items utilized for the factor analysis to 23.

In his study of television station Web users King (1998: 164) observed agreement on the 'Companionship' scale, indicating that 'TV station web users do not go online to find companionship'. For King's (1998) television station Web users, the need for 'Companionship' did not appear to drive their Web usage. The present study by and large seems to suggest that 'Faith items' (factor 3) is an underlying motive, which could possibly drive religious Web users in search of religious Web gratifications. As indicated above, respondents were asked 'What motivates you to visit religious websites . . .?' The highest item loading on factor three was 'I am seeking reinforcement for my personal beliefs'. A total of 94 per cent of the respondents indicated agreement with this response, with 60 per cent registering 'strong agreement'. When compared with the author's study this item had a mean of 2.22 as compared to Abelman's mean of 1.54, suggesting perhaps slightly different motives for Christian Web usage as opposed to religious television use. With 90 per cent of the respondents indicating agreement with the item 'I am attempting to explore my faith', this factor received a loading of 0.59.

The assigned item factor loadings employed in this study are roughly consistent with Abelman's (1988) study of religious television viewer motivations for viewing *The 700 Club*, Evangelist Pat Robertson's Christian programme. Thus, the four entertainment items utilized from the Abelman study also loaded on Abelman's factor one as well. These findings are

Table 11.4 Religious uses and gratifications rotated factor matrix for religious Web survey

Religious uses and gratifications rotated factor matrix	1	2	3	4	Valid N
Factor 1 (Religious entertainment and information items)					
For sacred verses and texts	**0.67**	0.00	0.12	0.06	912
Because this website is entertaining	**0.65**	0.06	0.18	0.14	912
For prayer requests	**0.64**	0.06	0.17	0.01	912
Inspirational music and graphics	**0.56**	0.22	0.01	0.25	912
Messages that are positive and uplifting	**0.53**	0.06	0.23	0.48	912
For information about religious community events	**0.52**	0.22	0.01	0.25	912
Alternative family oriented activities	**0.52**	0.17	0.11	0.04	912
Website has links to other websites I like	**0.51**	0.11	0.06	0.25	912
For research information	**0.45**	0.05	0.01	0.12	912
Factor 2 (Reaction items)					
Making a monetary contribution to this website's ministry	0.21	**0.68**	-0.01	0.26	912
Making a purchase from this website's ministry	0.17	**0.66**	0.03	0.30	912
I am interested in making a monetary contribution	0.08	**0.58**	0.21	-0.02	895
Factor 3 (Faith items)					
I am seeking reinforcement for my personal beliefs	0.11	0.06	**0.58**	0.10	912
I am attempting to explore my faith	0.06	0.11	**0.57**	0.06	895
I desire spiritual/religious training	0.09	0.02	**0.54**	0.12	898
I desire friendship with others who are spiritually minded	0.21	0.07	**0.49**	0.20	895
I desire personal spiritual or religious conversion	0.13	0.19	**0.46**	-0.01	896
Factor 4 (Alternative items)					
Agrees with my religious preference/denomination	0.34	0.08	0.13	**0.58**	912
Reinforcement and strengthens my spiritual beliefs	0.36	0.10	0.33	**0.57**	912
I am familiar with this ministry/organization	0.10	0.21	-0.03	**0.57**	912
Ministries selling products/resource materials	0.07	0.15	0.06	**0.57**	885
My beliefs influence my selection of programme content	-0.06	0.00	-0.10	**-0.55**	891
An alternative to traditional religious services	0.07	0.23	0.19	**-0.46**	912

Note: Responses are for agreement with statements 'I am motivated to visit a religious website because . . .'
1 – Strongly agree, 2 – agree, 3 – somewhat agree, 4 – disagree, 5 – strongly disagree.

different from Hamilton and Rubin's (1992) study on the influence of religiosity on television viewing. While both Abelman (1988) and Hamilton and Rubin (1992) identified entertainment-related items, they did not detect any underlying religious usage factor. Hamilton and Rubin (1992) also identified a factor labelled 'Voyeurism', which was eventually eliminated from the religious Web study. A comparison of the author's findings with those of Abelman and Hamilton and Rubin can be found in table 11.5.

In his religious television motivation study, Abelman (1988) utilized a factor known as 'Faith'. In that study 'Faith' loaded as factor three in a six-factor solution. The present religious Web study was consistent with Abelman's (1988) factor components in this area. His summated table does not provide the loadings per item in this factor, but a means comparison is provided in table 11.6. A comparison of the two tables points to a certain degree of consistency regarding the 'Faith Factor' as a driving motivation for the religious television user and religious website users as well. Over 94 per cent of the religious web respondents indicated agreement on a Likert scale of one (strongly agree) and two (agree) with utilizing religious websites as

Table 11.5 Comparison of religious television uses and gratifications items between Abelman (1988), Hamilton and Rubin (1992), and the present study

Items or factors	Abelman (1988)	Hamilton and Rubin (1992)	Present study
Entertainment items			
Because it entertains me	X	X	X
Because it relaxes me	X	X	–
Messages that are positive and uplifting	X	X	X
Alternative family oriented material	X	X	X
Reaction items and alternative items			
Making a purchase from this ministry	X	–	X
Making a monetary contribution to this ministry	X	–	X
I am interested in making a monetary contribution	X	–	X
An alternative to traditional religious services	–	–	X
Faith items			
For spiritual guidance	X	X	X
Prayer	X	X	X
For moral support	X	X	–
Reinforcement for religious beliefs	X	X	X
Agrees with my religious preference	–	–	X
Information items			
It helps me learn	X	X	X
Conduct personal research	X	X	X
It helps me learn about what could happen to me	X	X	–

Table 11.6 Comparison of ranked means of 'faith' between Abelman (1988) and the present study

Religious uses and gratifications items	Abelman (1988) Mean	Present study Mean
I am attempting to explore my faith	3.07	2.95
I desire spiritual/religious training	2.64	2.67
I desire friendship with others who are spiritually minded	2.87	2.68
I am seeking reinforcement for my personal beliefs	1.54	2.22

motivation as a result of their 'desire for spiritual/religious training'. Abelman (1988) noted that religious television users viewed the *700 Club* for many of the same reasons that Christian Web users browse. The opportunity that religious websites allow for users to 'explore their faith' found agreement on a Likert scale of one (strongly agree) and two (agree) with 90 per cent of the target audience.

Additionally, while both media offer some degree of reinforcement, the Web offers the advantage of interactivity with another person, a capability that is not widely resident in the average religious television user's home. Respondents in the religious Web survey, like religious television users, indicated high levels of agreement that they utilize religious websites because they 'desire friendship with others'. While over 94 per cent of religious Web users indicate agreement on a Likert scale of one (strongly agree) and two (agree) with seeking out companionship, when single items against single items were correlated, a negative relationship was observed for time spent in religious websites, against seeking friendship ($r = -0.15$), which was statistically significance at the $p < 0.01$ level. However, while statistically significant, this is numerically a fairly low correlation coefficient, so not much can be inferred from it.

Finally, 85 per cent of the respondents indicated a strong level of agreement with 'desire personal or spiritual or religious conversion' as motivation for Christian Web usage. This item received a factor loading of 0.46, which is an indication of some strength in relationship to the factor of faith. Overall, the exploratory findings of the survey indicate that a relationship exists between seeking reinforcement for personal motives and Christian website usage. Some of the quantitative data gleaned from this study suggest that some respondents clearly utilize Christian websites as a method of reinforcement of faith.

Concerning the 'reaction items', it should be noted, moreover, that this factor, in fact, had the highest loadings (see table 11.4). The majority of the respondents were not using the Web for 'making a monetary contri-butions' on Christian websites. With 79 per cent of the respondents indicating disagreement with making a contribution, the mean for this response was

4.8. Concerning the 'purchase of religious resources or materials from this website's ministry' item, it should be noted that this received a factor loading of 0.66. The most frequently occurring response was 4.4 with a standard deviation of 1.220, with responses from 80 per cent of the respondents. This finding is not completely unexpected. Abelman (1987: 67), in a study of the content of forty leading religious shows in 1987, examined monetary appeals by religious broadcasters as well as the levels of contributions by those who attend regular services. He observed

> that during one hour, a televangelist asked each viewer to donate $328.00. The person who watches two hours a week over the course of a year is subjected to direct appeal for a total of $31,400.00 a year. If one's two hour viewing fare consists only of revivals and preaching programs, that figure creeps up to an average of $33,361.00 per year.

One respondent's possible motive for using Christian websites was to obtain counselling and safeguard his privacy in the process:

> I had a serious problem that I could not share with anyone in my town. I needed to pray with someone about it, so I visited a Christian website, but the ministry never followed up and contacted me. I visited another site and got an automated response promising me that they would contact me within 48 hours, but they never did. I still need someone to pray with me.

Few individual respondents shared such detailed personal anguish concerning their possible motives for Christian Web use. However, the Web affords a degree of anonymity to those seeking to discuss sensitive issues. A respondent who noted 'The major reason I visit a Christian website is to grow in the Lord' (female Christian Web respondent) summarized the religious gratification that Christian websites appear to offer some respondents. 'Religious entertainment and information', which is an extracted factor, received some of the highest levels of agreement in regard to possible motives for Christian website use in this study. Several respondent comments appear to support this desire; for example, 'Christian websites provide me with information to make decisions for my family. It's great to be able to have religious websites. It makes the Internet time such fun' (female Christian Web respondent). Concerning the religious information gratifications being sought by visitors to Christian websites, these respondents remarked: 'Christian websites provide access to religious oriented news/information that the secular press refuses to discuss or elaborate on' (male Christian Web respondent). Access to religious information is clearly reported by these users as a major motivation that shapes and articulates their online experience. In this regard media-system dependency may provide some possible insights concerning what behaviours are being observed.

Ball-Rokeach and DeFleur's (1976: 7) media-system dependency theory assumes that the potential for mass media messages to achieve a broad range of 'cognitive, affective, and behavioural effects will be increased when media systems serve many unique information needs'. On the basis of these data, the Christian Web user may be attempting to utilize Christian websites to provide these 'many unique information needs'. Perhaps the Christian Web user is attempting to gratify needs other than the strictly informational ones alluded to by Ball-Rokeach and DeFleur (1976). Based upon studies of the relation between religion and community (Groothuis 1997; Goethals 1990; and Stout and Buddenbaum 1996) these elements provide some illumination on these submerged factors. Over 95 per cent of the respondents agreed that the opportunities to receive 'messages that are positive and uplifting', and 'alternative family oriented activities', are almost as important as 'inspirational music and graphics'. Additionally, 92 per cent of the respondents indicated agreement with functioning in an environment that 'agrees with my religious preference/denomination'. Over 88 per cent of the respondents indicated an interest in sites that provide 'sacred verses and texts'. While not as high, almost 77 per cent of the respondents identified religious website use as an opportunity for 'prayer requests'.

Over 94 per cent of the religious Web respondents indicated agreement with utilizing religious websites as motivation as a result of their 'desire for spiritual/religious training'. One respondent noted, 'Of course I want to strengthen my beliefs – but I want to be challenged also' (female Christian Web respondent). Another observed, 'I would like to see more academic Biblical research aids, better search engines to Christian web sites' (male Christian Web respondent). Abelman (1998: 116) noted that religious television users viewed *The 700 Club* for many of the same reasons that Christian Web users browse: 'salvation', and 'feeling close to God'. The opportunity that religious websites allow for users to 'explore their faith' found agreement with 90 per cent of the target audience respondents. This respondent noted, 'Fellowship and keeping in touch with others is greatly enhanced through the Internet. It helps one to realize just how many Christians are out there' (male Christian Web respondent).

Other motives received a lower score than the above: 49 per cent agreed that a motive for their religious Web use was 'searching for an alternative to traditional religious services', which received a mean response of 4.2 and a standard deviation of 1.36. When narrowing the the item to 'I am searching this website for a church, synagogue, temple, or mosque to affiliate with', less than 11 per cent indicated agreement but over 89 per cent disagreed, resulting in a 4.2 mean response and a standard deviation of 0.863. Further, when asked about their intentions within the next twelve months, whether they planned to 'visit a church, synagogue, temple, or mosque, now that I have visited their religious website', 86 per cent replied, 'No'. What the respondents appeared to be saying is that, while roughly half of them may be 'searching for an alternative', this quest may have been fulfilled for some of the respondents through the use of the religious website.

Conclusion

This study has attempted to determine whether there was a relationship between seeking reinforcement for personal motives and desires and Christian website usage, and such a relationship appears to exist. The employment of the factor analysis was to determine the factors contributing to Christian Web use as it relates to religious motives.

It is hardly surprising that the exploratory factor analysis seems to suggest that 'faith' is an underlying motive for Web users in search of religious Web gratifications. In his religious television motivation study, Abelman (1988) also utilized a factor known as 'Faith'. A comparison of the religious Web study and the Abelman (1988) study points to a certain degree of consistency regarding the 'faith factor' as a possible motivation for the religious television user and religious website users as well.

On the basis of the open-ended responses, these respondents appear to represent a community of Christian Web users who generally embrace the fundamentalist religious tradition. A key motive of the Christian Web user appears to be the value of the power of information coupled with the anonymity that the Internet provides, as well as the community of faith that cyberspace potentially embraces. These users are motivated to actively select their choices of Christian websites and state that they intend to tell others about what they have experienced online.

References

Abelman, R. (1987) 'Religious television uses and gratifications', *Journal of Broadcasting and Electronic Media*, 31, pp. 293–307.

Abelman, R. (1988) 'Motivations for viewing the 700 club', *Journalism Quarterly*, 65, pp. 112–118.

Abelman, R. and Neuendorf, K. (1985) 'Themes and topics in religious television programming', *Review of Religious Research*, 29, pp. 152–74.

Ball-Rokeach, S.J. and DeFleur, M.L. (1976) 'A dependency model of mass media effects', *Communication Research*, 3, pp. 3–21.

Beinhoff, L.A. (1997) 'What gratifications are sought from computers?' Paper presented at the 80th annual conference of the Association for Education in Journalism and Mass Communications, Chicago, IL, August 1997.

Blumler, J.G. (1979) 'The role of theory in uses and gratification studies', *Communication Research*, 6, pp. 9–36.

Buddenbaum, J.M. (1981) 'Characteristics and media-related needs of the audience for religious TV', *Journalism Quarterly*, 58, pp. 266–272.

Christians, C. (1985) 'Religion and communication', *Critical Studies in Mass Communication*, 2, pp. 282–305.

Dominick, J.R. (1996) *The dynamics of mass communication*, New York: McGraw-Hill Co. [Fifth edition].

Goethals, G.T. (1990) *The electronic golden calf: Images, religion, and the making of meaning*, Cambridge, MA: Cowley Publications.

Goshen (1998) 'Goshen net web directory of Christian sites', Available: http://www.goshen.net/WebDirectory/ [Accessed 6 June 1998].

Groothuis, D. (1997) *The soul in cyberspace*, Grand Rapids, MI: Baker Books.

Hamilton, N.F. and Rubin, A.M. (1992) 'The influence of religiosity on television viewing', *Journalism Quarterly*, 69, pp. 667–678.

Kaye, B. (1996) 'The uses and gratifications of the World Wide Web', Paper presented at the 79th annual convention of the Association for Education in Journalism and Mass Communications, Anaheim, CA, August 1996.

Kehoe, C., Pitkow, J., and Morton, K. (1998) 'GVU's 8th WWW Survey Results', Available: http://www.gvu.gatech.edu/user_surveys/survey-1997-10/#exec/ [Accessed 19 June 1998].

King, R. (1998) 'The uses and gratifications of the World Wide Web: An audience analysis for local television broadcasters', Knoxville: The University of Tennessee [Unpublished doctoral dissertation].

Lin, C.A. (1997) 'The relations of psychological gratifications factors and internet use', Paper presented at the 80th annual conference of the Association for Education in Journalism and Mass Communications, Chicago, IL, August 1997.

McMillan, S.J. (1998) 'Using the internet for content analysis and survey research', Paper presented at the 20th Annual Communications Research Symposium, Knoxville, TN, February 1998.

McMillan, S.J. and Downes, E.J. (1998) 'Exploring interactivity: toward a conceptual definition', Paper presented at the 20th Annual Communications Research Symposium, Knoxville, TN, February 1998.

Murphy, R.E. (1998a) 'Executive summary: UTK radio station web site survey', Available: http://web.utk.edu/~reggie [Accessed 5 June 1998].

Murphy, R.E. (1998b) 'Research on broadcasters on the web', Knoxville: The University of Tennessee, Knoxville [Unpublished doctoral dissertation].

O'Leary, S.D. (1996) 'Cyberspace as sacred space: Communicating religion on computer networks', *Journal of the American Academy of Religion*, 64, pp. 781–808.

Sheehan, K.B. and Hoy, M.G. (1998) 'The potential promise and pitfalls of E-mail surveys', Paper presented at the 20th Annual Communications Research Symposium, Knoxville, TN, February 1998.

Stout, D. and Buddenbaum, J. (1996) *Religion and mass media: Audiences and adaptations*, Beverly Hills, CA: Sage.

Chapter 12

Digital Waco

Branch Davidian virtual communities after the Waco tragedy[1]

Mark MacWilliams

Arjun Appadurai has argued that any understanding of the postmodern world must take into account the important role that electronic media play in 'the construction of imagined selves and imagined worlds' (Appadurai 1996: 3). One of the most important examples of that construction is 'virtual community', a term that Shawn Wilbur has described as 'certainly among the most used, and perhaps abused, phrases in the literature on computer-mediated communication (CMC)' (Wilbur 1997: 5). For cyber-enthusiasts such as Howard Rheingold, the great potential of cyberspace is that it is a 'not there' that frees people from the physical constraints of real-life places, where the home, office, or the neighbourhood street define the context of social relations. As an 'alternative social-space', the Internet has the power 'to unite individuals from all points of the globe, irrespective of geographic boundaries, age, sex, or race' through its power to foster communication and express powerful human feelings. As such, it 'frees people from the hierarchies of class, wealth, and gender that structure mainstream social spaces' that fragment modern society (Urban 2000: 273). In his seminal study, *The Virtual Community: Homesteading on the Electronic Frontier*, Rheingold argues that the power of this new space is the possibility of creating virtual communities within it, which he defines as 'social aggregations that emerge from the Net when enough people carry on public discussions long enough with sufficient human feeling to form webs of personal relationships in cyberspace' (Rheingold 1993: 5).

Others, however, are not so sure. For example in his essay 'The Internet and its Social Landscape' Steven Jones asks what kinds of webs of personal relationships are fostered through CMC, and questions whether being online provides 'some of the things we desire offline, things like friendship, community, interaction, and public life' (Jones 1997: 9). As a cyber-pessimist, Jones concludes that it is an illusion to think that one can construct a 'community from *communication*'. He envisions the Internet along the same lines as the 'imagined communities' that Benedict Anderson says arise with the advent of print journalism. Like a newspaper, the Internet creates a 'discontinuous narrative space' that temporarily unites diverse groups 'by means of mass communication and mass production. The imagined world that is created is 'a silent world, [where] all conversation is typed. To enter it, one forsakes both body and place and becomes a thing of words alone' (Jones 1997: 15). Despite list serves, bulletin boards, Usenet groups, and chat rooms that offer 'some semblance of a place for "being"', the only social formation that the Internet offers, Jones concludes, is the virtual analogue of a public library's reading room, which, like Richard Hoggart's bleak description of it, is filled with 'eccentric[s] absorbed in the rituals of . . . monomania . . . exist[ing] on the periphery of life, seeing each other daily but with no contact'. Internet communities are, he continues, at most, a grouping of people 'headed in the same direction for a while, but who live an isolated existence before their computer screens being *among* and not *with* others who are aimlessly connected online' (Jones 1997: 14). As such, they profoundly differ from real-life communities where people are *part of* the place, where there is 'human occupancy, commitment, interaction and living among and with others. We require a counterbalance to the spectacle that is created when one thing is juxtaposed among different others as in a newspaper or a department store' (Jones 1997: 16).

The debate over the reality of virtual communities, to state the paradox clearly, is important for the field of religious studies. First, some have argued that, despite the fact that cyberspace is a technological byproduct of the new physics, it has its conceptual roots in religion, particularly in a Christian spatial dualism that conceived of a 'soul space' of Heaven and Purgatory that were non-physical spaces that existed 'outside' the material world (Wertheim 1999: 67). If we wish to call such a 'soul space' a virtual reality, it is important to note that in this case 'virtual' does not mean illusory, intangible, or the opposite of real, but something that is symbolically real. Bellah argues that 'reality is never as real as we think'. Since for human beings reality is never simply 'out there', but always also involves an 'in here 'and some way in which the two are related, it is almost certain that anything "out there" will have many meanings' (Bellah 1970: 254). Religion is neither subjective nor objective but is a symbolic world that evokes the reality of a 'felt whole'.

In religious communities examples of such symbolically real 'virtual communities' abound. For example, in the key statement of Presbyterianism, the Westminster Confession of Faith (1663–1646), Chapter 25 defines 'the catholic or universal church' as an 'invisible' church consisting of 'the whole number of the elect, that have been, are, or shall be gathered into one, under Christ the head thereof; and is the spouse, the body, the fullness of him that filleth all in all'. Such an invisible church is an imaginary but nonetheless symbolically real 'church' for those Calvinist Presbyters who wholeheartedly accepted it. It was no mere dogma but was a felt whole for those who believed that only Christ had the spiritual power to elect those for salvation in the past, present, and future. As such this church of the eternally predestined saints transcended any local church 'out there' whose membership included the eternally reprobate as well as the saved. As the real universal or 'catholic' church, it had authority over the visible institutions of the Roman Catholic church that Calvin and the other reformers had emphatically rejected. In effect, the invisible church is a kind of virtual community in which those choosing to believe in it could dwell.

In this chapter, I will argue that cyberspace offers a symbolically real space in which religious communities can imaginatively dwell. Within its electronic 'soul space' constructed from words, images, and texts, religious communities create their own symbolic worlds that may be all but invisible to mainstream society and its mass media. Within its electronic architecture, religious communities find a 'place on which to stand' by establishing virtual communities by communicating on the Internet. Can we find such virtual religious communities that fit Rheingold's definition? Does the Internet provide an alternative social space that fosters specific kinds of religious experiences, expressions, and conversations? Can religious websites offer a medium for communication and evoke 'sufficient human feeling' to create a 'web of personal relationships' that link people together in new ways? What roles can these virtual communities play in religious life? These questions remain theoretical unless we study actual communities online.

I answer these questions through a study of the Branch Davidians and Waco Internet sites. My thesis is that Waco websites form a virtual community by creating a web of personal relationships in two ways. First, they constitute a community through communication. As such, they reveal a complex discourse that M.M. Bakhtin has called *heteroglossia*, a diverse mixture of voices on Waco consisting of insiders and outsiders, friends and foes, scholars and survivors, political activists and devout revivalists (Bakhtin 1981: 269–270). In the beginning of the twenty-first century, we still find people online eagerly disputing and discussing the 'the truth' of the Waco tragedy. As the space that is no place, cyberspace also opens up the limitless possibilities for communication with outsiders – critics, questioners, sympathizers, and even with academics such as myself. In sum, the Internet provides a powerful medium for marginalized groups, like the Branch Davidians, because it offers an electronic place for them to communicate with the outside world – to challenge powerful government and mainstream views of what and who they are. Second, the electronic frontier of cyberspace, wild, unregulated, and free as a medium for communication, creates a place in which to meet – to commune with each other and share visions of the sacred. For the survivors, Mount Carmel – the sacred home of the Davidian community with David Koresh as its spiritual leader – is gone after that fateful day, 19 April 1993, after the FBI raid of the 'compound', as they called it. The authorities had wanted to get access to 'Mount Carmel' in the first place in order to investigate accusations of sexual abuse of children and the possible possession of illegal weapons within the community. All that was Mount Carmel became 'the ashes of Waco'. Today, cyberspace is an arena where the surviving Davidian splinter groups can express their vision of Waco and David Koresh's legacy.

Branch Davidian and Waco sites on the Internet

The Branch Davidians are a splinter group originally founded by Victor Houteff who broke from the Seventh-Day Adventist Church in 1942. While they share the basic beliefs of the Seventh-day Adventists on the inerrancy of the Bible, certain dietary prescriptions, and the faith in the imminent return of Christ, they also have several distinctive theological doctrines and practices. The Branch Davidians believe in an ongoing line of prophecy based on the inspired interpretation of the Bible, especially the Book of Revelation. They also believe that 'the lamb' mentioned in Revelation 5: 2 was David Koresh himself, whose prophetic duty was to open the Seven Seals that should have triggered the sequence of events that would end the world as we know it. Their theology is a 'post-tribulationist' view that the apocalypse and the Second Coming would be preceded by years of turmoil (the tribulation) where the forces of Christ would battle the anti-Christ and his minions, the godless contemporary world that they identified as 'Babylon' (Barkun 1993: 599). In that war of Armageddon, which Koresh taught would begin in Jerusalem in 1995, the Davidians would play a major role culminating in their ascension to heaven to be with God (Tabor and Gallagher 1995: 23–80). Of course, the Branch Davidians are famous because of the horrific events that took place at Mount Carmel, their sacred centre near Waco, Texas, from 28 February to 19 April 1993. This began with their initial shoot-out with the Bureau of Alcohol, Tobacco and Firearms (BATF), who mounted an aggressive search and seizure operation that led to the deaths of six Davidians and four agents, the fifty-one-day stand-off with the FBI, and had its disastrous end with the FBI's tank and Bradley assault vehicle attack, the injection of a large quantity of CS gas into the buildings, and the still unexplained wild-fire that led to the deaths of David Koresh (Vernon Howell) and many of his followers.[2] Subsequently, there were many investigations: a wrongful death suit lodged against the government by Branch Davidians' families (denied by Judge Walter Smith on 21 September 2000), two congressional subcommittee hearings (1995), and an independent inquiry led by special counsel (and former senator) John Danforth. His final report, issued on 8 November 2000, completely exonerated federal law enforcement for the fire and deaths at Waco. Unlike Heaven's Gate, a new religious movement who committed collective suicide on 23 March 1997, the Branch Davidians did not control the place, time, and the meaning of their destruction. They found themselves at the mercy of forces beyond their control, and, at least initially, perhaps beyond their comprehension.

Branch Davidian and Waco sites are ubiquitous on the Internet. This is so ten years after the fire that consumed Mount Carmel during the FBI raid in

1993. Indeed, as we shall see, Waco sites have proliferated on the Internet because of the destruction of Mount Carmel, the deaths of Koresh and many of his flock, the incarceration of many of the survivors, and the controversial government investigations of the BATF and FBI's handling of the incident.

What sites are out there, and why were they created? Generally, these sites fit Anastasia Karaflogka's category of religion *on* cyberspace (2002); they are 'information sites' uploaded by various groups, individuals, and organizations from real life in reaction to the tragedy. According to Karaflogka, these sites use the Internet as a 'tool' for communication, from giving basic information to promulgating their own interpretation of what happened at Waco.[3]

There are five basic types of sites that make up the basic contours of the map of the Branch Davidian and Waco virtual community (see fig. 12.1). The first type consists of government and mainstream media sites. Waco was a mass-media event that riveted the nation. With its scenes of Bradley armoured vehicles, the Mount Carmel 'compound' with its defiant Star of David flag flying, David Koresh himself, who was often portrayed as a maniacal 'cult leader', and its tragic end in the flames that consumed the Branch Davidians, Waco was a made-for-television event. Moreover, since it involved the questionable use of lethal force by the BATF and FBI, it also led to several newsworthy criminal, civil, and congressional investigations.

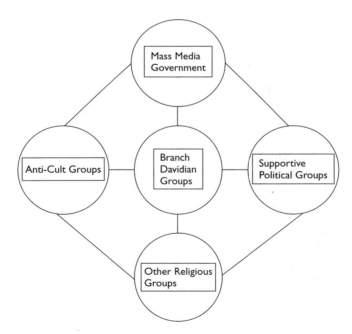

Figure 12.1 Branch Davidian and Waco Internet sites.

What appeared on television and newsprint, made its way on to the Internet mainly in the form of archives. One example is the Texas Department of Public Safety with its evidence archives on the Waco tragedy.[4] The main-stream media also publish their print, photographic, and video archives on the tragedy. The *Dallas Morning News*, for example, with its online site, Dallas News.com (see http://www.dallasnews.com/waco/), has a list of newspaper articles about the ongoing investigations.[5] The reason for these sites is obvious. Waco was a newsworthy event with the government deeply involved in both the tragedy and its legal aftermath of gathering evidence, prosecuting cases, and investigating the culpability of federal agencies.

The second type of Branch Davidian web presence is made up by Branch Davidian survivor sites. In many ways this is deeply ironic. Before 19 April 2003, computers and the Internet were not at the centre of the Branch Davidian world.[6] Koresh did not use the Internet to spread his message.[7] According to Waco amateur expert Mark Swett (personal communication, 21 October 2001),

> The Seven Seals message was a spoken message. No question about it. David did have aspirations to attract others to his message through music. All of the songs that he wrote and recorded were Biblical in nature and had a thread of the seven seals message running through them. One of the key things to remember was that the messenger of the seven seals was as important as the message. The means of reaching out to others (mostly Seventh-Day Adventists) was through meetings and Bible studies. Koresh would send Breault or Steve Schneider to pave the way. They would conduct some Bible studies as a teaser and David would follow.

All this changed after the destruction of Mount Carmel and the death of David Koresh. For Davidian survivors, the Waco tragedy was catastrophic not only because their sacred home, Mount Carmel, went up in flames, but because their spiritual leader and inspired interpreter was killed. This experience of loss is poignantly expressed by Ron Cole, a second-generation Branch Davidian convert. In his essay, 'Mt. Carmel: Then and Now' on his 'Messiah Cyrus Productions' website (http://www.cyrusproductions.com/), Cole describes his dream-vision on his last day at Mount Carmel, two years after the event. It was Christmas 1995, and he had walked out to the ruins of the former chapel when he saw David Koresh appear before him leading a Bible study:

> The Bible study began with David singing one of his original songs called *Shoshanahim* which is a Hebrew word for the Holy Spirit. 'I see the sun, rise up in the morning. I see the king, sittin' on the throne, He's sittin' there wondering why he's lonely and why he has, he has to reign alone.

Shoshanahim, she's the only one for him. *Shoshanahim*, she's the only song to sing.' *Shoshanahim*, what does it mean? As David sang and played his guitar, I closed my eyes and felt the cool wind blowing by; I felt the rocky floor of the chapel that I was sitting on. I felt the presence of 80 spirits all around me, sitting with me, in the chapel pews that were no longer there. The faces of my spiritual companions were clear, and then the details of the inside of the chapel became as real as reality . . . As David started his study that dealt with the revelation of Cyrus (not King Cyrus, but the Cyrus spoken of in Isaiah, the Book of Psalms and other prophesies) I noticed the feeling of burnt wood and ash on my hands as I opened my eyes. There was no chapel, no David, no room full of eager Bible students. There was only a dream, a voice, and a barren wasteland.

Cole's experience of the silent 'barrenness' of Mount Carmel after its destruction describes what other survivors probably experienced as well. Branch Davidian survivors found themselves displaced, leaderless, and, in some cases, incarcerated in Federal penitentiaries with only their memories and the ruins of what they perceived as their sacred home at Mount Carmel that remained.

There are two important official home pages posted by survivor groups. Both sites are typical of those of many new religious movements on the Net in that they are not adversarial, and do not attack anti-cult critics, the government, or the mass media (Mayer 2000: 260–261). Nor do they aggressively attempt to recruit new members online.[8] Rather, both sites focus on presenting basic information that would be of interest for those wanting to learn more about them. They are also a virtual outlet for the prophetic successors of Koresh who in real life find themselves displaced from Mount Carmel since they are behind bars in federal penitentiaries. Both deal with the difficult theological questions for the post-Holocaust Davidian communities. What is the theological legacy of Koresh? Who is the legitimate successor of the community? What is the future direction that should be taken by the community?

As sites established by different second-generation Branch Davidian factions, they reflect the schisms that have divided the Davidian community in the post-tragedy period. The first site is 'Mt. Carmel – The Branch Davidians' (http://start.at/mt.carmel), the website of the survivors associated with Clive Doyle's group, who have tried to re-establish the Branch Davidian Church at Waco.[9] The site has a ten commandments page, links to free study tapes of Koresh's teachings and his interpretation of the first seal of the Book of Revelation, visitors to Mount Carmel information page, memorial pages for Branch Davidians and links to a several Libertarian and pro-Davidian sites. The key part of this site, located at the centre of the home page, is devoted to Livingstone Fagen. Fagen, imprisoned in the federal penitentiary at Marion, Illinois, left Mount Carmel with Koresh's blessing during the siege to serve as the external theological spokesperson of the group. Many of his prison writings are posted on this site, which reveal him as theologically orthodox. Fagen accepts Koresh as the Lamb mentioned in Revelation 6 and his inspired interpretations of the Seven Seals. This site, therefore, reflects Fagen's own intent of representing 'Koresh's teaching in the hope of gaining more adherents before the Final Judgment' (Gallagher 2000: 304).

The other site is run by another survivor group known as Hidden Manna. Unlike the Mount Carmel Branch Davidians, they support another spiritual leader, Renos Avraam, a survivor who is also currently incarcerated in federal prison. Avraam sees himself as the 'Chosen Vessel', the living prophet and the true spiritual successor to David Koresh.[10] His site, called 'The Seven Seals Revelation Library' (cf. http://www.sevenseals.com/ and http://www. branchdavidian.com), is exactly that – a virtual library that describes itself as containing the 'NEW LIGHT (New Truth)' of Avraam's own inspired exegesis of the Seven Seals that 'opens the vaults of prophecy that have been locked since the beginning of creation'. As Gallagher has noted, Avraam 'offers a largely implicit critique of both Koresh and the Mount Camel community, while simultaneously acknowledging Koresh's crucial role in God's plan for salvation' (Gallagher 2000: 304). The site is aniconic. It contains the Book of Revelation with a line-by-line exegesis by Avraam. Without using flashy graphics and images, the sacred text with Avraam's inspired gloss is enough to convey the truth. This kind of web page design reflects implicitly a theological view of the centrality of the word – firstly, in biblical revelation and, secondly, in its prophetically inspired interpretation.

The third type of Branch Davidian Web presentation consists of religious sites that share some Branch Davidian theological views, communitarian lifestyle, and a critical political stance against mainstream society. Some are supportive, but others use their home pages to differentiate themselves carefully from the Branch Davidians. An important example of the latter is 'The Twelve Tribes' (http://www.twelvetribes.com/index.html), which describes itself as '*Messianic* community, for we live in the hope of Messiah and are being made ready for Him'. While having commonalities theologically and in their communitarian lifestyle with the Branch Davidians, the Twelve Tribes take great pains to distinguish their band of messianism from David Koresh's. Quoting from scripture to legitimate their points, they are critical of them, noting that 'it is clear that the Branch Davidians were not living an open and accessible life, keeping their behaviour *excellent among the Gentiles*, as the people of God are commanded to do' (1 Peter 2:12). The people of Waco, Texas, 'hardly considered the stockpiling and use of combat weapons by David Koresh and his followers to be *excellent behaviour*. Their master, *Yahshua*, the true Son of God who we follow, said that if you live by the sword you will die by the sword' (Matthew 26:52).

The fourth type comprises sites of political supporters, from libertarian, first amendment rights activists to the pro-gun, second amendment groups, and militia movements. All call attention to the government's unjustified use of force at Waco, and demand justice – sometimes even rebellion against the government. As an anarchical space free from official censorship and control, these sites use cyberspace to exercise their free speech to challenge what they perceive to be an assault on religious freedom, and because of the many unanswered questions about Waco that still remain. Despite the fact that the Danforth report claimed that doubts about official wrongdoing were unwarranted given the 'overwhelming evidence' exonerating the government of wrongdoing, an August 1999 *Time* magazine poll revealed that over 61 per cent of the American people blame federal authorities for the fire at Waco. Stephen O'Leary (2000: 1) argues that not just the lunatic fringe but 'reasonable people and responsible scholars' continue to have grave doubts about official version of Waco:

> The death of David Koresh and his followers is no longer only a matter for forensic investigation; for those who remain concerned about what really happened at Waco, the events of March and April 1993 have attained the status of myth. The Davidian religious community – a multi-racial and surprisingly liberal group – has been transformed into the unlikely martyrs for a variety of causes; patriots, militia sympathizers, Second Amendment activists, would be revolutionaries, and full-blown apocalyptic paranoiacs.

These many questions and conspiracy theories have created what Mark Swett calls 'never ending battle' in which the Internet has proved to be a key outlet for Waco activists to voice their doubts and outrage. A notable example of this is libertarian Daniel R. Tobias's A Brief Stop at Mount Carmel (or what's left of it) and Return to Mt. Carmel pages (http://www.dantobias. com/davidian.html). Tobias's perspective, he states, is summed up by 'Ted Nelson's Four Maxims': '(1) Most people are fools; (2) Most authority is malignant; (3) God does not exist; and (4) everything is wrong.' Tobias (personal communication, 30 September 2001) describes himself as

> a computer geek, agnostic Jew and Libertarian with some personal interest in politics, especially the politics of 'fringe' groups and their battles with the 'mainstream' . . . I have no connection with Waco or David Koresh, but my position is that, as wacky as their religious beliefs may be, the Branch Davidians had the right to peacefully practice them . . .

His site is a photo diary of his visits to Mount Carmel on two occasions, in May of 1995 and a few years later. Sometimes, libertarian sites also develop their own viewpoint with reference to the Davidian tragedy. Such is the case with Carol Moore, whose Davidian Massacre pages are among major libertarian sites on the Internet that deal with the injustices of Waco.[11] Within her pages one finds chapters of her book, *The Davidian Massacre*, the libertarian Committee on Waco Social Justice's and Branch Davidian prisoners' information. However, Moore's site is interesting because it offers a religious New Age vision along with the libertarian political one. She describes herself as 'a long-time student of consciousness and libertarian pacifist, activist, and writer' whose site

> is offered to all freedom-loving, open minded people of good will, whatever ideological, religious, ethnic, and racial, lifestyle or other labels they may apply to themselves. We are all souls, spirits, and conscious beings seeking truth. And in one way or another we are all students of consciousness. Hopefully, those of very different beliefs may find some spiritual and political insights here – as well as a basis for action upon a minimal set of political principles. Please check out Secession.Net!!

Moore sees her quest for the truth of Waco in not just political but also spiritual terms. It is part of her quest to raise human consciousness towards a new order, free of the oppression caused by the old established authoritarian order of God and country, the power that was behind the Waco massacre. Moore's deeply held spiritual hope is that 'the truth' can set humanity free:

> Can we move from a world ruled by God and State to a world alive with Consciousness and Community? Can we experience the one consciousness underlying the many faiths? Can we create networks and confederations of autonomous, self-governing communities to replace violently unified, warring nation states?

The fifth type is sites created by anti-cultists. A key example is Rick Ross's home page, 'Cult Expert, Lecturer, and Intervention Specialist' (http://www.rickross.com/).[12] Like other Waco sites, Ross's is styled as informational. It is 'created to offer the public a resource of information concerning controversial and/or potentially unsafe groups, which may have drawn some concern, attention, and interest'. Ross claims that he 'has no message per se', but rather offers an 'archive of information' (Ross, personal communication, 29 September 2001). Indeed, the site has an enormous news archive on Waco tailored to Ross's approach of deprogramming cultists.

The overall point of view, however, as illustrated on his FAQ page, is that groups like Waco are dangerous 'destructive cults' that use techniques of mind control and regimentation to 'abuse and exploit their members. This abuse may occur in the areas of finances, physical labour, child abuse and neglect, medical neglect, sexual exploitation and/or psychological and emotional abuse.' Anyone who describes the Branch Davidians as a religious movement is dismissed as a 'cult apologist' by Ross.[13]

The conflict of interpretations

What do we make of all these different sites? Do they qualify as a virtual community at all, or are they just a buzzing cacophony of information? The sociologist of religion David Chidester (1998: 8) has tried to answer this question. Overwhelmed by the vast number of sites dealing with Koresh, he is most intrigued by the 'conflict of interpretations' on the Net:

> Information is embedded in separate, distinct, and mutually exclusive sites – at home on a particular home page – that might be 'linked' to but not necessarily in conversation with other sites. In the case of information about David Koresh, it is clear that the sites maintained by anti-cult activists are not linked in any kind of meaningful contact or exchange with those maintained by the Committee for Waco Justice, expositors of Branch Davidian doctrines, or academics engaged in research projects. As a result information is disembedded from social relations, in which differences of interpretation might be engaged and adjudicated. Not only the 'lessons of Waco' but also basic matters of fact – what crimes were alleged, who fired first, how the fires started, and so on – are given entirely different renderings depending on which site you happen to visit. On one site, you will find that religious fanatics, at war with the United States, committed mass suicide when they realized that they were losing the war. On another, you will learn that an unconventional religious group, which the United States was bent on suppressing, was brutally massacred by a military assault.

It is clear from this quotation that Chidester takes Steven Jones's bleak view of the possibility of forming virtual communities on the Internet. What Chidester sees in digital Waco are different home pages monadically frozen in cyberspace, trumpeting their views without engaging in any 'meaningful conversation' with each another. He sees this as evidence of the fragmentation of postmodern American society where the whole concept of 'home' and 'community' has become a problematical category even in real life.[14] Is Chidester correct in his characterization of digital Waco? Is what we have here only a disparate collection of informational sites where disparate real-life institutions, groups, and individuals simply publish their views on Waco and leave it at that? If so, such isolated nodes spread throughout the electronic wilderness of the Internet would hardly qualify as a web of social relations – a virtual community – according to Rheingold's definition.

Digital Waco: community from communication

Chidester is right that there is in fact very little 'meaningful contact and exchange' on the Net between, for example, an anti-cult deprogrammer, like

Rick Ross, and the Branch Davidian survivor groups on the Net, even though his site does includes a link to the Hidden Manna Branch Davidian home page. But does that necessarily mean that cyberspace is so different from real-life communities? While social theorists often define communities in functional terms, as interdependent groups where 'different interpretations can be engaged and adjudicated', the reality is often quite different. Even in real-life society, conflict and dysfunctionality exist (Fernback 1999: 209).

In real life, there is no possibility of dialogue between a Rick Ross, who is an anti-cult deprogrammer, and members of, for example, Hidden Manna, whom he would dismiss contemptuously as part of a destructive doomsday cult. In the case of the Waco tragedy, this real-life inability to communicate was at the heart of the disaster, according to James Tabor and Eugene Gallagher in their book *Why Waco?*. Tabor and Gallagher argue that the conflict that ultimately resulted in death and destruction at Mount Carmel largely resulted from mutual misunderstanding – two groups who spoke a completely different language and understood what was happening 'on the ground' in profoundly contradictory ways. The FBI dismissed Koresh as a Bible-babbling lunatic and 'con man' who was holding his followers either against their will or through deceit in the Mount Carmel 'compound'. Koresh was a liar not a prophet, and the Branch Davidians were hostages in need of rescuing. By contrast, those inside Mount Carmel saw Koresh as an inspired interpreter of the Bible who revealed its truths; he was the designated lamb of God who would save those chosen from the demonic forces that were loosed at the end of history, the time of the apocalypse as foretold in the Book of Revelation. The BATF and the FBI, with their Bradley armoured vehicles, assault rifles, their PA system blasting the screams of dying rabbits, and CS gas, were the forces of 'Babylon' of the anti-Christ. Those inside saw Mount Carmel as a refuge rather than a prison, a place of safety from the demonic forces gathering outside. It was this deep conflict of interpretations between the FBI and the Branch Davidians that led to the disaster.

Nevertheless, the Internet can be a functional place where communication can 'take place.' The Internet as a communication tool is not one-way, like television; it is interactive. It can establish a web of personal relationships. Despite their appearance as isolated and separate information sources, there are many ways home pages can provide a dynamic, vital arena for mutual discussion that leads to involvement, and, in some cases, a place for community building. James Costigan has argued that the Internet's power is that it allows ease of access, allowing users to be embedded in social relations that would otherwise be difficult, if not impossible, in real-life community situations (Costigan 1999: xxii):

The medium has such an effect on community as to define it. Community relationships formed on line allow an access and an intimacy not transferred to other situations. On-line messages can be sent at any time and to anyone and can be responded to when time is available. This level of access does not transfer to face-to-face situations where different social, personal, and community rules exist.

In the case of Waco, it is a mistake to see the pages as 'separate, distinct, and mutually exclusive'. Almost all of them have email addresses to contact and website links that tie the reader via hypertext to a network of related pages.[15] Many of them have guest books, discussion groups, bulletin boards, and list serves that anyone can join and post messages on. Looking at these pages, one finds substantial evidence of 'access and intimacy', if not mutual understanding, that is basic to any community both in real life and in CMC.

A few examples will suffice. The Mount Carmel survivors' site (http://start. at/mtcarmel) shows the Web literally in its links sidebar on the home page. There you can find links to most of the key survivor, libertarian, and talk show supporter sites on the Net, such as Sharlene Shappart, Carol Moore, Alex Jones, and Carl Klang. These sites are linked together on every site to create a web of discourse on the Waco tragedy. Another example of this is Waco the Rules of Engagement (http://www.waco93.com/), the site authored by the filmmakers of the important Waco documentary film by that name, which includes page links to Alex Jones, a Texas radio talk show host who has volunteered to rebuild the Mount Carmel church. The pages not only give updated information on the progress of the construction, but give a listing of donations that are needed. Many Waco supporter sites throughout the Internet circulated a petition to the President of the United States to issue pardons to the imprisoned Branch Davidians. Given the power of the Internet these charitable and political campaigns have the chance of reaching a global audience.

Moreover, conversations that foster community-building occur regularly online. In the guestbook of David Thibodeau, a Waco survivor who has also become a leading voice of the Branch Davidians in the post-tragedy period, dated 4 September 2001, we find this poignant example in an excerpt from a letter of a Branch Davidian supporter, pastor Michael Treis, who reminisces about the last day of the siege:

> Greetings in the name of our Saviour Yahshua Messiah! I am sorry I could not have charged in like a knight on a big horse on April 19th, 1993, although I did try. At that time I was driving long haul out of North Dakota. I saw what was happning [sic] and tried to get a load to Texas. I was stopped at every turn. I warned my boss if I didn't, I may just take the rig to Texas anyway. He warned if I deveiated [sic] from my route he would report the truck stolen. I told him well I may just leave it at a truck stop. He quoted law and warned I would be arrested for abandonment of truck and cargo (also federal offence). I told him to get me back to Fargo or else. It took him three loads I arrived 2 days to

[*sic*] late to make any difference April 21. I have never forgiven myself for not taking the truck there or leaving it or something. I started ministry Yahshua Messiah's Sabbath Day Ministry in 2000. Satan has faught [*sic*] me every step of the way. I sold my house in Minnesota and turned a school bus into an RV to minister at truck stops. Satan has near bank-rupted me along the way being fought by police, local officials, etc. I am back in Ft. Worth, where I spent 22 years, my wife and son are from here. I would like to meet you sometime if possible especially if you are in the area.

This letter, posted by a man whose ministry has strong connections with Branch Davidian belief, reached out to Thibodeau and other interested parties through the guestbook. As a man literally on the road, with a truck driver's ministry, there is no place for 'inhabitance and being' where he can find his religious community. Community, though perhaps tenuous and fragile, is maintained through the 'non-place' of the Internet.

Important debates also occur on Waco sites that foster a sense of community. On the Rules of Engagement discussion board (http://waco93. com/wwwboard/index.html), people have posted messages on the Taliban and Koresh. One author, naming him or herself 'Imam', writes, 'The Taliban refused to give up Bin Laden and David Koresh refused to come out of Mt. Carmel. Justice rained down on them both' (9 October 2001). A day later, another correspondent posts a follow-up that engages the issue: 'Gassing infant children with Methylene Chloride, CS gas, and suffocating them with CO_2 is not justice. They did no wrong and yet they were intentionally singled out and targeted for destruction. That's just plain wrong.' Is Koresh equivalent to Osama bin Laden? Can you call Koresh a 'religious fanatic'? What is the proper governmental response to the Branch Davidians' activi-ties? To what extent can we tolerate different religious worlds? Are there important religious and ethical issues being considered here? The answer of course is yes, and the discussion board allows the opportunity for people to meet to exchange views in a meaningful way to 'take place'.

The Internet also has the power to break down the barriers between people who, in real-life society, may be able to keep themselves separate. For example, academics studying Waco from the outside can find themselves challenged by the very people they analyse if they publish their work on the Internet. A case in point is John Mann's An Introduction to the Branch Davidians site (http://www.fountain.btinternet.co.uk/koresh/index.html). Mann's is an 'amateur expert' site that tries 'to provide an overview and context' for the huge amount of information on Waco on the Net, including summaries of each document that Mann has read, and provides a provocative analysis of Branch Davidian teachings. Mann argues that, no matter what the defects of Koresh's personality that lead to possible child abuse etc., it is finally his own amazing ability to create a pastiche of linked Biblical passages into a meaningful whole that justifies his work. Mann lends a distinctly postmodern stamp to Koresh's abilities:

> Koresh developed very little of what could properly be called theology – he has no time for lengthy and complex philosophizing, yet he certainly did have time for lengthy and complex Bible studies. If one wanted, it would be possible to understand his 'philosophy' behind his thinking as a highly hermeneutical, post-structuralist, post-Nietzschian maze of codes, symbols, over determined meanings and an intricate inter-relating of Bible, language, and power . . . Koresh's juxtaposing disparate elements of language and Bible creates a powerful field of symbolism and meaning. Derrida was thought to have revealed an extra level of meaning to Hegel and Genet when he placed their texts in parallel columns, but Koresh does this all the time with the Bible. His mastery of the Biblical symbolic is astounding; he is a Christian Crowley, able to conjure up an extensive range of indexes of life from the Bible as Crowley did from Tarot, Astrology and Kabbala.

But this intellectual assessment of Koresh's hermeneutical poetics, which makes him in Mann's eyes 'a second Blake with his visions of God, his apocalypse or revelation', does not go unchallenged. What follows on his site is the first of several disturbing emails (from 29 June to 28 July 1999) from David Bunds, a former Davidian and arch-critic of Koresh. Bunds challenges Mann on every point:

> I disagree with you that Vernon's personality is not an issue in evaluating his writings. On the contrary, unless you understand Vernon's personality and understand it very well, you will never fully understand his teachings. This is because the various obsessions and carnal desires that Vernon suffered from was a major force in shaping his beliefs and teachings. This is something I know from experience. I was there.
>
> For example, Vernon was a pedophile. We normally think of pedophiles as men who like to have sex with little boys but it applies to any adult who likes to have sex with children, regardless of sexual orientation. It is a documented fact that Kiri Jewell (Sherri Jewel's daughter, she testified before Congress) was no more than 11 years old when Vernon had sex with her and she might have been as young as ten. I cannot remember for sure. I think a majority of people would consider a 10 or 11 year old a child. I sure do because I have children myself of this age. Some may be offended that I would label Vernon a pedophile but it is only logical to do so in my opinion. Most people are disgusted by such behavior and rightly so. So why did Vernon insist on doing such things? Because he said that it was God's will. If he had not believed that

he had permission from God to engage in sex with young girls he would never had done it because he could not have handled the guilt.

What we have here is digital discussion about several important issues: What authority does an outsider have to interpret events that an insider has personally experienced? What role does personality play in the creation of a theology? How should one assess that theology ethically in light of what we know about the theologian? How do we go about interpreting it? Are Koresh's writings a sad reflection of his sexual obsessions or a brilliant exposition of the divine will? The interactive power of the Internet brings Mann and Bunds together to debate these questions.

These examples of conversation, if you will, are particularly striking. Here the Internet creates an arena for different types of people to discuss a wide variety of important moral and spiritual issues. Pierre Levy (1998: 29) would see the above as examples of 'affinities' forming on line that are the basic building blocks of a virtual community:

> A virtual community can, for example, be organized on the basis of its affinities through the intermediary of telematic communications systems. Its members are reunited by the same centers of interest and the same problems: geography being contingent, is no longer a starting point or constraint. Although it is strictly speaking 'not there', this community is guided by passions and projects, conflicts and friendships. It exists without a stable point of reference: wherever its mobile members happen to be . . . or nowhere at all. Virtualization reinvents a nomadic culture, not through a return to the Paleolithic or to the early pastoral civilizations, but by creating a medium of social interaction in which relations reconfigure themselves with a minimum of inertia.

What we have being constituted in the digital Waco conversations discussed above is evidence of what Robert Bellah has called a 'real community'. They are 'communities of memory' that are no different from the religious groups Bellah studied in his book *Habits of the Heart*. Like the real-life ethnic, racial, regional, and religious communities from which they come, online members of the digital Waco community do not forget their past because they are involved in retelling their story (Bellah 1985: 152–155). Here the story is about David Koresh, a person who is remembered in different ways, to be sure, but none the less embodies and exemplifies important meanings for the community.

Notes

1 An earlier version of this chapter can be found on my website (see http://it.stlawu.edu/~mmac/DigitalWaco.htm).

2   Seventy-four of his followers (including twenty-three children) died. Nine members were outside at the time of the events. Fourteen adults and twenty-one children exited during the siege. Nine followers survived the fire. Of these, seven were later convicted criminally, including on voluntary manslaughter and firearms violations.

3   By contrast, Karaflogka's second type, religion *in* cyberspace, is 'a religious, spiritual, or metaphysical expression that is created and exists exclusively in cyberspace where it enjoys a considerable degree of virtual reality'. These are the sites that she thinks are best described as 'cyber-religions' (Karaflogka 2002).

4   The website can be found at http://www.txdps.state.tx.us/director_staff/public_information/branch_davidian.

5   There are also private academic sites that try to provide 'objective' information and analysis. The most famous of these, of course, is the CESNUR site (www.cesnur.org) of the Center for the Study on New Religions in Italy. CESNUR was established in 1988 by a group of religion scholars from leading universities in Europe and the Americas. The centre currently has an extensive Waco, FBI, and the Branch Davidians 'update file' of news and scholarly articles. There are also sites run by 'amateur experts'. Perhaps the most important of these is the now defunct site of Mark Swett, 'David Koresh: Saint or Sinner, Angel or Devil, Man or Prophet. You Decide!' (see http://home.maine.rr.com/waco/). Swett, whose day job is in medical insurance, calls himself a 'student of comparative religious theology', and is well known for having one of the most comprehensive and up-to-date Net 'archives' of Branch Davidian documents. Swett sees his site as an 'information tool' that transcribes what Koresh/Branch Davidians 'said and say in their own words/ unedited with as little commentary as possible' (Swett, personal communication, 1 October 2001).

6   Branch Davidian Wayne Martin might have had a Bulletin Board that was Internet accessible and other Davidians may have searched the Internet for information about Ruby Ridge, but there is no evidence to support this. While there was a 'computer room' at Mount Carmel, it was probably just an ordinary room with a computer in it that belonged to Marc Breault, a member who left the group in 1989 (Swett, private communication, 21 October 2001).

7   While Koresh seems to have used a word processor to type out the first part of his manuscript unlocking the Seven Seals, he and his followers seemed far more interested in weapons than computer technology. The computer floppy disk brought out of Mount Carmel by Ruth Riddle on 19 April 1993 is another mystery of the tragedy. Swett sums up the relevant questions: 'The Seven Seals manuscript was first written in long hand by David, then proofread by Schneider (or at least that is what he was supposed to do). David later dictated some of the manuscipt. But the Branch Davidians were using a manual typewriter to type it – one that had ribbon problems that last weekend, which forced Steve Schneider and his wife Judy to ask the FBI for some Casio typewriter ribbons so that they could continue working on the manuscript. The FBI did deliver some ribbons (as well as bugs) to them the early evening of 18 April 1993. It is interesting to note that Judy had initially requested a laptop to speed up the process, however, the FBI commanders refused her request. The Davidians did have a generator, but if it could have been used to power a computer why the request for the Laptop and then ribbons? Stalling tactic? I do not know. That is one of those little known things that most people do not mention or question. How did the manuscript get on that disk? Who put it there? When?' (Swett, personal communication, 21 October 2001).

8   According to Swett, 'The surviving Davidians do not proselytize for new "converts." Those that have come to join them have done so for a myriad of

reasons, but not because of any effort on the part of the Davidians to try and attract them. In fact it is just the opposite' (Swett, personal communication, 21 October 2001).

9 This site is authored by webmaster Tom Cook, a second-generation Branch Davidian who knew Koresh and studied with other Davidians, such as Perry Jones, but he was not 'in the message' until after 1993.

10 This is not accepted by Clive Doyle's group. See for instance Clive Doyle's letter to William McGivers on the Issop site (http://www.everett.net/users/rorim/iss/clivex.htm). On the theological particulars of this dispute see Gallagher '2000: 303–319'.

11 The website can be found at www.carolmoore.net. Moore, who has written extensively on Waco, is highly critical of Carol Valentine's conspiracy theories at her Waco Holocaust museum (see http://serendipity.magnet.ch/waco/valen.html).

12 Another similar site is called the Apologetics Index (http://www.gospel.com.net/apologeticsindex). As its name suggests, the information, while reflecting a variety of theological and sociological perspectives, is based upon an exclusivistic perspective; it is given to 'equip Christians to logically present and defend the Christian faith'.

13 According to Ross, his site receives seven thousand hits a day. Interestingly, perhaps in response to his role as a deprogrammer and government expert on cults at Waco, and successful lawsuits against CAN (the former Cult Awareness Network), Ross is very careful in his use of language. For example, he says that some of the groups, including the Branch Davidians presumably, 'may popularly be referred to as cults'. However, he adds the following disclaimer that 'the mention and/or inclusion of a group or a leader within this web site does not define that group as a "cult" . . .'. His comment page on Waco also seems edited to emphasize visitor comments that the site is objective and informative. On the conflict over what constitutes objective information and the anti-cultists' attack on academic 'cult apologists' see Mayer (2000) and the chapter by Massimo Introvigne in this volume.

14 Chidester draws an interesting conclusion about how all this reflects deep-seated conflicts between the definition of the sacred home in mainstream society and the Branch Davidians. He sees it as part of a 'growing problem of location itself in American society'. 'Home' for the Branch Davidians was the communitarian celibate lifestyle at Mount Carmel: a life that endorsed Koresh's sexual practices of marrying children and taking followers' spouses as his 'spiritual wives' as the fulfilment of his New Light revelation and part of God's plan in preparation of Armageddon. Such a form of domesticity reflected the power and religious meaning that was at the centre of Mount Carmel's definition as a sacred place, a home. But it was also seen as an 'abomination' by a number of people in America who saw it as violating the generally accepted norms of home. The 'conflict of interpretations' is over the question, what is a home? Home becomes a 'contested space of social relations, gender relations, and generational relations'.

15 See, for example, the Dreambook-related website links on Waco at http://books.dreambook.com/wyla/links.html and John Mann's introduction to the Branch Davidians at http://www.fountain.btinternet.co.uk/koresh/index.html.

References

Appadurai, A. (1996) *Modernity at Large: Cultural Dimensions of Globalization*, Minneapolis: University of Minnesota Press.

Bakhtin, M.M. (1981) *The Dialogic Imagination*, Austin: University of Texas Press.

Barkun, M. (1993) 'Reflections after Waco: Millennialists and the State', *Christian Century*, 110, pp. 596–600.

Bellah, R.N. (1970) *Essays on Religion in a Post-Traditional World*, Berkeley: University of California Press.

Bellah, R. (1985) *Habits of the Heart: Individualism and Commitment in American Life*, New York: Harper and Row.

Chidester, D. (1998) 'Forum: Interpreting Waco', *Religion and American Culture*, 8, pp. 1–30.

Costigan, J. (1999) 'Introduction: Forest, Trees, and Internet Research', in S. Jones (ed.) *Doing Internet Research: Critical Issues and Methods for Examining the Net*, Thousand Oaks, California: Sage Publications, pp. xvii–xxiv.

Fernback, J. (1999) 'There is a There There: Notes toward a Definition of Cybercommunity', in S. Jones (ed.) *Doing Internet Research: Critical Issues and Methods for Examining the Net*, Thousand Oaks, California: Sage Publications, pp. 203–220.

Gallagher, E. (2000) 'The Persistence of the Millennium: Branch Davidian Expectations of the End after Waco', *Nova Religio*, 3, pp. 303–319.

Jones S. (1997) 'The Internet and its Social Landscape', in S. Jones (ed.) *Virtual Culture: Identity and Communication in Cybersociety*, London: Sage Publications.

Karaflogka, A. (2002) 'Religious Discourse in Cyberspace', *Religion*, 32, pp. 279–291.

Levy, P. (1998) *Becoming Virtual: Reality in the Digital Age*, New York: Plenum Press.

Mayer, J.-F. (2000) 'Religious Movements and the Internet: The New Frontier of Cult Controversies', in J.K. Hadden and D.E. Cowan (eds) *Religion on the Internet: Research Prospects and Promises*, Amsterdam, London, and New York: Elsevier Science, pp. 249–276.

O'Leary, S. (2000) 'Waco Fire Continues to Burn on the Web', *USC Annenberg Online Journalism Review*, 13 October 2000. Available from: http://ojr.usc.edu/.

Rheingold, H. (1993) *The Virtual Community: Homesteading on the Electronic Frontier*, Reading, Massachusetts: Addison-Wesley Publishing Company.

Tabor, J. and Gallagher, E. (1995) *Why Waco: Cults and the Battle for Religious Freedom in America*, Berkeley: University of California Press.

Turner, V. (1969) *The Ritual Structure: Structure and Antistructure*, Ithaca, New York: Cornell Paperbacks.

Urban, H. (2000) 'The Devil at Heaven's Gate: Rethinking the Study of Religion in the Age of Cyber-Space', *Nova Religio*, 3, pp. 268–302.

Verhovek, S.H. (1995) 'No Martyrs in Waco: The Surviving Branch Davidians Resent Being Used by Militias Eager to Exploit Their Cause. God will Provide Vengeance Enough', *New York Times*, 9 July, pp. 33–35.

Wertheim, M. (1999) *The Pearly Gates of Cyberspace: A History of Space from Dante to the Internet*, London: Virago.

Wilbur, S. (1997) 'An Archaeology of Cyberspaces: Virtuality, Community, Identity', in D. Porter (ed.) *Internet Culture*, London: Routledge, pp. 5–22.

Index